The Social Embeddedness of Industrial Ecology

The Social Embeddedness of Industrial Ecology

Edited by

Frank Boons

Erasmus University Rotterdam, The Netherlands

and

Jennifer Howard-Grenville

University of Oregon, USA

Edward Elgar

Cheltenham, UK • Northampton, MA, USA

Published by
Edward Elgar Publishing Limited
The Lypiatts
15 Lansdown Road
Cheltenham
Glos GL50 2JA
UK

Edward Elgar Publishing, Inc.
William Pratt House
9 Dewey Court
Northampton
Massachusetts 01060
USA

A catalogue record for this book
is available from the British Library

Library of Congress Control Number: 2009928600

Mixed Sources
Product group from well-managed
forests and other controlled sources
www.fsc.org Cert no. SA-COC-1565
FSC © 1996 Forest Stewardship Council

ISBN 978 1 84720 782 1

Printed and bound by MPG Books Group, UK

Contents

Figures and tables

FIGURES

TABLES

Contributors

Weslynne S. Ashton is the Director of the 'Industrial Ecology in Developing Countries' program at Yale University's Center for Industrial Ecology. She holds PhD and master's degrees in Environmental Science from Yale and a bachelor's in Environmental Engineering from MIT. Ashton has worked as an environmental engineer and has been an independent environmental consultant to clients such as the Inter-American Development Bank and United Technologies Corporation. Her interests are in the area of sustainable industrial development, inter-firm collaboration and corporate environmental strategies and performance. She was born and raised in Trinidad and Tobago and resides in the United States.

Henrikke Baumann is an Associate Professor in Environmental Systems Analysis at Chalmers University of Technology in Göteborg, Sweden. Her research interests include life cycle assessment and organization theory. As a spin-off, she developed an interest in interdisciplinarity, for which she received a Royal award in 2004. She has followed the developments in the LCA research community since 1991 and published an LCA textbook in 2004. Baumann's own research focuses on the practices of LCA in industry. The influence of organization on environmental performance is a more recent interest. Here, she leads a multi-disciplinary research program on Organizing for the Environment.

Claudia R. Binder is Assistant Professor for Social and Industrial Ecology, at the Department of Geography at the University of Zurich, Switzerland. Her main research interests are: (a) development of interdisciplinary approaches for modelling the dynamics and the impact of human activities on the environment; (b) development of integrative sustainability assessment tools; and (c) analysis of regulatory mechanisms and structures within human-environment systems. Binder's empirical research areas include sustainable development of rural and urban regions including resource and waste management systems both in Switzerland and developing countries. She is section editor for material flow analysis in the *Journal of Industrial Ecology*.

Frank Boons is Senior Researcher at the Public Administration department of Erasmus University Rotterdam, The Netherlands. His work addresses

the way in which firms deal with ecological impact from an interorganizational perspective. He has published research on industrial ecology in
international journals such as the *Journal of Cleaner Production, Journal of
Industrial Ecology, International Studies in Management and Organization,*
and *Emergence: Complexity and Organization.* He is currently finalizing
a book on the ecological strategies of firms entitled *Creating Ecological
Value,* to be published in 2009.

Marian R. Chertow is Associate Professor and Director of the Industrial
Environmental Management Program at the Yale School of Forestry and
Environmental Studies. Her teaching and research focus on industrial
ecology, business/environment issues, waste management, and environmental technology innovation. Her most recent research involves the
study of industrial symbiosis – geographically-based exchanges of energy,
water, and material by-products within networks of businesses. Chertow
is on the founding faculty of the Masters of Science in Environmental
Management Program at the National University of Singapore and is a
Visiting Professor at Nankai University's National Center for Innovation
Research on Circular Economy in China.

Anthony Chiu works in the fields of Cleaner Production (CP), Operations
Strategy, and Eco-Industrial Development (EID). He has conducted
EIP workshops for 30 governments with UNEP, UNIDO, UN ESCAP,
InWEnt, Asian Productivity Organization, and other international organizations. Chiu first experienced EIP projects at UNDP in 1999, and
pursued this discipline. His latest publication was an UNEP kit on CP
and EID. Aside from being a professor, he has served the government as
a Pollution Adjudication Board Member; and as editor in journals including the *Journal of Cleaner Production* and *Progress in Industrial Ecology.*
Chiu holds BS Mechanical Engineering, MS Industrial Engineering, and
Doctor of Business Administration degrees.

John Ehrenfeld is Executive Director of the International Society for
Industrial Ecology. His research focus is sustainability and culture change.
He is the author of *Sustainability by Design: A Subversive Strategy for
Transforming our Consumer Culture.* He currently serves on the Council of
the Society for Organizational Learning. Ehrenfeld retired in 2000 as the
Director of the MIT Program on Technology, Business, and Environment.
In October 1999, the World Resources Institute honored him with a lifetime
achievement award. He holds a BS and ScD in Chemical Engineering from
MIT, and is author or co-author of over 200 papers, and other publications.

David Gibbs is Professor of Human Geography and Director of the
Graduate School at the University of Hull. His main research interests

are in the field of local and regional economic development, with a focus on the environmental implications of such developments. He has published widely from this work in journals such as *Environment and Planning A*, *Geoforum*, *Regional Studies*, and *Local Environment*, as well as several book chapters. He is the author of the books *Government Policy and Industrial Change* (1989), *Local Economic Development and the Environment* (2002) and *The Sustainable Development Paradox* (2007).

Jeremy Hall is an Associate Professor in the Faculty of Business Administration, Simon Fraser University, Canada, and a fellow of The Centre for Innovation Studies. His research interests include sustainable development innovation, stakeholder ambiguity, inter-firm innovation dynamics and the social impacts of entrepreneurship and innovation. Hall's recent research has been published in *Entrepreneurship: Theory & Practice*, *Harvard Business Review* (Latin American edition), *Greener Management International*, *Industrial & Corporate Change*, *Journal of Business Ethics*, *Journal of Business Venturing*, *Journal of Cleaner Production*, *Journal of Operations Management*, *MIT Sloan Management Review*, *R&D Management*, and *Research Policy*.

Jennifer Howard-Grenville is an Assistant Professor of Management at the University of Oregon's Lundquist College of Business. She studies processes of organizational and institutional change and is particularly interested in how people change their organizations in response to environmental and social demands. Her work has been published in *Organization Science*, *Organization & Environment*, *Law & Social Inquiry*, *California Management Review* and several other journals. She is the author of *Corporate Culture and Environmental Practice* (Edward Elgar, 2007), which documents her ethnographic study of a high-tech company. Howard-Grenville received her PhD at MIT, her MA at Oxford University, and her BSc at Queen's University, Canada.

Timothy M. Koponen is a Lecturer in Public Policy at Indiana University, based in Indianapolis. He has been interested in political economy and economic development, having written his dissertation on 'Maize in Zimbabwe'. His focus is the realization of technology and physical (not financial) economic development. He is also interested in 'Civic Engagement' pedagogy. Koponen is the author (or co-author) of two books, *Partnerships that Work* (forthcoming), and *Making Nature, Shaping Culture* (1995) and his articles have appeared in *Sociological Review* and the *Journal of the Indiana Academy of the Social Sciences*.

Yan Liu studies business administration and economics at the University of Shanghai, China, and the Carl von Ossietzky University of Oldenburg, Germany. Currently, she is a PhD student at the University of Kassel, Germany, holding a Scholarship of the German Academic Exchange Service (DAAD). Her research interests are sustainability and supply chain management with a special focus on supply chain integration.

Stelvia Matos is a Research Associate, the Centre for Policy Research on Science & Technology (CPROST) and an Adjunct Professor at the Faculty of Business Administration, Simon Fraser University, Canada. Her research areas include engineering policy, sustainable development innovation, social entrepreneurship, information and communication technologies in rural areas, environment management tools, life cycle assessment and social aspects of innovation dynamics. Matos' work has been published in the Latin American edition of *Harvard Business Review*, *International Journal of Technology, Knowledge & Society, Journal of Business Ethics, Journal of Operations Management*, and *Research Policy*.

Cynthia Mitchell is Professor of Sustainability at UTS' Institute for Sustainable Futures. Cynthia's goal is to create change towards a restorative economy – that is, development (in its broadest sense) that goes beyond no net negative impact. She is fundamentally intrigued by how learning and change happen. Her practice-led work for change is based on principles from her engineering and science training, overlaid with ideas and insights from transdisciplinarity, futures and systems thinking, diffusion of innovation, socio-technical landscapes, economics, and learning in all its forms (personal, organizational, social . . .). Mitchell holds a Bachelor of Engineering degree from the University of Queensland, and a PhD from the University of New South Wales. She holds an Honorary Doctorate in Technology from Chalmers University and is an Australian Learning and Teaching Council Fellow.

Romy Morana is Professor of Environmental Management at University of Applied Sciences (FHTW), Berlin. She studied business administration and environmental sciences at the Technical University of Berlin and Humboldt University of Berlin. She completed her PhD (2005) on closed-loop supply chain management at the Carl von Ossietzky University of Oldenburg, Germany. Morana's research interests include environmental management, supply chain management, and closed-loop supply chain management. She has published a number of papers in journals including the *International Journal of Production Research*.

Raymond Paquin is an Assistant Professor of Management at the John Molson School of Business at Concordia University. His research focuses on organizational issues around environmental practices in business, industrial symbiosis, interorganizational relations, and social networks. Paquin received his doctorate in organizational behaviour from Boston University School of Management.

Stefan Seuring is Professor of International Management at the University of Kassel, Germany. Previously he held positions at the University of Waikato, Hamilton, New Zealand and the Ossietzky University of Oldenburg, Germany. He was Visiting Professor at the Copenhagen Business School, Denmark, in 2004. He obtained his PhD (2001) and habilitation (2004) in business administration at the Carl von Ossietzky University of Oldenburg, Germany. Seuring's major research interests are supply chain management, sustainability and management accounting, where he has conducted joint projects with a range of companies. Sustainability and supply chain management related publications have appeared in journals including the *Journal of Cleaner Production* and *Business Strategy and the Environment*.

Bart van Hoof holds an MSc in Industrial Engineering. van Hoof's research interests include the greening of industry in developing countries with emphasis on Latin America. Bart is currently a researcher and teacher at the School of Management in Los Andes University Bogotá, and a PhD student in the program on Industrial Ecology at Erasmus University in Rotterdam. He worked for more than ten years as a consultant on the design and the implementation of cleaner production projects in a broad range of programs and companies in Colombia, Mexico, Panama and Chile.

List of abbreviations

APELL	awareness and preparedness for emergencies at the local level
APO	Asian Productivity Organization
BRWTP	Barceloneta Regional Wastewater Treatment Plant
CAS	complex adaptive systems
CP	cleaner production
CTNBio	National Technical Commission for Biosafety
EID	eco-industrial development
EIE	eco-industrial estate
EIPs	eco-industrial parks
EMS	environmental management system
EPI	environmental performance indicators
FAO	Food and Agriculture Organization
GMB	Grain Marketing Board
GMOs	genetically modified organisms
IDEC	Institute for Consumer Defense
IE	industrial ecology
IEAT	Estate Authority of Thailand
IOA	Input–Output Analysis
IS	industrial symbiosis
ISF	Institute for Sustainable Futures
LCA	life-cycle analysis
MFA	material flow analysis
MITI	Ministry of International Trade and Industry
NEP	New Ecological Paradigm
NEPP	National Environmental Policy Plan
NGO	non-governmental organization
NISP	National Industrial Symbiosis Programme
OECD	Organization of Economic Cooperation and Development
PRIDCO	Puerto Rico Industrial Development Company
PRIME	Private enterprises Involvement in the Management of Environment
PRIOS	Puerto Rico: an Island of Sustainability
PRMA	Puerto Rico Manufacturers' Association
QFD	Quality Function Development
RGS	Rio Grande do Sul

SAA	Structural Agent Analysis
SET	Sciences, Engineering and Technology
SETAC	Society of Environmental Toxicology and Chemistry
SMEs	small and medium-sized enterprises
SNA	social network analysis
STS	Science and Technology Studies
TBL	triple bottom line
TEP	techno-economic paradigm
TWG	Technical Working Group
UNDP	United Nations Development Program
WISP	West Midlands Industrial Symbiosis

Preface

We like prefaces to be short. The message is in the book, and as writing the preface is usually the last task to be completed, it tends to lead into reflections on this message that we think are better left to the reader. Maybe it suffices to state that we see this book as a starting point rather than a finish line. After finding a mutual interest in communicating the relevance of the social sciences to members of the industrial ecology field, we invited people whose work we appreciated to contribute to an edited volume. These people became the authors of the book. We were sensitive to the difficulties of communicating the social science perspective to the many industrial ecologists who have a science or engineering background. For this reason, we invited a number of people to act as 'intermezzo' authors. We see these authors as central to one of our goals which is to initiate a dialogue that we hope others will take up and continue. Of course, a book is no substitute for face to face interaction among people with different disciplinary backgrounds. So we hope the book will, in one way or the other, provide the incentive for readers to engage in such interactions in other fora.

A book is also a physical product: text needs to be edited, formatted to certain standards, and then converted into a physical object. We thank Scott Martin and Simon Sanchez, our student assistants at the University of Oregon, USA, for their help in this process. We also thank Alan Sturmer and colleagues at Edward Elgar for enabling this conversion process and supporting this project from its inception. Finally, we greatly appreciate the work of all our authors, and their sharing of their research, ideas and, in some cases, personal journeys with us so that this book can capture a diversity of ideas and reflect critically on our collective work on industrial ecology.

Frank Boons
Jennifer Howard-Grenville

PART I

An outline of the social science potential

1. Introducing the social embeddedness of industrial ecology

Frank Boons and Jennifer Howard-Grenville

In the last 15 years, industrial ecology has proven to be a powerful label for scientists, policymakers and practitioners to develop new perspectives on and ways of dealing with the ecological consequences of industrial activities. Scientists from various disciplines, including the natural and technical sciences as well as social and management sciences, have been inspired by the label. While from its inception industrial ecology has displayed a technological bias, its development, diffusion and application has implications that can fruitfully be studied from social science perspectives. Indeed, industrial ecology at its basis is a social construction (Cohen-Rosenthal 2000). However, social science contributions to the field are scattered throughout the literature, and only loosely connected with technical and natural science approaches. As with other attempts to combine insights from different disciplines, the industrial ecology field displays a tendency to develop islands of knowledge with infrequent visitors from other areas.

In this book, we focus on perspectives that address the social embeddedness of industrial ecology: the ways in which material and energy flows are shaped by the social context in which they occur. Our purpose is threefold. First, we bring together empirical work that explores this social context of industrial ecology. Much of this work can fruitfully offer insights into the complex interactions between individuals and organizations that have material and energy streams as their consequence. Major questions include: what is the social context in which material and energy flows are produced, how does this social context enable or constrain envisioned transformations in production and consumption, and, in more practical terms, what role do business, governmental, and other organizations play in developing industrial ecology approaches? The contributions in this book seek to demonstrate the conditions under which industrial ecology arrangements form, the mechanisms and processes by which they unfold, and their broader consequences in a social system. In general, such questions have received considerably less attention in the research literature than have questions surrounding the technological aspects of industrial ecology.

A second key goal of the book is to inspire and develop the dialogue in the field between academics and researchers with different disciplinary backgrounds. Through a number of intermezzo chapters, authoritative researchers with a background in natural Sciences, Engineering and Technology (SET) comment on selections of chapters and offer their views on how the approaches outlined in the chapters can contribute to the developing field. They also observe gaps in the research and push authors and others towards greater clarity in the project of interdisciplinary research.

Finally, our third goal is to offer suggestions and direction for scholars who seek to build on our understanding of industrial ecology through social science and, ideally, interdisciplinary approaches. The two final chapters (10 and 11) explore challenges to and opportunities for such approaches.

This chapter begins with a sketch of the development of the field, including, critically, the definition of its subject matter. We describe the development of this body of knowledge as an emerging social field, with all the consequences of diversity in motives, impact of communication structures, and the development of idiosyncratic language, norms and values. Section 2 defines the core concept of social embeddedness, which we use as an organizing framework for social science contributions to industrial ecology. Section 3 develops the argument for the second goal of the book: that of dialogue between social and other scientific disciplines. The chapter closes with an overview of the remaining chapters.

1.   DEVELOPMENT OF THE FIELD: DEFINING INDUSTRIAL ECOLOGY

In defining a concept, different routes can be taken. One is to logically develop a definition by establishing relationships with other concepts. In the case of industrial ecology, these concepts would include material and energy flows, ecological impact, symbiosis, industrial metabolism, industrial food webs and eco-industrial parks. A different route starts from the recognition that the concept of industrial ecology has been constructed by human beings, and is used to study certain human activities in relation to their natural environment. This leads to a genealogy of the concept as it is currently used, and includes a description of the groups of individuals that use the label to describe their activities. This translates roughly into a 'sociology of knowledge' approach. In this chapter we will take the second route. This has the added value of providing a first glimpse of a sociological perspective in action. A core concept in sociology is that of institutionalization, the process through which a set of norms, values and routines becomes established among a group of social actors. The emergence of industrial ecology as a field can be regarded as an institutionalization process (Ehrenfeld 2002, 2004; Cohen and Howard 2006).

A genealogy starts in the present, so we need a description of core elements of the industrial ecology concept as they are currently acknowledged by members of the field as well as outsiders. These core elements can be derived from influential definitions in the field (White 1994; Graedel and Allenby 1995; Lifset and Graedel 2002). Core elements include:

- the analysis of material and energy flows that result from human activities in industrial societies;
- the metaphor of a natural ecosystem as a basis for the normative goal of closing material cycles related to economic activities, and thus contributing to sustainability/decreasing ecological impact;
- the use of somewhat standardized tools such as Life Cycle Analysis, Materials Flow Analysis, and Design for Environment to measure and compare environmental impact; and,
- a systems perspective, with implicit or explicit consideration of geographical or other boundaries in assessing systemic flows and impacts.

It is the combination of these elements that distinguishes the label of industrial ecology from other approaches to the ecological impact of economic activities. In order to adequately describe the impact of industrial activities on the natural environment, the label communicates the message that we need to look at patterns of relationships that exist between economic actors, rather than focus on individual firms. The normative insight is that it is desirable that patterns of industrial activity are changed such that material and energy loops are closed. This derives from an analogy with natural ecologies, and an understanding of their metabolisms as representative of closed material cycles. Although this is a problematic position to start with (Boons and Baas 1997; Isenman 2002; Wells 2006), this metaphor has been important in communicating and diffusing the industrial ecology label.

The genealogy of the industrial ecology label is complicated by the fact that there are partially overlapping labels such as industrial metabolism, industrial ecosystems and industrial symbiosis. We will look at the ways in which scientists have started to consider linkages in industrial activities in relation to ecological impact, and the usage of the metaphor of a natural ecology. For pragmatic reasons, at the end of this section we will provide the definitions that will be used throughout this book.

Antecedents to Industrial Ecology

Comparing society with nature is certainly not new. Around 1850, Thoreau wrote in his notebooks: 'In our workshops, . . . we pride ourselves on discovering a use for what had previously been regarded as waste, but how partial and accidental our economy compared with Nature's. In Nature, nothing is wasted' (cited in Worster 1977: 64–5). This analogy was used in the latter half of the nineteenth century by several authors to stress the possibilities of wastes as an input for production processes. However, at that time the economic possibilities seem to have been the sole focus; concerns over the ecological consequences of these waste streams were not taken into consideration (Boons 2008a). Related to this, several economists developed views on the ubiquitousness of firms seeking to put to use the by-products of their production processes (Kurz 1986, 2006).

In the same period, the concept of metabolism was used by the founding fathers of the social sciences (including Marx, Spencer and Comte) to address the relationship between material society and nature. Metabolism in that era referred to the exchange of energy and substances between organisms and the environment, and society was thought to conform to the definition of an organism (Fischer-Kowalski 2003: 37). The idea further evolved through work of ecological anthropologists that sought to understand the social organization and culture of specific populations as functional adaptations which permit populations to exploit their environments successfully without exceeding their carrying capacity (Orlove 1980: 240).

The concept of ecology was coined in 1866 by Ernst Haeckel (Worster 1977). Throughout the early years of its use, debates raged over whether human beings and their societies should be included in this new field of study. Eventually, the study of what came to be called human ecology developed in parallel to biological ecology, with many cross fertilizations. Human ecology actually is a collection of insights dispersed over the disciplines of social geography, anthropology and sociology (see Chapter 2).

The connection between the ideas of nature's economy, societal metabolism and human ecology on the one hand, and the ecological consequences of the development of modern society was only made in the early 1960s. Increasing public concern over ecological problems was fuelled by the work of scientists who provided mounting evidence of the substantial negative consequences of society for ecosystems. This coincided with the development of a systems approach in ecology as well as in other sciences, providing a stimulus to interdisciplinary work. Boulding's paper on the coming spaceship 'Earth' (1966), Ayres and Kneese's 1969 paper on 'Production, consumption, and externalities', and the report for the Club of Rome (Meadows et al. 1972) were the first efforts to develop ideas that we can consider to be at the heart of the subject matter of industrial ecology.

In *The Closing Circle*, Barry Commoner (1971) analysed the impending ecological crisis in terms that are remarkably similar to those of industrial ecology. However, it was Preston Cloud who first coined the term *industrial ecosystem* in a paper presented at the 1977 Annual Meeting of the German Geological Association. Based on the second law of thermodynamics and the work of Georgescu-Roegen, he aimed to show the inaccuracy of dominant economic view of industrial production. In many ways, in the paper he formulated ideas that would later form the core of the concept of sustainable development, including the need to consider impacts on future generations.

The industrial ecology label was used in other academic and policy settings. In Japan, the term industrial ecology was used in a Ministry of International Trade and Industry (MITI) program to decrease dependency of the national economy on materials in the early 1970s (Watanabe 2002). Around the same period, Belgian scientists also used the label in their analysis of the material flows of the Belgian economy (Billen et al. 1983).

Simultaneously, shifts were occurring in the field of sociology and related disciplines. In the 1970s and 1980s, scholars began to embrace new ways of representing and analysing social life. Key among these was attention to relational perspectives, which emphasized the presence and importance of interaction between individuals or organizations rather than the discrete characteristics of these entities. Social network analysis was central to this relational approach and has become highly influential in sociological and organizational studies. While some of the precursors to social network analysis are found as far back as the 1920s (e.g., the work of Georg Simmel), it was only in the 1970s that the conceptual and methodological groundwork was laid that allowed it to firmly enter the mainstream (Smith-Doerr and Powell 2005). The 1970s and 1980s saw a dramatic rise in network approaches following some key empirical studies. For example, Granovetter's (1973) work on how individuals found jobs in a period of economic recession revealed the 'strength of weak ties', or the importance of accessing non-redundant information from a variety of sources. Granovetter's work led to networks being seen as a 'third way' that avoided both undersocialized (individual, atomistic behaviour) and oversocialized (determined by culture and social structure) accounts of social action (Granovetter 1985). At the organizational level, networked forms of organization were posited as new organizational forms, distinct in their modes of operating from both markets and hierarchies. The biotech industry was found to epitomize this form, where innovation occurred through the collaboration of university researchers, small biotech companies and large pharmaceutical companies (Powell et al. 1996). While some work in industrial ecology draws directly on work in this relational tradition of economic sociology (for example, regional agglomeration and clustering), it is important to note that in the sociological literature at that time networks were rarely used to analyse ecological problems.

Related to this shift in the social sciences were two other developments. First, dynamic representations of processes as opposed to states became more common place. In organization studies this shift in emphasis from 'nouns to verbs' (Langley 2007: 275) can be summed up by Weick's call for understanding *organizing* as opposed to organizations (Weick 1969). The emphasis, at least among some scholars, moved to how things came to be, as opposed to how things 'are'. Social mechanisms through which both apparent stability and change were created and recreated over time began attracting more attention (Anderson et al. 2006). Second, scholars began to abandon concepts and methods that focused on understanding linear, simply causal processes and sought more complex descriptions of social life. This shift away from thinking in terms of a 'general linear reality' (Abbott 2001) and towards accepting other dynamics – shocks, jolts, oscillations around equilibrium, and accumulation of small effects to create large scale change – began to appear in the organizational literature, but only quite recently. Lessons from complexity theory became important as assumptions of equilibrium were dropped and the possibilities of small events leading to unpredictable but significant change were entertained and explored (Meyer et al. 2005; Plowman et al. 2007).

In sum, these developments each draw attention to the nesting of individual and organizational action within multiple levels of other social or temporal structures. Taken together, they imply that, for certain problems, it is neither possible nor helpful to view an organization's, group's, or individual's actions in isolation. Nor is it desirable to view actions as responses to static background 'contexts'. Rather, it is essential to take a multi-level view that scrutinizes influences on action that stem from other levels of analysis or other domains of action. In other words, a company's actions may well be influenced by the norms at play within its industry, or by the expectations of local communities. Furthermore, norms and expectations may take on distinct forms, and carry distinct sanctions, depending on the domain in which they are generated.

The Emergence of an Industrial Ecology Field

An institutionalized field emerges through the increased interaction of actors which can result in a distinct pattern of domination and coalition developing. Actors are confronted with an increase in information, establish communication channels and eventually develop a mutual awareness that they are involved in a common enterprise. Defined in this way, it is clear that the preceding ideas had not yet provided a basis for the development of a distinct field of industrial ecology. They were not subject to discussion by a distinct group of actors; instead, each of them emerged in more or less separate (sub)disciplines.

For the industrial ecology field, such interaction is generally thought to have been sparked by the publication of a paper by Robert Frosch and Nicholas Gallopoulos in the popular science journal *Scientific American* in 1989. Gallopoulos (2006) has later described in some detail how that paper developed; an interesting insight into the way in which ideas are constructed by humans. According to Erkman (1997), an article by Tibbs from 1992 played a similar catalytic role in the business community.

One of the first traceable increases of interaction around the concept was the establishment of a group of US scientists under the name of the Vishnu Group, who started to exchange ideas to further develop the concept (Wernick and Ausubel 1997).

Also, tools such as Life-Cycle Analysis (LCA) were developed and standardized in order to provide the information input for these studies (Heiskanen 2000). In Europe, the Society of Environmental Toxicology and Chemistry (SETAC) launched an effort to develop a standard for LCAs, fuelled by the increased demand from governments and firms to be able to assess the ecological impact of products throughout their life cycle. In the US, a Congressional Committee was assigned to develop the concept. Quickly, books began to be published which further developed the concept. A few years later, there was already an emerging field, as a special issue from the *Journal of Cleaner Production* in 1997 testifies. A milestone was reached in 1997 with the first issue of the *Journal of Industrial Ecology*, a dedicated journal for the new field.

Although intuitively intriguing, a concept such as industrial ecology needs real life examples in order to be communicated successfully. The evolution of collaboration between a number of companies in the Danish town of Kalundborg became such an icon. Although Kalundborg was introduced to the 'international environmental community' at the Rio Conference in 1992, this regional network had only been sporadically mentioned in the industrial ecology-related literature in the early 1990s. Indeed, according to Chertow (2000), it was only in the late 1980s that the firms in Kalundborg realized the environmental implications of the exchange relationships that had evolved among them since 1970. It is Gertler's (1995) study supervised by John Ehrenfeld that appears to have been extremely instrumental in the spreading of the Kalundborg story as a success story of industrial ecology:

> Kalundborg, Denmark is home to a system of arrangements by which four large industries and a town share material and energy resources and reuse waste materials. Industrial symbiosis, as this practice has come to be called, has significantly reduced the environmental impact of industry in the area while decreasing its need for energy and raw materials. Although it was not explicitly intended as such, this beneficial arrangement forms the most highly developed implementation of the industrial ecosystem concept to be found anywhere in the world. As a result Kalundborg has become the prototype for the application of industrial ecology. (Gertler 1995, p. 23)

Gertler continues by describing the concept of symbiosis, the symbiosis results and linkages, and the requirements in more detail. These requirements include that the industries fit together, are geographically close, and that the 'mental distance' between the participants is short. He also highlights the cultural and regulatory pressures encouraging companies to embark on such an endeavour. Gertler's study, and the related article that appeared in the first issue of the *Journal of Industrial Ecology* (Ehrenfeld and Gertler 1997), also elaborate on the label industrial symbiosis for such a pattern of exchanges. In fact, it was the wife of one of the managers at Kalundborg who coined this term in 1989 for the linkages that had been established.

Kalundborg was also important in conveying the idea of the possibility of a geographically bounded type of industrial ecology (Boons and Baas 1997). This proved to be attractive for scientists and governments in several countries. In the US, the President's Council on Sustainable Development (1994) and EPA developed the related idea of eco-industrial parks. In Canada, researchers from Dalhousie University made a development handbook (Coté et al. 1994). In The Netherlands, a national government program was initiated to stimulate the development of 'sustainable business parks' (Boons and Janssen 2004).

The Kalundborg case, as it was immortalized by Gertler and Ehrenfeld, has been important not only in providing a stimulating success story, but also in highlighting the fact that the linkages promoted by industrial ecologists require human decisions to be actually implemented. Up until then, this 'human side' of the field had received only scant attention.

Although social scientists have contributed to the field from its early years, in 2000 Ed Cohen-Rosenthal could still legitimately plead for more attention to the social side of the field. He pointed out that increased information on possible linkages between industrial processes does not necessarily mean that they will be established (Cohen-Rosenthal 2000). Industrial systems do not self-organize automatically in such a way that loops are closed; it requires decisions made by policymakers and managers that need to overcome existing organizational structures and ingrained ways of perceiving the world. The research presented in this book shows that, since 2000, these themes have become more established in the field.

The field further institutionalized with the establishment of the *International Society for Industrial Ecology* in 2001. A second dedicated peer-reviewed journal, *Progress in Industrial Ecology*, was launched in 2004. These institutions help the members of the field to further develop linkages, ideas and research projects. A further indication of the maturation of the field is the publication of articles in non-dedicated journals which explicitly state that they originate from a field called industrial ecology (that is, Gibbs 2003; Hoffman 2003; Boons 2008b).

Criticism and Disputes

We can thus conclude that, at least as a scientific field, industrial ecology has become institutionalized. Although this requires some consensus on core concepts, approaches and results, it does not preclude debate and disputes. In an initial phase, these serve as mechanisms through which the field can establish itself; later on they function as necessary vehicles for development and innovation. We briefly describe three major debates that are still relevant today.

In the early phase, there has been some criticism of inherent flaws of the concept of industrial ecology. Commoner argued that industrial ecology has 'a strong tendency to trivialize the problem [of ecological impact of industrial activities] by emphasizing small, internal components of the industrial system rather than its larger, more basic interactions with the environment' (1997: 125). There is ample evidence that industrial production, and the way it has developed after the Second World War has resulted in severe impact on ecological systems. The incompatibility of current industrial activities with natural ecosystems is such that a fundamental restructuring, involving national industrial policy, is deemed necessary by Commoner. A similar criticism is voiced by Oldenburg and Geiser (1997), who state that industrial ecology can imply improvement of local efficiencies which at the same time obstruct preventative efforts that are more important. Commoner also addresses the technological focus of industrial ecology, and argues that it is necessary to consider the governance of the basic design of major systems of production, that is, the market mechanism and decision-making routines within governments and corporations. We will return to this important issue in the final chapter.

A second recurring theme is that of the desirability of an 'objective' industrial ecology. Ehrenfeld observes that the field of industrial ecology has two distinctive shapes: one is descriptive and analytical, seeking to understand the material and energy flows in industrial societies (2000). The other is normative and metaphorical, aiming at changing existing practices. As one of us has argued elsewhere (in collaboration with Nigel Roome), this distinction is too rigid. The 'objectivity' desired by some (see Allenby 1999) is itself a normative position; it refers to a set of norms about what constitutes accepted scientific practice. Moreover, the metaphor on which the field is based is evoked because of its alleged exemplarity in closing loops. If this crucial element of the metaphor is left aside, there seems little reason to use the label industrial ecology at all for the study of material and energy flows (Boons and Roome 2000). Nevertheless, the discussion concerning the 'objectivity' of the field continues to be relevant, which can be viewed as a valuable asset because it keeps industrial ecologists sensitive to the way in which they adhere to more general norms about what constitutes good research.

A third theme touches upon one of the founding elements of the field; the idea of using natural ecologies as a metaphor for industrial systems. As will be shown in Chapter 2, several social scientists have turned to ecology to borrow concepts to enrich their study of societies, networks of organizations, and industrial systems. Over the years, several members of the industrial ecology field have reflected on the extent to which the application of ecological concepts is useful, or should be improved (Bey 2001; Johansson 2002; Isenmann 2003; Ayres 2004). This goes to the heart of the validity of metaphoric reasoning. A metaphor is useful in two ways. By applying ecological concepts to industrial systems, the observer is led to new observations about such systems that she otherwise would not make. At the same time, the metaphor never fits completely. This 'boundary' of the metaphor is insightful because it leads the observer to reflect on the specific way in which the industrial system differs from natural ecologies. The result of the thoughtful application of a metaphor thus can have valuable heuristic results.

A Definition of Industrial Ecology

Debate and variation in perspectives and methods are normal characteristics of a developing scientific field. Nevertheless, for reasons of clarity, we need to provide some definitions that will be used throughout this book. We define industrial ecology in the following way:

Industrial ecology is the study of the material and energy flows resulting from human activities. This study provides the basis for developing approaches to close cycles in such a way that ecological impact of these activities is minimized.

We distinguish between two lines of research in this book. Under the label of regional approaches, we will group the analysis of industrial ecologies that are geographically bounded networks of social actors. Under the label of product chain approaches, we group analysis of industrial ecologies that deal with human activities related to a (set of) product(s) throughout their material life cycle.

Although inherently a social construction, industrial ecology has been developed almost exclusively from arguments with a technological and scientific emphasis. The theoretical and practical closing of material streams has gained considerably more attention than the role of social processes (including economic perspectives; see Van den Bergh and Janssen 2004) in shaping possibilities and constraints. As Cohen-Rosenthal suggests, the main rationale for most scientists involved can be construed as (implicitly) that associated with a neo-classical economic point of view. That is, the view that acquiring information will lead to its application, and that governments should change incentive structures to direct actors in markets to establish linkages between industrial processes. The social science based research that is available shows clearly that this is an untenable position. The actions of individuals and organizations that create energy and material flows can only be understood by taking into account the social context in which they operate, and government policy and/or a free market mechanism are only aspects of such a context. In the next section, we propose to use the concept of social embeddedness to develop a systematic frame of reference for ordering the various aspects of this broader social context.

2. THE SOCIAL EMBEDDEDNESS OF INDUSTRIAL ECOLOGY

In our view, at the core of industrial ecology is its focus on energy and material flows in industrial processes. For a social scientist, the immediate question is: how are these flows shaped through human interaction? This basic question can then be refined and elaborated upon using a large variety of theories that characterize the social sciences in general. In developing this book, we took the position that it would be most useful to allow for this diversity and see it as a strength, rather than discuss it in terms of a weakness, or draw comparisons among competing theoretical perspectives. For this reason, we did not propose a specific theoretical framework to guide the authors in writing their chapters. Instead, we use the meta-theoretical concept of 'social embeddedness' to frame the diversity that can be found in social science approaches to industrial ecology.

The term embeddedness was introduced by Polanyi (1944) but has come into increasingly popular use in the social sciences since the publication of Granovetter's (1985) classic article linking economic activity with the structure of social relations. Since then, scholars in the fields of sociology, organizational theory, political science, anthropology and even psychology have used embeddedness to refer to the contextualization of economic and organizational activity in broader social arrangements and processes. Importantly, embeddedness is multi-level (Dacin et al. 1999; Hagedoorn 2006). This means that one may regard individual managers and decision makers as embedded in networks of information, friendship, and trust relations, yet, at the same time the companies to which they belong are embedded in legal, regulatory and political regimes. Each of these shape action by affording certain opportunities and constraints.

While much of the literature on embeddedness focuses on the embeddedness of economic and market exchange, we take a somewhat broader view, consistent with others who seek to counter explanations for organizational action that are grounded in assumptions of rationality, efficiency and intentionality (Marsden 1981; Dacin et al. 1999). Embeddedness in this sense accounts for the contextualization of organizational activity more broadly, and it also draws attention to how social structures and processes enable, rather than simply constrain, particular activities (Powell 1996; Dacin et al. 1999). We include in our use of the term embeddedness not only the contextualization of organizations' activities in social processes, but also the contextualization of decisions about material and energy flows and technical processes. Relating this to industrial ecology, each of the mechanisms described below contribute to an explanation of the ways in which energy and material flows come into existence, are reinforced, or may be redirected. Viewed in this way, the social embeddedness of industrial ecology is at the heart of the field, both in terms of analysis and in terms of the possibilities for changing these flows (that is, closing loops).

Six Mechanisms of Embeddedness

Zukin and DiMaggio use the term embeddedness to 'refer to the contingent nature of economic action with respect to cognition, culture, social structure and political institutions' (1990: 15). To these mechanisms we add two more that are particularly important to industrial ecology: spatial and temporal, resulting in six dimensions of the social context of economic activities. These dimensions can be meaningfully applied to the field of industrial ecology (Baas and Boons 2006).

Cognitive embeddedness

This form of embeddedness refers to the limits on individuals' mental processes that arise from decision making under conditions of uncertainty, complexity and limited information (Zukin and DiMaggio 1990). Building on findings from cognitive psychology and decision theory, cognitive embeddedness resembles the concept of 'bounded rationality' which has been used to explain limits to rational action within organizations. Individuals use a number of heuristics to make day-to-day decisions and rely on other shortcuts when the information requirements or cognitive capacity to make fully 'rational' decisions would be overwhelming. Patterns of habitual action result and people no longer question – even if they have the ability and information to do so – certain causal relationships deeply.

The idea of cognitive embeddedness – if not the term itself – arises in some of the research so far on sustainability, environmental management and industrial ecology. On the most basic level, changes in how material flows, waste, and energy are conceptualized forces in some cases revision of ideas about what constitutes waste itself and asks individuals to bring to the foreground activities that may have long receded into the background and become habitual organizational activities (for example, energy provision, wastewater treatment). In the research literature, recent work demonstrates the difficulties that individuals have in making decisions around complex environmental problems whether these are considered 'new' or not. For example, Wade-Benzoni finds that people have difficulty making decisions about the allocation of resources as a result of cognitive limits in performing inter-generational discounting (Wade-Benzoni 2002). Others have argued that individuals and their problem-solving strategies are ill-suited to conceptualizing and addressing systemic problems, such as those associated with sustainability (Roome and Sweet 2002). Particular tools used by individuals and organizations also reinforce and perhaps blind their users to cognitive biases. Several scholars have critiqued life-cycle analysis (LCA) tools for their implicit assumptions of rationality and their limitations when users have different value interpretations and cognitive frames for using the tools (Bengtsson 2000; Heiskanen 2000a).

Cultural embeddedness

Cultural embeddedness captures the influence of collective understandings and shared norms on economic and organizational behavior (Zukin and DiMaggio 1990). It operates at a collective, rather than individual, level and is thus distinct from cognitive embeddedness. Cultural understandings may be shared at a national level, regional level or on smaller scales, but they help to define what is legitimate and valued within a certain sector of economic, organizational and social activity. For example, consumer preferences are highly influenced by culture, as are norms for what comprises socially acceptable business operation. Cultural norms of course interact with legal and regulatory norms, and also over time tend to influence individual's cognitive biases. For these reasons, the influence of cultural embeddedness is most fruitfully seen in comparative studies (between regions or nations with different cultures), or through longitudinal studies that probe either long-term changes or dramatic events that shift cultural norms (Zukin and DiMaggio 1990).

The idea of cultural embeddedness is particularly important as industrial ecology has become increasingly concerned with addressing aspects of the consumption, not simply production, of goods (Hertwich 2005). Sociological work on consumption locates it in a cultural frame, but stops short of critiquing or problematizing the cultural embeddedness of consumption (Zukin and Maguire 2004). The relationship between consumers, company's marketing activities, and corporate social responsibility has also been explored (Bhattacharya and Sen 2003; Drumwright 1994). Clearly, cultural influences are significant when conceptualizing alternative arrangements that could radically alter the environmental impacts of products and their production. Some recent work explores the relationship between cultural values and ethical or fair trade practices, pointing out that cultural values can constrain the introduction of potentially valuable practices (Blowfield 2003) but also that new practices can infuse new norms into traditional production arrangements (Raynolds 2002). These different analyses remind us that culture, often seen as a constraint, is somewhat dynamic and mutable and can be regarded as a mechanism for certain types of change.

Structural embeddedness

This form of embeddedness is closest to Granovetter's early use of the term, and refers to 'the contextualization of economic exchange in patterns of ongoing interpersonal relations' (Zukin and DiMaggio 1990: 18). Here the structure of social interactions between actors shapes whether and how information and influence flow, and ultimately shapes economic and other forms of exchange. Actors in this case can be either individuals or organizations, or some combination of the two. Giving rise to the now significant attention to social network analysis by economic sociologists and organizational theorists (Smith-Doerr and Powell 2005), this form of embeddedness was also regarded by Zukin and DiMaggio (1990) as more important than the cognitive and cultural forms. Structural embeddedness is appealing partly because it enables the mapping and quantitative analysis (using social network analysis methods) of interactions between actors. The density of interactions within a network of actors, their concentration around a certain actor or set of actors, and changes in these over time, can tell a great deal about how influence is exercised and who is central to information and other forms of exchange. However, attention to structural embeddedness alone can miss important dimensions of the social processes at work. For example, the content of the interactions is often far more important than the existence of an interaction between parties, but this is rarely captured in empirical studies (Smith-Doerr and Powell 2005; Kilduff et al. 2006). The direction and reciprocity of interactions can also be critical. Some of these factors can be influenced strongly by cognitive, cultural or political embeddedness which may be less easily represented in a model.

Despite these potential shortcomings, the concept of structural embeddedness and its associated techniques of social network analysis have been extensively used and are increasingly entering literature on industrial ecology and environmental management more broadly. For example, Ashton (2008) uses social network analysis to quantify and analyse patterns of relationships associated with industrial symbiosis in the Barceloneta industrial park in Puerto Rico. Many others have used the idea of networks as a conceptual or analytical tool to discuss the development of industrial ecology and draw attention to learning and change (or the lack of it) through networks (Jacobsen and Anderberg 2004; Malmborg 2004; Boons 1998; Baas and Boons 2004; Howard-Grenville and Paquin 2008).

Political embeddedness
Zukin and DiMaggio (1990: 20) refer to political embeddedness as 'the manner in which economic institutions and decisions are shaped by a struggle for power that involves economic actors and nonmarket institutions, particularly the state and social classes'. By pitting market actors against political actors this definition reflects a certain view of power that is perhaps more appropriate for broad policy questions (for example, around the nature of patent law) and less useful for other aspects of industrial ecology. However, this definition reminds us that a plethora of other actors – apart from businesses and their managers – have significant influence over corporate practices. Regional development agencies, advocacy organizations, communities, labour unions, and others can all shape how companies and industries act. Furthermore, power is distributed unevenly at both macro levels (states) and micro levels (individuals) which has a strong influence on how other forms of embeddedness actually 'play out' in practice. For example, regulatory and legal norms

are constructed, negotiated and enacted through the interplay of organizational and governmental actions, with companies themselves creating norms of compliance rather than simply accepting them (Edelman et al. 1999; Gunningham et al. 2003).

The policy aspects of political embeddedness have been treated in the literatures on environmental management and industrial ecology. Often these papers consider how a particular policy shapes organizational action or suggest how policy might be developed or implemented at the municipal, regional or national level to influence corporate environmental activities (for example Burstroem and Korhonen 2001.) Other work considers how nongovernmental organizations have influenced companies' actions.

Spatial and temporal embeddedness

Relatively neglected in the work on embeddedness (Dacin et al. 1999), spatial and temporal considerations are particularly important to industrial ecology because every product or process is connected in some way to physical material flows (be they of material, energy, other resources, or all of these). These dimensions draw attention to the ways in which geographical proximity and time influence interaction. The dimensions of space and time are implicit in many accounts of industrial ecology, yet we believe they deserve explicit treatment. Physical proximity has been identified as a crucial catalysing factor in, for instance, the occurrence of complex forms of learning and the building of trust. Time is important as the evolution of industrial systems typically involves long time periods. Furthermore, time also matters because it is the 'measure' by which we see accumulations in other dimensions of embeddedness. For example, repeated interactions over time can be associated with growing trust and learning.

Interesting questions that bring in the spatial and/or temporal dimensions of industrial ecology include: What are the appropriate boundaries for analysis and implementation of material or energy loop closing efforts? How does physical proximity enter into global production and consumption chains? Can these be viewed as interconnected regional systems? How are we to make sense of and alter the inherent dynamics of institutionalization in the development of industrial systems over time? As we return to in the final chapter, the spatial and temporal embeddedness of industrial ecology remains poorly understood and offers great opportunity for further study.

Linking Dimensions of Embeddedness

The dimensions of embeddedness as described above serve to introduce the scope of social science contributions to the field of industrial ecology. But it is possible to take things a step further by exploring how the different dimensions of embeddedness interact and with what consequences (Zukin and DiMaggio 1990; Dacin et al. 1999). To do this, one has to move beyond a concern with the broad *mechanisms* of embeddedness and consider the *outcomes* of embeddedness and how these outcomes shape the choices/*options* available to actors (individuals or firms) (Dacin et al. 1999).

In order to fully understand the influence of embeddedness on organizational actions and decisions related to industrial ecology, one must treat the forms of embeddedness outlined above as operating simultaneously, though not with equal strength and salience in all cases. The intensity of embeddedness can differ between actors and situations, and the interaction across the levels of embeddedness take on different forms (Dacin et al. 1999). Ultimately, the influence of the embeddedness of particular organizations in particular contexts must be explored with attention to a particular outcome of interest. For example, one recent paper develops theoretical hypotheses around the influence of different levels of embeddedness (dyadic, interorganizational and environmental) on the particular issue of interfirm partnership formation (Hagedoorn 2006). Similarly, such influences could be explored for the development of industrial symbiosis arrangements. However, the types of embeddedness and their relative influence might be quite different when exploring questions of consumption of products.

3. INTERDISCIPLINARITY: BUILDING BRIDGES THROUGH DIALOGUE

Industrial ecology is an interdisciplinary field due to its connection of the analysis of material and energy flows with the analysis of the ways in which such flows are generated by social actors in industrial societies, and in its attempts to provide insight into the ways in which such flows can be changed to minimize impact on natural ecosystems (Ehrenfeld 2004; Fischer-Kowalski 2003; Howard and Cohen 2006). Although the exploration of social embeddedness is the core matter of this book, we see it as vital that these insights are connected to work from scientists with other disciplinary backgrounds.

Interdisciplinary fields have their own problems. Despite the fact that members share a common object of study, they use different languages and cognitive maps to study it. Rather than discussing the consequences of interdisciplinarity in abstract terms, we simply note that industrial ecologists will benefit from a better understanding of the respective cognitive maps that their colleagues bring to the field. As Flood (1999) has noted, a systemic perspective requires prismatic thought; the bringing together of different perspectives.

In this book, we have chosen to facilitate such understanding through including *intermezzos*; short contributions in which members from the field with a Science, Engineering and Technology (SET) background reflect on a set of chapters written by social scientists. We hope these intermezzos contribute to the emergence of a dialogue among industrial ecologists with different disciplinary backgrounds. The essence of dialogue is the uncovering of assumptions and deeper layers of thought. As these assumptions are shaped throughout a person's career, we have asked the authors of the intermezzos to tell us something about their personal paths. The essence of dialogue is not to criticize or defend positions; the purpose is for the participants to search within themselves for their assumptions, and to try to empathize with the uncovered assumptions and cognitive maps of others.

4.   OUTLINE OF THE BOOK

The operation, interaction and outcomes of social embeddedness and its influence on industrial ecology can be uncovered by asking empirical questions. The mechanisms of embeddedness can be used as sensitizing instruments and understood theoretically, but ultimately any consideration of embeddedness must engage with what is happening 'on the ground' within a social system. Accordingly, the chapters in this volume largely explore particular empirical settings, focusing on what is most salient in these settings to probe forms of embeddedness that seem to be at play.

Prior to the empirical chapters and the intermezzo commentaries on them, we continue this introductory section with two chapters that aim to orient the reader to the potential value of social science approaches to industrial ecology. In Chapter 2, Frank Boons reviews various ways in which social scientists have related to the study of ecology. He categorizes work at the intersection of ecology and social science in three ways: (a) social theories that use ecological metaphors; (b) theories that consider social and ecological systems as separate entities and examine their interactions; and (c) theories that consider nature and ecology as socially constructed. Boons concludes the chapter by pointing to implications of studying industrial ecology through each of these three lenses. In Chapter 3, Henrikke Baumann shares her reflections on the reality and challenges of doing research that crosses disciplinary boundaries. In this provocative essay, she explores and contrasts how engineers/natural scientists and social scientists approach cross-disciplinary work, and concludes with some suggestions for facilitating such work. Based on her own experience, Baumann suggests that performing cross-disciplinary work is less about the optimistic image of 'breaking down barriers' to shared understanding, and more about 'crossing fences' between domains of understanding, and mastering the language of multiple fields. The first intermezzo, written by Frank Boons, follows Chapter 3 and introduces the idea of dialogue that informs the intention of the other intermezzos.

The next two parts of the book explore broad themes within the industrial ecology literature: Regional Approaches, and Product Chain Approaches. In each part, three empirical chapters present research results and offer interpretations that draw attention to the social embeddedness of the industrial ecology phenomena explored. Following the empirical chapters, two separate authors comment in intermezzos on the value of such approaches, drawing on their own experience in the field, and raise larger questions.

The empirical chapters in the Regional Approaches part (Chapters 4, 5 and 6) all look at geographically-bounded settings where industrial ecology principles are either intentionally being applied or have been observed operating. In Chapter 4, David Gibbs explores eco-industrial parks and asks whether they might serve as 'strategic niches' from which innovation and disruption of established technological regimes may originate. Drawing on the field of Science and Technology Studies (STS), he concludes that industrial ecology principles, as instantiated in existing eco-industrial parks, provide only a partial solution to overcoming established technological regimes. Chapters 5 and 6 focus on industrial symbiosis as opposed to eco-industrial parks, but similarly observe that progress is complicated by the larger social forces at play. In Chapter 5, Raymond Paquin and Jennifer Howard-Grenville use a sociological lens and the method of social network analysis to look at the evolution over time of industrial symbiosis in one region of the UK. They find that a facilitating body, the National Industrial Symbiosis Programme (NISP) was critical in enabling significant and rapid growth in industrial symbiosis activities over the course of only a few years. However, the nature of the industrial symbiosis changed somewhat over time as the facilitating body and others responded to broader political and economic incentives. Finally, in Chapter 6, Marian Chertow and Weslynne Ashton compare the development, or lack of development, of industrial symbiosis within a number of industrialized regions on the island of Puerto Rico. Through interviews with numerous firm members in four industrial parks, researchers mapped material and energy flows, learned about inter-firm synergies and identified other sources of business or social exchange (for example local business associations). In contrast to two other industrialized areas that displayed significant material and resource interchanges, Chertow and Ashton found low levels of synergies of any type in the four parks studied, and attributed this to a lack of communication and inter-personal ties within these parks. Their findings suggest that inter-personal communication may be particularly important to the development of industrial symbiosis among geographically co-located firms; without communication, information flow and motivation for collaboration are severely hindered.

Anthony Chiu and Cynthia Mitchell each comment in intermezzos following the Regional Approaches part on some common themes across the chapters. They also bring their perspectives – Chiu's as a practitioner involved in a number of industrial ecology efforts in the Asia Pacific region and Mitchell's as an academic who knows well the challenges and rewards of interdisciplinary and applied research – to bear to outline further challenges and questions around the use of social science methods to inform work on industrial ecology.

The empirical chapters in the Product Chain Approaches part continue and expand on the idea that industrial ecology researchers and practitioners must engage with a 'messy reality' in order to appropriately apply traditional tools like Life Cycle Assessment. In Chapter 7, Hall and Matos explore how complex scientific and technological decisions get made when a variety of social and political stakeholders are involved. Exploring the case of transgenic crops in Brazil, they draw on organizational theory to argue that 'satisfactory' rather than 'optimal' solutions, often driven by analogical reasoning, may be the most appropriate in highly ambiguous situations. Koponen echoes this cautionary stance in Chapter 8 where he reminds us of the reductionist traps of mathematical optimization as a key tool for economic theory. Instead, Koponen argues for a 'commodity chain' approach to understanding production and markets, and illustrates the power of such an approach by following and contrasting the production of maize/corn in Zimbabwe and the US. A variant on the sociological approach of actor network theory, commodity chains draw attention to the actors, their values and interests, and how these are expressed (or not) as the commodity itself moves between them. In Chapter 9, Seuring, Morana and Liu introduce key models from the sustainable supply chain management literature and identify where and how they relate to industrial ecology. They find that two seemingly opposing strategies used by firms to manage their supply chains (namely, greening the process of supply by monitoring suppliers, or recrafting supply chains to develop new material sources and green products) can nonetheless be regarded as complementary. Doing so brings attention to the multiple pressures for and barriers to change that come from within supply arrangements and external stakeholders. Taken together, these chapters offer not only a critique of 'industrial ecology as usual' but also demonstrate some ways that might better integrate social concerns into the analysis of product chains.

Two intermezzos, written by Claudia Binder and Bart van Hoof, comment on the Product Chain chapters. Claudia Binder frames her comments in terms of three ways in which she feels social scientists can contribute to industrial ecology: increasing system understanding, reducing uncertainty and providing knowledge on processes of management and transformation. She also proposes an interesting link between regional and product chain approaches. Trained as an engineer, Bart van Hoof provides an insiders' account of the value of social science insights in working with small and medium sized firms. Drawing on his work in Latin America he is also able to shed light on the importance of being sensitive to cultural differences.

Finally, the last section of the book includes an invited chapter by John Ehrenfeld which reflects on the development of the field of industrial ecology and confronts some of the problems it has faced as a developing interdisciplinary field. These include the role of industrial ecology as a science, a set of problem-solving practices, and as a normative frame. Ehrenfeld offers some observations on the development of dialogue within the field, its importance and its limitations. The final chapter by editors Jennifer Howard-Grenville and Frank Boons summarizes at a high level some key themes raised in the empirical chapters and what they reveal about the social embeddedness of industrial ecology. This chapter also reflects on insights from the intermezzos and other reflections (Chapters 3 and 11) and offers some directions for future research and practice.

REFERENCES

Abbott, A. (2001), *Time Matters*, Chicago: University of Chicago Press.

Allenby, B. (1999), 'Culture and industrial ecology', *Journal of Industrial Ecology*, **3**(1): 2–4.

Anderson, P., R. Blatt, M. Christianson, A. Grant, C. Marquis, E. Neuman, S. Sonenshein and K. Sutcliffe (2006), 'Understanding mechanisms in organizational research: Reflections from a collective journey', *Journal of Management Inquiry*, **15**(2): 102–13.

Ashton, W. (2008), 'Understanding the organization of industrial ecosystems: A social network approach', *Journal of Industrial Ecology*, **12**(1): 34–51.

Ayres, R. (2004), 'On the life cycle metaphor: where ecology and economics diverge', *Ecological Economics*, **48**(4): 425–38.

Ayres, R. and A. Kneese (1969), 'Production, consumption, and externalities', *The American Economic Review*, **59**(3): 282–97.

Baas, L.W. and F.A.A. Boons (2004), 'An industrial ecology project in practice:

exploring the boundaries of decision-making levels in regional industrial systems', *Journal of Cleaner Production*, **12**(8), 1073–85.

Bey, (2001), 'Quo vadis industrial ecology? Realigning the discipline with its roots', *Greener Management International*, **34**: 35–42.

Bhattacharya, C.B. and S. Sen (2003), 'Consumer–company identification: a framework for understanding consumer's relationships with companies', *Journal of Marketing*, **67**(2), 76–88.

Billen, G., F. Toussaint, P. Peeters, M. Sapir, A. Steenhout and J. Vanderborght (1983), *L'Écosystème Belgique: Essai d'Écologie Industrielle*, Brussels: Centre de Recherche et d'Information Socio-politique.

Blowfield, M. (2003), 'Ethical supply chains in the cocoa, coffee and tea industries', *Greener Management International*, **43**: 15–24.

Boons, F.A. (1998), 'Caught in the web: the dual nature of networks and its consequences', *Business Strategy and the Environment*, **7**(4): 204–12.

Boons, F. (2008a), 'History's lesson. A critical assessment of the Desrochers' papers', *Journal of Industrial Ecology*, **12**(2): 148–58.

Boons, F. (2008b), 'Self-organization and sustainability: The emergence of a regional industrial ecology', *Emergence: Complexity and Organization* **10**(2).

Boons, F. and L. Baas (1997), 'Industrial ecology: The problem of coordination', *Journal of Cleaner Production*, **5**(1–2): 79–86.

Boons, F. and M. Janssen (2004), 'The myth of Kalundborg: social dilemmas in stimulating eco-industrial parks', in J. Van den Bergh and M. Janssen (eds), *Economics of Industrial Ecology*, Cambridge, MA: MIT Press, pp. 337–55.

Boons, F. and N. Roome (2000), 'Industrial ecology as a cultural phenomenon: on objectivity as a normative position', *Journal of Industrial Ecology*, **4**(2), 49–54.

Boulding, K. (1966), 'The economics of the coming spaceship Earth', in K. Boulding and H. Jarret (eds), *Environmental Quality in a Growing Economy*, Baltimore: The Johns Hopkins Press.

Burström, F. and J. Korhonen (2001), 'Municipalities and industrial ecology: reconsidering municipal environmental management', *Sustainable Development* **9**(1): 36–46.

Chertow, M. (2000), 'Industrial symbiosis: literature and taxonomy', *Annual Review of Energy and Environment*, **25**: 313–37.

Cloud, P. (1977), 'Entropy, materials, and posterity', *Geologische Rundschau*, Bd. **66**(1): 678–96.

Cohen, M. and J. Howard (2006), 'Success and its price: the institutionalization and political relevance of industrial ecology', *Journal of Industrial Ecology*, **10**(1–2): 79–88.

Cohen-Rosenthal, E. (2000), 'A walk on the human side of industrial ecology', *American Behavioral Scientist*, **44**(2): 245–64.

Commoner, B. (1971), *The Closing Circle: Nature, Man, and Technology*, New York: Knopf.

Commoner, B. (1997), 'The relation between industrial and ecological systems', *Journal of Cleaner Production*, **5**(1–2): 125–9.

Coté, R. and J. Hall (eds) (1994), *The Industrial Ecology Reader*, Halifax: Dalhousie University.

Dacin, M.T., M. Ventresca and B. Beal (1999), 'The embeddedness of organizations: dialogue and directions', *Journal of Management*, **25**(3): 317–56.

Drumwright, M. (1994), 'Socially responsible organizational buying: environmental concern as a noneconomic buying criterion', *Journal of Marketing*, **58**(3): 1–19.

Edelman, L., C. Uggen and H. Erlanger (1999), 'The endogeneity of legal regulation: grievance procedures as rational myth', *American Journal of Sociology*, 105(2): 406–54.

Ehrenfeld, J. (1997), 'Industrial ecology: a framework for product and process design', *Journal of Cleaner Production*, 5(1–2): 87–96.

Ehrenfeld, J. (2000), 'Industrial ecology: paradigm shift or normal science?' *American Behavioral Scientist*, 44(2): 229–44.

Ehrenfeld, J. (2002), 'Industrial ecology – becoming a new field?' Paper prepared for presentation at AIChE 2002 Annual Meeting, 3–8 November 2002, *Sustainable Engineering*.

Ehrenfeld, J. (2004), 'Industrial ecology: a new field or only a metaphor', *Journal of Cleaner Production*, 12(8–10): 825–31.

Ehrenfeld, J. and N. Gertler (1997), 'Industrial ecology in practice: the evolution of interdependence at Kalundborg', *Journal of Industrial Ecology*, 1(1): 67–79.

Erkman, S. (1997), 'Industrial ecology: a historical review', *Journal of Cleaner Production*, 5(1–2): 1–10.

Fischer-Kowalski, M. (2003), 'On the history of industrial metabolism', in D. Bourg and S. Erkman (eds), *Perspectives on Industrial Ecology*, Sheffield: Greenleaf Publishing, pp. 35–45.

Flood, R. (1999), 'Knowing of the unknowable', *Systemic Practice and Action Research*, 12(3): 247–56.

Frosch, R. and N. Gallopoulos (1989), 'Strategies for manufacturing', *Scientific American*, 261(3): 144–52.

Gallopoulos, N. (2006), 'Industrial ecology: an overview', *Progress in Industrial Ecology*, 3(1–2): 10–27.

Gertler, N. (1995), 'Industrial ecosystems: developing sustainable industrial structures', Master's Thesis, Cambridge, MA: Massachusetts Institute of Technology.

Gunningham, N., R. Kagan and D. Thornton (2003), *Shades of Green: Business, Regulation, and Environment*, Stanford, CA: Stanford University Press.

Gibbs, D. (2003), 'Trust and networking in inter-firm relations: the case of eco-industrial development', *Local Economy*, ISSN 02690942, 18(3), 222–36.

Graedel, T. and B. Allenby (1995), *Industrial Ecology*, NJ: Prentice Hall.

Granovetter, M. (1973), 'The strength of weak ties', *The American Journal of Sociology*, 78(6): 1360–80.

Granovetter, M. (1985), 'Economic action and social structure: the problem of embeddedness', *The American Journal of Sociology*, 91(3): 481–510.

Hagedoorn, John, (2006), 'Understanding the cross-level embeddedness of inter-firm partnership formation', *Academy of Management Review*, 31(3): 670–80.

Harper, E. and T. Graedel (2004), 'Industrial ecology: a teenager's progress', *Technology in Society*, 26: 433–45.

Heiskanen, E. (2000), 'Institutionalization of life-cycle thinking in the everyday discourse of market actors', *Journal of Industrial Ecology*, 4(4): 31–45.

Hertwich, E. (2005), 'Consumption and industrial ecology', *Journal of Industrial Ecology*, Winter/Spring, 9(1–2), 1–6.

Hoffman, A. (2003), 'Linking social systems analysis to the industrial ecology framework', *Organization & Environment*, 16(1): 66–86.

Howard-Grenville, J. and R. Paquin (2008), 'Organizational dynamics in industrial ecosystems: insights from organizational behavior theory', in M. Ruth and B. Davidsdottir (eds), *Dynamics of Industrial Ecosystems*, Cheltenham, UK and Northampton, MA, USA: Edward Elgar.

Isenmann, R. (2002), 'Further efforts to clarify industrial ecology's hidden philosophy of nature', *Journal of Industrial Ecology*, **6**(3–4): 27–48.

Jacobsen and Anderberg (2004), 'Understanding the evolution of industrial symbiotic networks: the case of Kalundborg', in J. Van den Bergh and M. Janssen (eds), *Economics of Industrial Ecology*, Cambridge, MA: MIT Press, pp. 337–55.

Johansson, A. (2002), 'Industrial ecology and industrial metabolism: use and misuse of metaphors', in R. Ayres and L. Ayres (eds), *Handbook of Industrial Ecology*, Cheltenham, UK and Northampton, MA, USA: Edward Elgar, pp. 70–77.

Kilduff, M., W. Tsai and K. Hanke (2006), 'A paradigm too far? A dynamic stability reconsideration of the social network research program', *Academy of Management Review*, **31**(4): 1031–48.

Kurz, H. (1986) 'Classical and early neoclassical economists on joint production', *Microeconomica*, **38**(1): 1–37.

Kurz, H. (2006), 'Goods and bads: sundry observations on joint production, waste disposal, and renewable and exhaustible resources', *Progress in Industrial Ecology*, **3**(4): 280–301.

Langley, A. (2007), 'Process thinking in strategic organization', *Strategic Organization*, **5**: 271–82.

Lifset, R. and T. Graedel (2002), 'Industrial ecology: goals and definitions', in R. Ayres and L. Ayres (eds), *Handbook of Industrial Ecology*, Cheltenham, UK and Northampton, MA, USA: Edward Elgar, pp. 3–15.

Malmborg, F. von (2004), 'Networking for knowledge transfer: towards an understanding of local authority roles in regional industrial ecosystem management', *Business Strategy and the Environment*, **13**(5): 334–46.

Meadows, D.H., D.L. Meadows, J. Randers and W. Behrens (1972), *Limits to Growth*, Universe Books.

Meyer, A., V. Gaba and K. Colwell (2005), 'Organizing far from equilibrium: nonlinear change in organizational fields', *Organization Science*, **16**: 456–73.

Oldenburg, K. and K. Geiser (1997), 'Pollution prevention and . . . or industrial ecology?', *Journal of Cleaner Production*, **5**(1–2): 103–8.

Orlove, B. (1980), 'Ecological anthropology', *Annual Review of Anthropology*, **9**: 235–73.

O'Rourke, D., L. Connely and C. Koshland (1996), 'Industrial ecology: A critical review', *International Journal of Environment and Pollution*, **6**(2): 89–112.

Plowman, D.A., L. Baker, T. Beck, M. Kulkarni, S.T. Solansky and D.V. Travis (2007), 'Radical change accidentally: the emergence and amplification of small change', *Academy of Management Journal*, **50**: 515–43.

Polanyi, K. (1944), *The Great Transformation: The Political and Economic Origins of Our Time*, Boston, MA: Beacon Press.

Powell, W., K. Koput and L. Smith-Doerr (1996), 'Interorganizational collaboration and the locus of innovation: networks of learning in biotechnology', *Administrative Science Quarterly*, **41**: 116–45.

Smith-Doerr, L. and W.W. Powell (2005), 'Networks and economic life', in N.J. Smelser and R. Swedberg (eds), *The Handbook of Economic Sociology*, 2nd edn, Princeton, NJ: Sage/Princeton University Press.

Tibbs, H. (1992), 'Industrial ecology: an environmental agenda for industry', *Whole Earth Review*, Winter: 4–19.

Van den Bergh, J. and M. Janssen (eds), (2004), *Economics of Industrial Ecology*, Cambridge, MA: MIT Press.

Watanabe, C. (2002), 'Industrial ecology and technology policy: the Japanese experience', in R. Ayres and L. Ayres (eds), *Handbook of Industrial Ecology*, Cheltenham, UK and Northampton, MA, USA: Edward Elgar, pp. 232–48.

Weick, K. (1969), *The Social Psychology of Organizing*, Reading, MA: Addison-Wesley.

Wells, P. (2006), 'Re-writing the ecological metaphor: Part 1', *Progress in Industrial Ecology*, **3**(1–2): 114–28.

Wernick, I. and J. Ausubel (1997), *Industrial Ecology: Some Directions for Research. Pre-Publication Draft*. New York: Rockefeller University for the Office of Energy and Environmental Systems, Lawrence Livermore National Laboratory.

White, R.M. (1994), Preface, in B. Allenby and D. Richards (eds), *The Greening of Industrial Ecosystems*, Washington, DC: National Academy Press, pp. v–vi.

Worster, D. (1977), *Nature's Economy: The Roots of Ecology*, San Francisco: Sierra Club Books.

Zukin, S. and P. DiMaggio (eds) (1990), *Structures of Capital: The Social Organization of the Economy*, Cambridge, UK: Cambridge University Press.

2. Ecology in the social sciences: an overview

Frank Boons

INTRODUCTION

Industrial ecology provides a specific perspective on the way in which human activities relate to the interacting abiotic and biotic elements that constitute natural ecologies. This relationship between human activity and ecologies (often referred to as natural environment or nature) has been addressed in different ways in several social science disciplines. In order to understand and further develop the social science perspective on industrial ecology, it is important to have insight into these attempts. I assume that the way in which social scientists have dealt with ecology is unfamiliar territory to readers with a science, engineering or technology (SET)-background. But from reading the work of social scientists to the field of industrial ecology I have the impression that they are not always familiar with this work either.

I distinguish three ways in which ecology and the social sciences intersect. First of all, the concepts of ecologists have been used by social scientists as metaphors for social phenomena. Of course, the field of industrial ecology is one example of the application of this metaphor, but there are many more. Second, if we take ecology as an encompassing way of looking at nature, there have been various approaches that seek to analyse the interaction between social phenomena and natural ecologies. One way is to look at society and nature as separate entities or systems, and analyse the interrelations between them. Finally, a distinct social science perspective which has become dominant especially in recent times takes ecology/nature into account as it is constructed in social interaction. Research in each of these three ways provides us with insights that are relevant for the further development of social science approaches to industrial ecology.

In the following sections of this chapter I present the material in each of the categories outlined above, which are respectively labelled as: society as ecology, society within nature, and nature as social construction. I will make no attempt to be exhaustive; this would result in a book-length treatise. Instead, I will present strands of research that are recognized as distinct within one or more social science disciplines. The aim is to provide some insight into the diversity of the work that has been done, and more importantly, to focus on ideas that are in some way relevant for the field of industrial ecology. I have also restricted myself by focusing on ecological rather than evolutionary approaches to the (a)biotic environment. For the purpose of this chapter, ecology is defined as the study of the interactions of species and the abiotic environment on which they draw for their resources.

SOCIETY AS ECOLOGY

Most of the practitioners and researchers in the field of industrial ecology are aware of the fact that the label under which they operate is the application of an ecological metaphor to society. What is perhaps less well known is that the ecology metaphor has been applied in several other areas of social science research. The exchange of concepts (which went both ways) between ecology and the disciplines of sociology and economics has been the subject of some research (see for instance Hodgson 1993 and Hannon 1997), but it is beyond the purpose of this chapter to look into this. The important observation is that the interaction between species and their abiotic environment, as studied by ecologists, has been perceived by many as holding clues for interaction among human beings.

Human Ecology (Chicago School)

One of the first distinct strands of research emerged at the University of Chicago and became known as human ecology. Robert Park, one of the leading scholars in this development, drew explicitly on the work of ecologists like Clements and Warming (Park 1936a, 1936b). In his view, society is organized at two levels, the biotic and the cultural. The biotic level, which follows the principles laid out by ecologists in concepts such as the succession of various developmental stages, is characterized by competition among species. Human societies differ from non-human ecologies in having a cultural level. In Park's view, this cultural level, consisting of symbols, norms and institutions, serves to restrict competition. Much of the empirical material with which Park and his associates worked dealt with the spatial distribution in American cities (Park et al. 1925). They built on the ecological insight that this distribution is not the result of planning, but emerges as the unintended result of the actions of its citizens.

The work of Park and his colleagues has received considerable criticism (Alihan 1964; Gettys 1940). Most problematic is the distinction between the biotic and the cultural level, which, as Park acknowledges, are aspects of human society rather than levels that can be separated for study. As a result, the application of ecological concepts becomes metaphoric, while theoretically human ecology builds on their direct use.

In my view, the Chicago School in human ecology is relevant for the field of industrial ecology for two reasons. Admirably, the work of its members made explicit use of then recent insights of ecologists, and scrutinized their relevance for the study of societies. Such explicit treatment of contemporary ecological theories would be desirable in industrial ecology. At the same time, the work of Park and others provides a warning of the difficulties associated with the application of ecological insights through analogous or metaphoric reasoning.

Organization and Management Studies

One of the major contributors to *marketing theory* is Wroe Alderson (1957). He sought to develop a theory of marketing from a systemic perspective. In his view, marketing science needs to build on an understanding of the way in which firms and consumers connect. Markets are heterogeneous; products and demand are not uniform but differ as a result of geographical dispersion, product differentiation and heterogeneous 'assortments' of products demanded by households. Given this heterogeneity, Alderson looked for the analogy with natural ecologies, in which species occupy specific niches. As Alderson included the supply chain in his analysis, he ended up providing a conceptual framework similar to Porter's concept of a value system (Priem and Rasheed 1997). While concepts such as niche have been incorporated into mainstream marketing theory, Alderson's integrated view of what industrial ecologists would call production and consumption systems has all but been forgotten (Tamilia 2005). It seems worthwhile to explore his work, as he deals explicitly with the consumer side of such systems, an area which recently has become much more important (Hertwich 2005).

A more recent strand of research builds explicitly on ecological theory and methodology. The *population ecology* approach in organizational sociology emerged in the late 1970s as a way of analysing the long-term development of groups of organizations that have similar characteristics, or operate in a similar social environment, such as sectors of industry (Hannan and Freeman 1977). Population ecologists apply the biological population ecology equations from Lotka and Volterra to study the birth and death of organizations in groups over long time periods. Their analysis provides insight into the characteristics of successful organizations, that is organizations that are able to survive over longer time periods, the existence of niches within industries, and the interaction of types of organizations in terms of predator-prey interaction patterns. Although this theoretical framework has led to a substantial body of research, it has distinct limitations. A major problem is the assumption that organizations are relatively inert, which is necessary in order to treat organizations as species (Hannan and Freeman 1984). This implies that managerial choice and organizational change are deemed to be largely irrelevant; organizational forms are selected by their social environment. The relevance of this research for the industrial ecology field seems limited; the research questions of industrial ecology do not fit very well into the requirements necessary for applying the methodology.

The development of network theories in sociology partly focused on organizations, as organizational sociologists started to view the social environment of an organization as an interrelated set of organizations (Benson 1975). Both interfirm networks and networks consisting of diverse organizational actors such as governmental agencies, knowledge institutes, NGOs, and firms became a major unit of analysis in the field. The work in this strand is especially relevant for industrial ecology in uncovering the way in which network structure and culture affect the actions of the organizations that constitute a network. Several authors have developed these insights into the study of *organizational communities*: sets of organizations from different populations (Astley and Fombrun 1983; Aldrich 1999). These authors explicitly use ecological analogies in studying network relationships, such as commensalism (populations that make similar demands on their environment), and symbiosis (mutual dependency between members of different populations). Aided by these concepts, the emergence and evolution of organizational communities can be studied. Examples of such studies include the emergence of the biotechnology industry, and more generally the emergence of networks around new technologies (see Baum and Singh 1994 for an early collection of work; Ruef 2000). In my view, it is extremely worthwhile for industrial ecologists to explore the possibilities of drawing on this work in analysing the dynamics of regional and product chain industrial ecologies.

A slowly emerging addition to the ecosystem analogies in the management sciences was introduced in 1993 by James Moore in his book *The Death of Competition*. This so-called business ecosystem approach focuses on the increasing relevance of the networks in which business firms are engaged for their competitive success. The approach moves away from a narrow focus on supply chains, which suggests a linear relationship between a firm and its suppliers, to a network of relationships where value is created (Hearn and Pace 2006). The authors who work within this approach make explicit use of biological concepts to make sense of this relationship.

Moore (1993: 76) defines a business ecosystem as the set of companies that 'work cooperatively and competitively to support new products, satisfy customers, and eventually incorporate the next round of innovations'. Interestingly, he defines such systems around a core company, and thus companies such as Apple and IBM each have their distinct ecosystem. Moore further develops the analogy by distinguishing different phases in the evolution of a business ecosystem (birth, expansion, leadership, self-renewal), and defines strategies that are best suited for each of these phases. Moore also stresses that the evolution of the business ecosystem is a result of co-evolution between the member firms. Such co-evolution can be competitive, mutualistic or exploitative (Peltoniemi 2006), with different results for the system as a whole.

Iansiti and Levien (2004) further develop this perspective by focusing on types of species within a business ecosystem. Several companies occupy specific niches in the system through exploiting specific capabilities that other firms lack. Other firms try to dominate the whole system, for instance through a strategy of vertical integration. In doing so, they threaten or exploit niche players, and destroy the variety that is crucial for the ecosystem's long term survival. An alternative to such a strategy is employed by so-called keystone firms. Like keystone species, they are crucial for the ecosystem's continued existence, as they provide resources that are vital to the other firms in the system. Such firms need to employ a strategy in which the development of the whole system is a focal concern.

These contributions provide several interesting insights for industrial ecology. Moore's successive stages and corresponding strategies indicate that, in the development of an industrial ecology, strategies may need to shift over time to match the evolution of the evolving system. The work of Iansiti and Levien is relevant as it indicates that in such systems, different types of firms operate with divergent (and to some extent competing) strategies. Importantly, the consequence of these strategies for the long term survival of the system as a whole is explored.

SOCIETY WITHIN NATURE

In addition to building on the ecological metaphor, industrial ecology deals with the linkage between society and its natural environment. This linkage has been the subject of research within the social sciences, and is often summarized under the heading of human ecology, even if it bears little resemblance to the work of the Chicago School discussed earlier. The core principle of this work is that human beings are a biological species. They depend for their existence and activities on their (a)biotic environment, and also to some extent are determined by their biological qualities. The relevance of this fact for the social sciences has been contested. In the nineteenth century, when disciplines such as sociology and psychology took shape, a strong movement to distinguish these from other scientific disciplines was present. One strategy was to define the social sciences as dealing with issues that were strictly social, separating them from the biological component of human behaviour. Social Darwinism took an opposite approach by applying the evolutionary ideas from Darwin directly to society, resulting in a questionable normative view with which many social scientists did not want to be associated. Nevertheless, ideas about the relationship between social phenomena as they relate to nature have a long history. In a comprehensive study, Glacken (1967) has shown how ideas about man's place in nature, as well as the influence of human societies on their natural environment, have evolved at least since the Ancient Greeks. Since the early twentieth century, scholars from different social science disciplines have built their own set of ideas on the relationship between nature and human society.

Anthropology

Already in the nineteenth century, anthropologists sought to understand the relationship between man and nature, as their study of small and less technologically 'advanced' societies made this embeddedness more visible. Ecological anthropology can be defined as 'the study of the relations among the population dynamics, social organization, and culture of human populations and the environments in which they live' (Orlove 1980: 235). Like anthropology in general, it seeks to understand cultural traits of human societies, such as kinship patterns, economic and political organization, and the way in which these are reproduced through rituals and social practices. But ecological anthropology is distinct in seeking the explanation of these traits in the relationship between society and its (a)biotic environment. In the ecological approach, the *human ecological complex* is studied in its entirety, through the linkages between natural environment, technology, population and socio-cultural life (Duncan 1964).

Julian Steward developed the first comprehensive statement of an ecological approach. His *cultural ecology* approach linked the possibilities of human habitats for exploitation to demographic patterns and social organization characteristics of primitive societies. He focuses on the cultural core, the set of features of human societies that are most closely related to subsistence activities and economic activities (Steward 1972: 37). This approach is applicable to any type of society, but as technological control over the natural environment increases, the relationship between culture and environment becomes less easy to establish; technological control increases the number of available exploitative patterns, and thus cultural diversity is less easy to explain in relation to the natural environment.

Steward's work, like many of his contemporaries, was fundamentally functionalist (Sanderson 1990). It explained the social organization and culture of specific populations as functional adaptations to their natural environment, in allowing them to exploit these environments successfully without exceeding their carrying capacity. Although followers like Harris (1975) and Rappaport (1967) further expanded his views by adding a focus on energy flows in ecosystems and explicitly using a systems perspective (Moran 1990), they initially did not depart from this equilibrium assumption (Orlove 1980). Later on, this assumption was discarded, which allowed anthropologists to focus on the dynamic interaction between society and ecologies, including responses to exceeding carrying capacity. Also, linkages between different populations and the ecosystems on which they draw were included, allowing for the analysis of linkages between developing and developed countries (Biersack 1999; Kottak 1999). In short, within anthropology ideas have developed to a point where the connection to industrial societies can more easily be made.

Such advances complicate methodological choices in ways similar to the ones that need to be made by industrial ecologists. In this respect, Vayda's (1983) method of progressive contextualization deserves mentioning. In order to analyse the interconnected systems of societies and natural ecologies, he proposes a method which does not build on an *a priori* system boundary, but starts from drawing the boundary around a small system, which may be enlarged to include elements that are found in the analysis to be indispensable for answering the questions the researcher seeks to answer.

History

Historians do not have a similar tradition in studying the interaction between human beings and their natural environment. Since the early 1970s, a number of them have started to explore this topic. Norgaard (1994) provides an overview of this work from a co-evolutionary perspective. Historical research enables him to analyse the ways in which changes in social organization, social values, knowledge and technology interact in complex ways with the evolving natural environment. For most of the thousands of years in which human beings have populated the earth, this interaction has been relatively direct, as human societies were dependent on their immediate surrounding ecologies and energy provided by the sun. Through hunting and gathering as well as developing forms of agriculture, human activities changed ecologies and the species therein, while the specific resources available in their environment influenced values and ways of social organizing.

The industrial revolution of the nineteenth century ended this direct relationship, mainly through the use of hydrocarbons as an energy source. Through technologies and social organization that enabled Western societies to exploit these resources, they 'freed themselves from many of the complexities of interacting with environmental systems' (Norgaard 1994: 45; see also Catton 1980). Of course, this is an illusion; the use of hydrocarbons merely means that Western societies interfere with ecological cycles on a larger geographical and time scale. But the time it took for this to become visible created the space in which organizational practices, sets of values, knowledge and technology could develop based on the idea that control over or separation from nature was possible.

This work is relevant as a longitudinal focus helps to uncover stable as well as changing factors in the interplay between human societies and the ecologies on which their activities have effects. It thus provides valuable insight for industrial ecologists in drawing attention to the long gestation periods of modern industrial practices, and the path dependencies that need to be taken into account when trying to change them.

Economics

While economics and ecology have developed as separate disciplines since the late nineteenth century, there has been considerable exchange of concepts and insights. Indeed, the first definition of the field of ecology as formulated by Haeckel in 1870 described this scientific field as the body of knowledge concerned with the 'economy of nature', a then popular way of expressing the amazement (as well as religious awe) with which students of nature approached their discovery of the many ways in which species and their environment were linked. Yet ecologists hardly studied human beings as part of natural ecologies, and economists abstracted more and more from the natural basis of productive and consumptive activities. The work of Kenneth Boulding and Nicholas Goergescu-Roegen, now considered as predecessors of ecological economics, took place in the fringes of mainstream economics. Also, environmental economics and natural resource economics developed, both treating nature in terms of the neo-classical paradigm, where natural resources are implicitly deemed to be abundant, natural resources and human capital are completely substitutable, and the impacts of economic activities on natural ecologies are dealt with in term of 'externalities' (Van den Bergh 2001).

Ecological economics is defined by Costanza (1989) as addressing the relationships between natural ecosystems and economic systems in the broadest sense. Instead of looking at ecological impact in terms of external effects, it takes a holistic perspective in which the dynamics of natural ecologies are connected to those of economic systems. Economic activities depend upon natural resources and the absorptive capacity of natural ecologies, which makes the extent to which such activities do not exceed the carrying capacity of the earth a central theme of ecological economics. A second theme is that of the implications of the laws of thermodynamics for economic activities and systems. Production activities involve the transformation of matter and energy, and result in an increase in entropy.

Making use of various disciplinary inputs, ecological economics advocates a transdisciplinary approach which is focused on solving the problems of modern societies and their ecological impact. Formulated in this way, the scope of ecological economics is extremely broad, as is indicated by the diversity of contributions to a dedicated journal and international society.

In a foundational text, Faber et al. (1996) present three major problem areas that are addressed within the field of ecological economics. A first one is that of measurement and policy. This concerns the development of tools to measure the impact of economic activities on natural ecologies, such as the ecological footprint (Wackernagel and Reese 1997). Such measurements serve as a basis for discussing alternative ways of defining economic growth. Also, it addresses the issue of how to value the services that are provided by natural ecosystems. Such measurements can then be introduced into cost-benefit analysis where trade-offs are made between nature conservation and developing parts of ecosystems for alternative uses. Measurement also concerns assessing the effectiveness of policies that are implemented to decrease ecological impact. A second problem area concerns ethical values. Ecological economics touches upon ethical questions such as the resource and pollution consequences of the growth of human population, the extent to which the value of human life exceeds that of plant and animal life, and the ways in which the needs of future generations can and should be taken into account. This is a crucial problem area, as methods of valuation are inherently based upon judgements with ethical consequences. A third problem area is that of developing tools and methods that can be used to analyse the dynamics of natural, physical and social systems and their interaction. One of the ongoing debates is about the way in which the laws of thermodynamics can be incorporated into economic analysis, but this problem area also concerns the distinct ways in which evolutionary processes can be seen to operate in social and natural systems.

There are many similarities between industrial ecology and ecological economics. Others have looked at the precise way in which these fields intersect (Kronenberg 2007). For the purpose of this chapter it is enough to note the overlap as an incentive to make critical use of the insights of ecological economists.

Sociology

The troublesome relationship between biology and *sociology* is reflected in the confusion that results from using the word 'environment' among sociologists: for them, the word environment refers to the social and cultural influences on human behaviour, explicitly excluding the physical and natural surroundings in which human beings act (Dunlap and Catton 1979). Although the founding fathers of sociology did not all neglect nature as an important factor, Durkheim's formulation of the sociological method in which social facts need to be explained by other social facts prevailed until the 1960s. Until that time, the natural environment and its influences on society were studied as specific examples of more general sociological areas of interest, such as social movements or wildland recreation as an example of leisure behaviour.

A 1979 paper by Dunlap and Catton was a specific attempt to propose a framework for a distinct environmental sociology in which the interaction between human beings and the natural environment was to be the focus of study. They formulated the New Ecological Paradigm (NEP), based on Duncan's concept of an 'ecological complex' (1959). This complex consists of population, organization, environment, and technology, and Dunlap and Catton are careful to stress that organization refers to the cultural, social and personality aspects of social behaviour (1979). The interaction between the physical environment on the one hand, and population, technology, culture, social systems and personality systems was to be the core focus of the NEP.

As Buttel noted in a review almost a decade later, the NEP was formulated to change the anthropocentric nature of sociology, but instead became the basis of 'just another' sociological specialization (1987). Research has focused mainly on the following areas:

1. the attitudes, values, and behaviours of individuals towards environmental problems, both through general survey research and applied studies that focus on the attitudinal and behavioural aspects of littering, participation in recycling programs, and energy conservation;

2. the environmental movement: what its support base is, what its strategies are for mobilizing resources and achieving political success, etc.;
3. the way in which individuals and societies deal with technological risks that are inherent in modern societies (Beck 1992), for instance those associated with nuclear energy production.

The field has produced two more specific theories that have achieved some status, and which deal more generally with the development of the social system and its relationship with the natural environment.

Ecological modernization theory (Spaargaren and Mol 1992) starts from the central sociological thesis that Western societies are subject to a process of modernization. This process involves increasing rationalization in all societal spheres. The central thesis of the ecological modernization perspective is that this process initially results in increasing ecological damage, but that at some point, through further rationalization and industrialization, societies are able to counter this trend and decrease their level of ecological impact. While this leaves the basic capitalist structure of these societies intact, it involves changes in its coordinative structures, with shifts in state policies and the balance between state and market. This perspective has a distinct European bias as its main developers come from Germany and The Netherlands, where in the last decades of the twentieth century such a transformation seemed to be taking place.

An alternative theory has been proposed by Schnaiberg (1980). His perspective revolves around the question of why the ecological impact of industrial activities has increased dramatically since the Second World War. He postulates the existence of a 'treadmill of production' which refers to the mechanism in which the continuous demand for increased productivity in industrial systems is narrowed down to labour productivity. In order to increase the output per unit of labour force, employers introduce more advanced production technologies, which imply an increase in necessary resource inputs. Increased labour productivity results in increased output, or alternatively results in firing obsolete employees. As these need to find work elsewhere, there is a need to develop more productive activities, which can only be competitive if they adhere to the same logic of increasing labour productivity. Although Schnaiberg does not consider services explicitly, the general trend within advanced capitalist economies fits with the mechanism he describes.

This work is mostly relevant for industrial ecology in providing insight into the possible longer term trends in the treatment of ecological issues in industrial societies. However, as these ideas were further developed, they moved more and more into the consideration of how environmental issues are socially constructed. This perspective will be discussed in the next section.

Complexity Theory

In the past decade, insights from complexity theory have become a basis for analysing the interaction between social and ecological systems. Although the scholars active in this growing field may not label themselves as social scientists, this work has been put forward as a promising basis for further developing the social science perspective on the society-ecology relationship (Abel 1998; Scoones 1999). Consequently, it provides interesting new avenues for industrial ecology.

Both societies and ecologies can be conceptualized as complex adaptive systems (CAS), sharing the following characteristics (Levin 1999, 12):

1. Diversity and individuality of components: components of the system are diverse and there are mechanisms for maintaining that diversity. In addition, components can act autonomously. A CAS consists of heterogeneous components.
2. Localized interactions among components, such as competition, collaboration, and information exchange.
3. An autonomous process of selection: a mechanism which accounts for the continuation of certain local outcomes and the elimination of other outcomes.

These features give rise to nonlinear interactions which makes the system's behaviour difficult to predict. Typically, the system's behaviour is not the result of planning by any one central actor, but instead emerges as the result of relatively autonomous actions of system members (biological species, or human beings and organizations). A group of researchers called the Resilience Alliance, with Holling and Folke as main members, has developed a framework for analysing the interaction between society and natural ecologies in terms of CAS (Gunderson and Holling 2002). Their work deals specifically with sustainability issues, and proposes approaches to developing governance structures for increasing the resilience of social-ecological systems. One of the interesting concepts that these researchers use is called the 'adaptive cycle'. This cycle models the four phases that a social-ecological system goes through in adapting to its wider environment: exploitation, conservation, release and reorganization (Holling 2001). The succession of phases is the result of the internal dynamics of the system as well as pressure on the system from its environment. Also, each of the phases has distinct implications for governance, that is, the way in which the activities of its members are coordinated.

The work from complexity theory is promising as it allows the analysis of both ecological and the social systems in similar terms, and as such, it could be of considerable relevance to the field of industrial ecology.

NATURE AS SOCIAL CONSTRUCTION

A final and distinct way of dealing with nature within the social sciences considers the way in which (collective) perceptions of nature are shaped by, and influence, social phenomena. This body of knowledge has more recent origins, building on the work of the sociologists Berger and Luckmann (1967). Their approach starts with the idea that human beings, as social actors, do not deal with the outside world directly, but rather through their images and beliefs about that world. Although the real world is not denied, Berger and Luckmann argue that it is these social constructions, their emergence and continuous confirmation, that hold the clue to understanding social phenomena. The simplest application to ecological phenomena is in recognizing that human beings act in response to their perception of ecological impact rather than to that ecological impact per se. As is clear from the impact of Rachel Carson's *Silent Spring*, it took her work and its recognition by many citizens to construct an image of human activities as harming the natural environment and endangering human life.

Anthropology

Before sociologists started to apply the insights of Berger and Luckmann, anthropologists had already developed interpretative approaches towards nature. *Ethnoecology* started out by emphasizing the analysis of verbal behaviour in describing the way in which people view their local natural environment, and is part of what Sturtevant calls ethnoscience, the system of knowledge and cognition typical of a given culture (Sturtevant 1964; Anderson 1973). The aim is to find out what people 'know' about nature, and how they use this knowledge as a basis for action.

Ethnoecological research increases our understanding of human action as such local knowledge may differ from our own perceptual schemes. Although we may view the latter as objective knowledge based on scientific principles, ethnoecological research reminds us that this is also a culturally bounded appreciation of truth. Looking at various conceptualizations of nature as they exist in different cultures is not simply comparison, but rather shows how local knowledge leads to specific behavioural patterns, and in that sense is 'true in its consequences'.

Research on local knowledge can take several forms. By understanding the linkage between belief and knowledge systems about nature, and the social practices that are based on them, we can increase our understanding of the ways in which people belonging to a certain culture are able to maintain a sustainable relationship with nature. One example is a study of the Yucatec Maya by Barrera-Bassols and Toledo (2005). Insight in local knowledge may also be of help in connecting existing practices of pest management and seeking ways of improving these rather than replacing them with agricultural practices that are based on Western industrial products (Altieri 1993). It also helps to define 'indicators of sustainability' that make sense to people from cultures other than the one where the concept of sustainable development emerged (Nazarea et al. 1998; see also Chapter 7).

Sociology

The social constructivist work in environmental sociology has been summarized by Hannigan (1995). His starting point is the study of social problems, of which environmental problems are a subset. Up until the early 1970s, social problems were considered in sociology to be objective conditions of a dysfunctional society. Spector and Kitsuse (1973) developed an alternative view in which such problems were approached as sequences of events based on collective interpretations of reality by social actors. A social problem is a situation which is evaluated by societal actors as undesirable, and about which they make claims. Rather than studying the validity of such claims, a social constructivist perspective focuses on the process by which collective problem definitions emerge, and the processes by which they arise on public and political agendas, resulting in action to deal with them.

While this work deals with the construction of ecological problems at the level of societies, applications have also been made at the level of organizations. Managers and employees of firms, as well as civil servants in public organizations, shape their strategy towards ecological issues based on their distinct set of beliefs and values about nature. Such work highlights the cognitive and cultural embeddedness which shapes organizational action (see Howard-Grenville 2007; Georg 2006 for a recent collection of work in this strand).

This work is valuable for industrial ecologists in pointing out the ways in which the beliefs and values of organizational members, politicians, consumers and citizens are shaped, and subsequently determine their actions. The relevance of this is illustrated by the concept of industrial ecology itself. This concept is itself a socially constructed way of looking at reality, and much of the work in the field builds on the idea that diffusing this specific conceptualization will bring practitioners to deal with their material and energy flows in a different way.

Political Ecology

The field of political ecology emerged in the early 1970s from cultural ecology as a distinct approach in which concerns over ecological problems were approached from a political economy perspective (Greenberg and Park 1994). Challenging the equilibrium stance of Steward and his followers, degradation of natural ecologies was analysed as a result of the power relations between human groups involved in the struggle over scarce resources. While cultural ecologists tended to focus on the interaction between ecology and human groups at the local level, political ecologists took a macro view, explaining ecological degradation from asymmetric power relations between national governments, local producers and consumers, and international economic actors. Colonialism and the global capitalist system were seen as important explanatory factors in the environmental degradation in developing countries.

Political ecology thus developed around three central concepts (Paulson et al. 2003): (1) marginality, the idea that economic, ecological and political marginalization may be mutually reinforcing; (2) pressure of production on resources, the social relations around production and consumption that result in increased demands for natural resources, and (3) plurality, the recognition that human actors have diverse interests, perceptions, and rationalities towards the natural environment.

In early studies, insights from social and ecological science were combined to analyse, and propose solutions to, ecological problems such as tropic deforestation in Amazonia and soil erosion in Nepal. During the 1990s, less attention was given to ecological dynamics, and the focus shifted towards the 'political' in political ecology. The global perspective of the 1980s was criticized as being overly deterministic, and researchers started to emphasize political processes at the micro level. Also, more emphasis was given to the symbolic aspect of political processes: the various ways in which human beings perceived ecological problems and possible solutions (Walker 2005). An example of this work is the 'deconstruction' of the concepts of sustainable development and biodiversity conservation by Escobar (1996). Here the focus is exclusively on the way in which these concepts reflect, and perpetuate, existing power relations, and how they miss any explicit link between human action and its effects on natural ecologies.

Given this development, early political ecology would fit better in the preceding section, while the later work moves closer to the social constructivist position. More important for our purposes is the fact that work under this label explicitly analyses the political embeddedness of economic activity and its relationship with nature. As power relations are seldom addressed by industrial ecologists, again this strand of research is useful to take into account in further developing the field.

CONCLUSION: SOME OBSERVATIONS

I want to emphasize that the collection of insights presented above does not aspire to completeness. Even within this selection, it is hardly possible to do justice to the work that forms the basis for this overview. I have described strands of research in a way that hopefully tickles the imagination of readers, spurring them on to read original texts. The references given are provided as starting points from which additional material can easily be found.

Despite its incompleteness, I want to draw some conclusions about this material in addition to the remarks made throughout on the usefulness for industrial ecologists. The metaphoric use of ecological concepts seems to provide a lot of inroads for industrial ecologists, especially drawing on the insights from organizational researchers. Their work relates directly to the structural embeddedness of industrial ecology in focusing on the network of relationships among groups of organizations. The ecological metaphor generally has inspired them to look at the dynamics of such communities, and given the interest of industrial ecology in the change of industrial ecosystems, this seems an important body of work. Also, the work presented here has in several ways a more developed way of using ecological concepts. Despite some exceptions (Levine 1999; Hardy and Graedel 2002), much of the work of industrial ecologists bases itself on a crude version of the ecosystem metaphor, and does not use to its full advantage recent developments in ecology. The recent advances in complexity theory are well suited to connect the analysis of social and ecological systems.

A second conclusion is that there is plenty of work in the social sciences that can be used to flesh out the various dimensions of embeddedness outlined in the first chapter. At the same time, the overview shows that distinct paths for research usually focus on one or two dimensions. This may be taken as a warning signal that we should not expect too easily that the interrelations between all forms of embeddedness can be incorporated into research.

Much of the anthropological and sociological work serves to indicate that human action, and thus the material and energy flows that result from it, is critically shaped by the social context in which it occurs. The cognitive maps that people have of their natural and social environment, the cultural values to which they aspire, the relational patterns in which they find themselves and the power asymmetries within these patterns – all contribute to their impact upon their natural environment.

REFERENCES

Abel, T. (1998), 'Complex adaptive systems, evolutionism, and ecology within anthropology: interdisciplinary research for understanding cultural and ecological dynamics', *Georgia Journal of Ecological Anthropology*, **2**: 6–29.

Alderson, W. (1957), *Marketing Behaviour and Executive Action*, Homewood, IL: Richard D. Irwin, Inc.

Aldrich, H. (1999), *Organizations Evolving*, London: Sage Publications.

Alihan, M.A. (1964), *Social Ecology: A Critical Analysis*, New York: Cooper.

Altieri, M. (1993), 'Ethnoscience and biodiversity: key elements in the design of sustainable pest management systems for small farmers in developing countries', *Agriculture, Ecosystems and Environment*, **46**: 257–72.

Anderson, J. (1973), 'Ecological anthropology and anthropological ecology', in J. Honigmann (ed.), *Handbook of Social and Cultural Anthropology*, Chicago: Rand McNally College Publishing Co., pp. 179–239.

Astley, W. and C. Fombrun (1983), 'Collective strategy: social ecology of organizational environments', *The Academy of Management Review*, **8**(4): 576–87.

Ayres, Robert U. and Allen V. Kneese (1969), 'Production, consumption, and externalities', *The American Economic Review*, **59**(3): 282–97.

Barrera-Bassols, N. and V. Toledo (2005), 'Ethnoecology of the Yucatec Maya: symbolism, knowledge and management of natural resources', *Journal of Latin American Geography*, **4**(1): 9–41.

Baum, J. and J. Singh (eds) (1994), *Evolutionary Dynamics of Organizations*, New York: Oxford University Press.

Benson, J. (1975), 'The interorganizational network as a political economy', *Administrative Science Quarterly*, **20**(2): 229–49.

Berger, P. and T. Luckmann (1967), *The Social Construction of Reality*, New York: Doubleday.

Biersack, A. (1999), Introduction: from the "new ecology" to the new ecologies', *American Anthropologist, New Series*, **101**(1) : 5–18.

Catton, W. (1980), *Overshoot: The Ecological Basis of Revolutionary Change*, Champaign: University of Illinois Press.

Costanza, R. (1989), 'What is ecological economics?', *Ecological Economics*, **1**(1): 1–7.

Duncan, O. (1964), 'Social organization and the ecosystem', in R. Paris (ed.), *Handbook of Modern Sociology*, Chicago: Rand-McNally, pp. 36–82.

Dunlap, R. and W. Catton (1979), 'Environmental sociology', *Annual Review of Sociology*, **5**: 243–73.

Escobar, A. (1996), 'Construction nature. Elements for a post-structuralist political ecology', *Futures* **28**(4): 325–43.

Faber, M., R. Manstetten and J. Proops (1996), *Ecological Economics. Concepts and Methods*, Cheltenham, UK and Brookfield, USA: Edward Elgar.

Georg, S. (ed.) (2006), 'Mobilizing and managing the environment', Special issue of *International Studies of Management and Organization*, **36**(2): 3–124.

Gettys, W. (1940), 'Human ecology and social theory', *Social Forces*, **18**(4), 469–76.

Glacken, C.J. (1967), *Traces on the Rhodian Shore: Nature and Culture in Western Thought from Ancient Times to the End of the Eighteenth Century*, Berkeley, CA: University of California Press.

Greenberg, J. and T. Park (1994), 'Political ecology', *Journal of Political Ecology*, **1**:1–11.

Gunderson, L. and C. Holling (eds) (2002), Panarchy. Washington, DC: Island Press.

Hannan, M. and J. Freeman (1977), 'The population ecology of organizations', *American Journal of Sociology*, **82**: 929–64.

Hannan, M. and J. Freeman (1984), 'Structural inertia and organizational change', *American Sociological Review*, **49**(2): 149–64.

Hannigan, J. 1995. *Environmental Sociology. A Social Constructionist Perspective*. London: Routledge.

Hannon, B. (1997), 'The use of analogy in biology and economics. From biology to economics, and back', *Structural Change and Economic Dynamics*, **8**: 471–88.

Hardy, C. and T. Graedel (2002), 'Industrial ecosystems as food webs', *Journal of Industrial Ecology*, **6**(1), 29–38.

Harris, M. (1975), *Culture, People, Nature: An Introduction to General Anthropology*, New York: Crowell.

Hearn, G. and C. Pace (2006), 'Value-creating ecologies: understanding next generation business systems', *Foresight*, **8**(1): 55–65.

Hertwich, E. (2005), 'Consumption and industrial ecology', *Journal of Industrial Ecology*, Winter/Spring, **9**(1–2): 1–6.

Hodgson, G. (1993), *Economics and Evolution. Bringing Life Back into Economics*, Cambridge, UK: Polity Press.

Holling, C. (2001), 'Understanding the complexity of economic, ecological, and social systems', *Ecosystems*, **4**: 390–405.

Howard-Grenville, J. (2007), *Corporate Culture and Environmental Practice: Making Change at a High-Technology Manufacturer*, Cheltenham, UK and Northampton, MA, USA: Edward Elgar.

Iansiti, M. and R. Levien (2004), 'Strategy as ecology', *Harvard Business Review*, March, 69–78.

Kottak, C. (1999), 'The new ecological anthropology', *American Anthropologist, New Series*, **101**(1): 23–35.

Kronenberg, J. (2007), *Ecological Economics and Industrial Ecology: A Case Study of the Integrated Product Policy of the European Union*, London: Routledge.

Levin, S.A. (1999), *Fragile Dominion. Complexity and the Commons*, Reading, MA: Perseus Books.

Levine, S. (1999), 'Products and ecological models: a population ecology perspective', *Journal of Industrial Ecology*, **3**(2–3), 47–62.

McIntosh, R. (1985), *The Background of Ecology*. Cambridge: Cambridge University Press.

Moore, J. (1993), 'Predators and prey: a new ecology of competition', *Harvard Business Review*, May–June, 75–86.
Moran, E. (ed.) (1990), *The Ecosystem Approach in Anthropology. From Concept to Practice*, Ann Arbor: University of Michigan Press.
Nazarea, V., R. Rhoades, E. Bontoyan and G. Flora (1998), 'Defining indicators which make sense to local people: intra-cultural variation in perceptions of natural resources', *Human Organization*, **57**(2): 159–70.
Norgaard, R. (1994), *Development Betrayed*, London: Routledge.
Orlove, B. (1980), 'Ecological anthropology', *Annual Review of Anthropology*, **9**: 235–73.
Park, R. (1936a), 'Human ecology', *American Journal of Sociology*, **42**(1), 1–15.
Park, R. (1936b), 'Succession, an ecological concept', *American Sociological Review*, **1**(2), 171–9.
Park, R., E, Burgess and R. McKenzie (1967 [1925]), *The City*, Chicago: University of Chicago Press.
Paulson. S., L. Gezon and M. Watts (2003), 'Locating the political in political ecology: an introduction', *Human Organization*, **62**(3): 205–17.
Peltoniemi, M. (2006), 'Preliminary theoretical framework for the study of business ecosystems', *E:CO*, **8**(1), 10–19.
Priem, R. and A. Rasheed (1997), 'Alderson's transvection and Porter's value system: a comparison of two independently-developed theories', *Journal of Management History*, **3**(2): 145–65.
Rappaport, R. (1967), *Pigs for the Ancestors*, New Haven: Yale University Press.
Ruef, M. (2000), 'The emergence of organizational forms: a community ecology approach', *American Journal of Sociology*, **106**(3): 658–714.
Sanderson, S. (1990), *Social Evolutionism. A Critical History*, Cambridge, MA: Blackwell Publishers.
Sargent, F. (ed.) (1974), *Human Ecology*, Amsterdam: North-Holland Publishing Co.
Schnaiberg, A. (1980), *The Environment*, New York: Oxford University Press.
Scoones, I. (1999), 'The new ecology and the social sciences: what prospects for a fruitful engagement?' *Annual Review of Anthropology*, **28**: 479–507.
Spaargaren, G. and A. Mol (1992), 'Sociology, environment, and modernity: ecological modernization as a theory of social change', *Society and Natural Resources*, **55**: 323–44.
Spector, M. and J. Kitsuse (1973), 'Social problems: a reformulation', *Social Problems*, **20**: 145–59.
Steward, J. (1972 [1955]), *Theory of Culture Change. The Methodology of Multilinear Evolution*, Urbana: University of Illinois Press.
Sturtevant, W. (1964), 'Studies in ethnoscience', *American Anthropologist*, **66**(3): 99–131.
Tamilia, R. (2005), *Placing Alderson and his Contributions to Marketing in Historical Perspective*, Cahiers de Recherche 02-2005, University of Quebec, Montreal.
Van den Bergh, J. (2001), 'Ecological economics: themes, approaches, and differences with environmental economics', *Regional Environmental Change*, **2**: 13–23.
Vayda, A. (1983), 'Progressive contextualization: methods for research in human ecology', *Human Ecology*, **11**(3): 265–81.

Vayda, A. and B. Walters (1999), 'Against political ecology', *Human Ecology*, **27**(1): 167–79.

Wackernagel, M. and W. Rees (1997), 'Perceptual and structural barriers to investing in natural capital: economics from an ecological footprint perspective', *Ecological Economics*, **20**(1): 3–24.

Walker, P. (2005), 'Political ecology: where is the ecology?' *Progress in Human Geography*, **29**(1): 73–82.

York, R. and E. Rosa (2003), 'Key challenges to ecological modernization theory: institutional efficacy, case study evidence, units of analysis, and the pace of eco-efficiency', *Organization & Environment*, **16**(3): 273–88.

3. Don't fence me in . . .

Henrikke Baumann

As I set out to write this chapter, I realize that after more than 15 years in what many call disciplinary no-man's land, a certain weariness of inter-disciplinary politics has set in. I've come to a point where I just want to get on with my work, whatever its disciplinary label. And at that point being asked to write a personal essay on interdisciplinary experiences, I argued with myself: what justification do I need to take time off from that work? Maybe the fact that I managed to get tenured on merits of interdisciplinarity counts for something?!

This book is about putting the 'social' into industrial ecology – through dialogues between disciplines. Yes, dialogue would have been nice, but that rarely happened during those 15 years – 'languages' were so different. There was more confusion and tension, and occasionally even open conflict. In my mind, dialogue entails a civil and constructive exchange, even when the participants are very different, as the research-ers within industrial ecology[1] are. Roughly speaking, there are the engi-neers (with their long-time allies the natural scientists) and there are the social scientists. And although both engineering and social scientists come in many different kinds and have their own internal debates, it is in the exchange between these two main groups where I've observed most misunderstandings.

Over the years I've noticed that when engineers initiate interdisciplinary work, it often resembles attempts at social engineering, while when social scientists put forward their work, it is not unusual that many engineers find it completely irrelevant. In preparation for this chapter, I found several articles on the troubles and joys with interdisciplinary research when combining the environmental and social sciences (one article is even dated back in 1972[2]). I found it strange that almost all articles mirror the same reflections, but hardly any deals with the topic of academic quality in interdisciplinary research. If, by reflecting on some hard-earned experiences from my research,[3] I could contribute to a dialogue on quality in interdisciplinary work in this field, the role of disciplines and disciplining, then that could be my calling.

'CROSSDISCIPLINARITY CAN MAKE EVERYBODY CROSS . . .'

For sure, there are many variants of interdisciplinarity (multi-, inter-, transdisciplinarity), some more fashionable than others, but I want to start by taking a step back: there are many disciplines, and when trying to deal with a mix of them, the researcher sooner or later ends up feeling mixed up . . . Not only do scholars of each field have their own ideas on what qualifies as good research, but many scholars also hold implicit and rather inflexible notions of what constitutes interdisciplinarity – as if there were only one way of mixing disciplines! The clash of academic values may be considerable. And I realized this sooner, rather than later, as a young academic – at the first meeting with my multi-disciplinary group of four supervisors.

The general plan for my PhD studies was that I should do something about life-cycle assessment (LCA) and decision making in companies. I knew it wasn't going to be easy, but I saw it as an exciting challenge and I thought I was pretty well prepared for the topic. I had already worked for more than a year as an assistant in various research projects – the most important one was a national packaging study (consisting of many LCAs) for the Swedish Ministry of Environment (SOU1991). My basic training had been in chemical engineering at Chalmers University of Technology, with a specialization in environmental chemistry. In addition, I had taken courses on, for example, business administration, economics, political science and history of technology, which had led me to contacts with the Swedish Ministry of Environment for whom I conducted my MSc diploma project on environmental investments in industry. On top of that, both the research agency funding my project and the environmental work group at the Swedish Federation of Industries were extremely positive to my project. A multidisciplinary group of supervisors was assembled, consisting of two researchers at the business school (a general management researcher and a specialist in decision making and business accounting) and two from Chalmers (the head of our environmental division and the LCA specialist who had led the great packaging project). And, at least two of them had experience with multidisciplinary projects. So, I had some familiarity with academic life, background training, and competent and enthusiastic support – at least so I thought.

At the first meeting with my four supervisors, one of the supervisors from the business school exclaimed: 'But this will never amount to anything of scientific value!' He continued: 'Drop whatever it is that you're writing on. You've got to take at least two years of courses here before you can have anything to say.'

This he exclaimed after having heard about the work we had done so far at my group at Chalmers: the writing of a couple of journal papers on LCA methodology about learning from the big packaging project, a tentative plan for my doctoral studies with a list of topics I thought I needed to learn more about. A purpose of the meeting had been to solicit from the business school supervisors what courses and readings they thought suitable for my needs. When he so flatly condemned what was being put forward, I gasped for words. Also my Chalmers supervisors seemed deflated by his assault – no one said a word in defense.

I struggled to comprehend the situation. The meeting ended without nothing much being decided. Afterwards, nothing really changed, and gradually I felt my situation grow insupportable. A couple of months later, I had to take time out from my PhD studies (that is, sick leave) to figure out whether or not to continue and, if so, how. The relative silence of my Chalmers supervisors at the meeting had surprised me, but it soon became clear to me that although I was a beginner at research, I was already the more experienced of talking to the 'other' discipline. Philosophers of science sometimes label interdisciplinarity as either 'big' or 'small', indicating 'distances' between academic fields, where 'small' typically means collaboration between fields within the same faculty (for example, within the engineering sciences) and 'big' refers to collaboration between different faculties (for example, the engineering and the social sciences). What we had at that first meeting was a case of big interdisciplinarity but with little awareness of the distances, and I sat amidst the resulting clash.

Looking back, I see the struggle for academic supremacy taking place during that meeting, but also the lack of some kind of interdisciplinary moderator. Somehow I decided to continue, but after that I only met with my supervisors one by one, never in a group, and never the dismissive one. (The irony is that he was chosen as supervisor for he was known as a kind, understanding and soft-spoken man.) I remember myself constantly explaining Chalmers ways to the remaining business school supervisor and vice versa. Thus I became the interpreter between the different disciplinarians, my supervisors. Strangely enough, I thought, but there I was, the young beginner, translating between my senior and more 'experienced' supervisors. I couldn't but lose some of the respect of my senior peers, but I also gained a sense of self-confidence – whatever I would achieve under such crossfire, it would be more than they ever had. (Another irony is that the articles I was supposed to give up are among my most cited ones.) The supremacy issue was resolved technically – I was after all a PhD student at Chalmers where the PhD curriculum was flexible. Instead of having to take a compulsory set of courses as one did at the business school, I could take elective courses at my own pace, letting research projects, knowledge needs and curiosity define course selection. The issue of quality, however, was never really raised again by any. Nevertheless it continued to haunt me. I had realized that such assaults on interdisciplinary research were to be expected. So, if I was to continue, I had to learn as much as possible about different academic disciplines and their scholars in order to be able to defend my ideas academically. Thus started my amateur ethnographic study of academia and nomadic criss-crossing across its different fields.

UNTANGLING CROSS CONFUSION

By now, I can see several reasons for what happened at that meeting and on other similar occasions. For example, I've seen similar questioning of the work of my doctoral students, even from other environmental and interdisciplinary researchers. What I didn't realize in the beginning was that the type of interdisciplinary research I started with my PhD is rather uncommon.

One reason, I think, why both I and my PhD students are met with suspicion despite interdisciplinarity being so fashionable, is that the organizing of our interdisciplinarity deviates from what is considered 'normal' interdisciplinarity. 'Normal' interdisciplinarity typically takes place when researchers of different backgrounds take part in a multidisciplinary project. That is what I call *collaborative* interdisciplinarity, while what I did for my PhD was more solitary and integrative. In this *integrative* interdisciplinarity, the researcher, not a (multi-people) project, has to harbor and synthesize the different types of knowledge as well as choose between different academic norms and conventions. By doing so, I immediately deviated not only from any of the disciplines I attempted to integrate, but also from 'normal' interdisciplinarity, the collaborative kind.[4] Unless one's work fits into the 'normal' mould, one is often met with suspicion and sometimes even blunt rejection, but that is nothing that good academic self-defense and discussion cannot resolve. My trouble was that I was too inexperienced at that first critical meeting.

Another reason is related to processes for judging the quality of research and a curious absence of this among industrial ecology researchers. Engaging in interdisciplinary collaborations is for most a positive experience, although strange things happen too. The meeting with other disciplines and scholars is, according to them, most interesting, rewarding, a great learning, and so on. They had, as I see it, (only) engaged in friendly conversation over a neighbourly fence, sometimes borrowing a tool or two. The conversation is not without misunderstandings, and there is usually quite a bit of bad-mouthing behind the back of one's academic neighbour. This crossdisciplinary behaviour is strange in that it somehow confirms and reinforces the idea of a fence. An engineer with such an interdisciplinary experience is often still foremost an engineer (and so is the social scientist). The interdisciplinary conversation even seems to have induced a crippling politeness concerning discussions on academic quality. The engineers typically don't get involved in the quality assessment of the neighbour's work (nor let the neighbour evaluate them either) – they are mainly concerned with what is done in their own plot (and vice versa). This evasive behaviour can be observed for example in relation to PhD theses and their examination. Many times I've observed engineering PhD candidates who have carried out some piece of qualitative research being evaluated by an examination committee without any competence on qualitative research. Alternatively, I've observed uncritical borrowing from other academic fields resulting in extensive application of outdated or contested theories where caution should have been advised but nothing was said. When raising issues related to quality (justification for methods chosen or theories applied, internal consistency), the typical answer I hear is: 'But this is such a young field, and we're only just learning.' The trouble, as I see it, is that such an excuse is quickly exhausted and we should be better at defending our research. Somehow this lack ought to reflect on processes related to wider academic recognition – I don't think it is only a desire for independence that has led so many multidisciplinary environmental research groups to locate themselves organizationally outside the regular faculty organization. It is after all there one finds the longest traditions of discussing and judging research quality. If we cannot justify our IE research within academia, then maybe it doesn't belong there . . . ? In contrast to collaborative researchers, I've had to cross fences, trespass, try to blend in, try hard not to be exposed as an impostor or a fake when doing integrative research. Still, I revert constantly between different academic identities and orientations. By not honouring disciplinary fences, I've become an unusual crossbreed, even among other environmental interdisciplinarians. At the technical university people address me as the 'social scientist' while at the business school people refer to me as the 'engineer'. That means that I am constantly cast as the 'other'. This used to sadden me because I felt no one really understood my research, nor appreciated my efforts, but by now I can derive some pleasure from not having to have conformed, from not having been 'disciplined' into established expectations and behaviours. Simultaneously, I realize that if my integrative work does not have a clear academic home, how can its quality be judged? In fact, I've had the same piece of research evaluated as 'completely unscientific' by an interdisciplinary environmental research council; as 'unserious and opportunistic' by an interdisciplinary environmental research assessment panel; it received a best poster award at an interdisciplinary environmental conference; it has received a royal distinction from an interdisciplinary environmental committee; and with a basic research council, the same research was characterized as 'world-leading'. How does one make sense of such contradictory evaluations? Whom can I take seriously?

The third reason has to do with overall purposes of research. The urgency of the environmental problem has so far mostly led to a focus on practical recommendations, measures and remedies in research – this is why transdisciplinary research (as it has come to be understood within this environmental field[5]) has become so popular. Environmental urgency has also led to interdisciplinary and environmental research mainly being esteemed on grounds of its practical and direct usefulness – not so much by its contribution to theory, whatever the type of theory. But is it so that a focus on practical relevance can outweigh inattention to theoretical advancement? One trouble with focusing on solving practical problems in IE is that the research often ends up with measures and remedies resting on the researchers' inarticulate and common-sensical assumptions about how society works (for example, on roles of actors in society, what decision making is, how companies operate, and so on). The focus on practical problems also means that much of the interdisciplinary research mainly consists of applied research, which in turn, presumes that there is basic research that can be applied to the practical problems. But how many of us haven't found existing theories lacking, inadequate, somehow incomplete or too narrow in scope? That doesn't mean that we should give up on theories. So I ask: what if there is a need for more *basic*, interdisciplinary environmental research that focuses on a rich understanding of the environmental problem of society and on a more integrative development of theoretical knowledge in the field? To paraphrase Latour (1993): Reality is not divided in disciplines, so why study it through disciplines? And when I aim at either understanding the social organization of environmental efforts in industry or try developing some integrative socio-environmental theory, I have to deal with the irritation from colleagues whose hidden assumptions[6] I have exposed or those who think that my research is not useful enough. I don't want urgency, nor crossdisciplinary politeness, to become excuses for dodging issues related to academic quality, forthright dialogue and theoretical advancement. Why isn't there room for all these issues?

Sense and Orientation?

My first interdisciplinary experience was upsetting and took some hard reflecting to recover from. I've used it as a lens to make sense of meetings between scholars of different denominations. While much written about interdisciplinarity discusses it on a conceptual level (for example whether concepts are borrowed, added to each other or synthesized), my perspective is more organizational and people-oriented (for example, about organizational practices and routines, communities, interests, norms and behaviour), which is why I mainly distinguish between collaborative and solitary/integrative interdisciplinary research. Many of the tensions I've observed over the years stem from such differences. The interdisciplinary combination of concepts is a type of problem that can be resolved, but is academic organization a problem to be solved? For me, it came down to developing navigation strategies in order to find my orientations around the many academic fields. To carefully think out the grounding of my research became very important and then to defend it, like all researchers do. The difference is in the nature of the defense. In more established research fields, one can learn the art of academic self-defense by 'imitating' one's peers and by learning the 'scripts' of the debate within the field. In my case, that was insufficient. Who was there to imitate? And it was almost impossible to predict what direction critique would come from. Doing integrative interdisciplinary research, I realized, requires a multidisciplinary understanding of how researchers understand (and don't understand), the overall philosophy of their research and to be able to introduce and explain very basic premises of research and concepts to many different types of researchers in ways that are meaningful to them. The problem is, one can never learn enough . . . and situations when one is uncomfortably speechless and simply unable to get across should only be expected. Now, I do what I can to also help my PhD students to prepare for academic self-defense of the higher school, to support them through periods of feeling lonely and to encourage them to seek out their own academic allies and sources of influence.

My academic vagabonding together with my ethnographic studies[7] made me quite knowledgeable about academia and the roles of university in society in general. I often find myself interpreting, explaining and mediating between different disciplinarians, something that has come to be appreciated in contexts such as the faculty senate at Chalmers, although it took me a couple of years before I realized how an outsider like myself could have insights central to discussions there. But, as I said in the beginning, I'd rather get on with my research, so I'll use this opportunity to hand over observations from my academic explorations. I start with a description of the 'tribes' before turning to the travelling tips. I hope these descriptions can guide anyone engaging in interdisciplinary research by informing them *about* the 'other' and the peculiarities to be expected, or even propel them to learn *from* the 'other'. While the learning *about* other research communities supports effective collaborations, the learning *from* other research communities can lead to more integrative forms of research. This means that for integrative interdisciplinarity, academic mixing goes further. By learning *from* the 'other', one replaces some of one's practices by those of the other. This can result in new kinds of mongrelized researchers.[8]

In any case, my first travelling tip is to develop communication skills, and here the term 'interdisciplinary' acquires a special meaning. 'Interdisciplinary' in this particular sense is understood as a skill of *interpreting between* different disciplines. Interdisciplinarity, in this literal meaning, is a very useful skill in multi-disciplinary collaborations to facilitate communication and learning. With greater interdisciplinary skills comes a deeper knowledge about different academic communities, their forms of reasoning and methodologies, thereby enabling the putting together of more integrated forms of research.

A word of caution to the reader is probably in place, here. I paint my descriptions of the engineering and social scientist with a broad brush, bordering on stereotype caricatures. My description of engineering researchers is perhaps more critical than that of the social scientists, but it might help the reader to think many of the flaws I describe are my own that I've had to deal with during my interdisciplinary journey. When comparing the reasoning and methods in different academic milieus, I uncovered thought patterns and values that had been bestowed upon me (and everyone else) through education (for example, reductionism) – it was a kind of 'intellectual, academic therapy' that I underwent. Some realizations did not come easy, but they allowed me to avoid 'auto-pilot' thinking. This doesn't mean that I don't have any critical remarks about social scientists, only that those remarks are fewer.

Kings of Things

Perhaps the most distinctive feature of engineers is their love for practical problem solving. There is even a book with the title 'The existential pleasures of engineering' wholly devoted to the deep-felt satisfaction stemming from solving complicated problems, usually technical problems. To master complicated physical conditions and technical objects is the height of engineering. The more complicated, the more satisfying – hence Kings of Things. This also means that the engineering sciences are mainly applied sciences, using more basic science to develop solutions to all sorts of problems, including the environmental problems in our societies.

The sense of environmental urgency goes down well with the engineers' love of practical problem solving. It even gives them a feeling of responsibility for seeing to environmental problems. However, this is also a major source of frustration in relations with social scientists. Especially those social scientists who aim at understanding and explicating the many dimensions of a problem are particularly difficult for engineers to stomach. With the social scientists' rich understanding of problems, the engineers don't understand why social scientists don't use it for developing solutions, and not even for putting forward practical recommendations. Most of the bad-mouthing taking place behind the backs of social scientists concerns the engineers' frustration with this: 'They don't contribute with anything useful; the point in their research is practically irrelevant.'

One must remember that the type of knowledge engineers are used to applying is that of the natural sciences (mainly physics and chemistry) and this has several side effects complicating their communication with social scientists. Reality is often seen by engineers as objective, possible to describe in a general way, possibly even with a grand unifying theory. With this perspective on reality follows a strong tendency to generalize. There is for example one law of gravity, and it applies everywhere in the universe. Although appropriate when it comes to the laws of nature, engineers tend to bring this inclination for generalization into other realms, such as social realities, as a matter of course. Generalization together with their focus on practical solutions makes them typically very goal-oriented, and it is not unusual to hear engineers discuss problems related to work organization or gender equality as if there were a single, commonsensical, natural, objective (and optimal) practical solution. It might go as far as having a unified understanding of society, enabling the formulation of grand solutions, a gung ho mentality ready to take on any kind of problem, and ensuing a slight hubris.

With this in mind, it might not be strange to understand that engineers often have difficulties in seeing and understanding that problems are perceived differently by different actors, and that there can be many ways of dealing with problems. It is not unusual for them to become frustrated when confronted with social processes ensuring equal value to a plurality of perspectives. When it comes to environmental problems, they often seek broad technical solutions to these, putting a lot of energy into persuading policy-makers and the public about the suitability of these. The extent to which they bring social scientists into their work is to have them design information campaigns that educate people about the necessity for the identified (usually technical) solutions. Simon Guy and Elizabeth Shove describe these processes extensively in their book *The Sociology of Energy, Buildings and the Environment: Constructing Knowledge, Designing Practice* (2000).

Engineering researchers interested in environmental problems realize that there are social dimensions to environmental problems, and that social scientists might not be interested in the afore-mentioned information campaigns. So, instead of collaborating with social scientists, engineers are not afraid of doing a bit of social science themselves. Since engineering is basically an applied science, it is quite natural for engineers to think that also social science should be possible to apply to their problems. And together with their gung ho and commonsensical mentality they will approach the social sciences, fully convinced that they are capable of that too. However, they will not readily give up their objective understanding of reality and their tendency to broad generalization, and it is likely that they will miss out on important subtleties and the point in plurality. 'Engineers are good at doing bad social science' as an observant colleague once said.[9]

Engineers may learn to use the methods of social scientists, mainly surveys and interviewing, but when it comes to taking stock of theories, that is a whole different matter. To begin with, engineers are not likely to use their empirical findings for formal theorizing, because, as I've said, engineering is basically an applied science. They may, however, use their empirical findings for more commonsensical reasoning. When they do work with theories, they look for a theory from which they can draw out recommendations for problem solving. But, without an overview of theories and schools of theories in the social sciences, the engineers may pick one 'from the pile' and be happy with that, not really knowing the full implications of their selection. Often engineers feel comfortable with theoretical schools in the social sciences that have a similar logic as engineering: rational and objective. This means that they prefer to collaborate with certain kinds of social scientists: economists, and possibly also psychologists. Sociologists, however, especially those with a social constructivist perspective are difficult for engineers to understand. Although engineers can understand some of the messages from a social constructivist, it will be extremely difficult for engineers to take the consequences of such insights in relation to their own knowledge perspective (epistemology).

Speaking of epistemology, it is also worth remembering that the engineering scientists within industrial ecology have almost all experienced an intellectual revelation when they got in contact with systems thinking. Systems thinking is a school of thought that actually fits very well with the engineer's understanding of the chemical process industry, automated production facilities, computer systems, and so on but their education rests strongly on the heritage of the basic sciences and their tradition of a reductionist school of thought. Discovering systems thinking is usually therefore described by industrial ecology engineers in exhilarating words, as if all pieces have fallen into place.

It is of course a good insight for a researcher to come to grips with different schools of thought. However, there are two aspects that are somewhat problematic. One is their rather inconsistent application of systems thinking. A most telling example is the formulation of the allocation rules in the LCA standard (ISO14041, 1998). The teleological principle, that methodological choices and the design of the model depend on the purpose of the model, is completely set aside by a strict and prescribed hierarchy of methodological options, irrespective of the purpose of the LCA. The teleological principle, however, is expressed in the opening paragraph of the standard that methodological choices depend on the purpose of the LCA. I explain such inconsistencies as an incomplete understanding of systems thinking, or that the full consequences of that logic are not taken. The other problem is that although the engineers have another school of thought besides reductionism, they are not fully prepared to accept and understand yet another school of thought, namely social constructivism. So they just leave it at that and stay with systems thinking which is supportive to problem solving and, if not for generalizations, then at least for broad overviews. I sometimes wonder if there is not a slight feeling of overview, authority and control (not to say omnipotence) fuelling the passion for systems thinking. How else can one explain the presentation on an industrial ecology blog: 'Industrial Ecology – The Science of Sustainability'?

Seismographs of the Social

Referring to the social scientists as a single group is a too sweeping a characterization, but engineers who find it hard to distinguish one type of social scientist from another often do this. However, the group of social scientists is more heterogeneous than the group of engineers. The differences are made up by not only different areas of research and interest, but also by the representation of different schools of thought and theories. There are systems thinkers among them too, but also social constructionists, post-colonialists, structuralists, post-modernists, essentialists, feminists, to list a few. This results in a pluralism among social scientists, un-paralleled and poorly understood among engineering researchers. This pluralism in knowledge perspectives fosters an open-minded and allowing culture among social scientists, but the engineer should not believe that everything is met with friendly acceptance. I would say that there are more conflicts among social scientists than among engineers. A management scholar about economists: 'No way I'll work with them – it's such an imperialistic science!' or an anthropologist about a management scholar: 'Postmodernists are such opportunists . . .' Such conflicts are often rooted in fundamental differences in views on the individual's agency in society and knowledge perspectives. There are usually ideological dimensions to these differences. Although differences can be stark to social scientists, they appear often vague to engineers, who usually have a rather inarticulated or naive position on these matters. The trouble is, at least for engineers, that the social scientists are not clearly 'labelled'. Nevertheless, the social scientists have their codes for informing others about their position, but these are too subtle and abstract for engineers. I still have trouble to separate different sorts of social scientists, even after more than 15 years, so I've taken the habit of asking them directly: 'What is your position on postmodernism?' or 'What types of theories are you interested in and why?'

Pluralism has its effects on the cross-disciplinary exchange between engineers and social scientists. Social scientists tend to show great patience with engineers, no matter what simplistic or authoritarian suggestions for social change they put forward. I sometimes understand their patience as listening to yet another voice in the pluralistic choir. On other occasions, it is more a matter of listening and observing the engineers and their doings as objects of study, thereby allowing the engineers to be as 'engineery' as they like. Either way, this comes across to the engineers as the social scientists not seeming particularly engaged and feeds an insecurity in the engineers about whether or not the social scientists really are interested in cross-disciplinary exchange.

What the engineers might not register is the social scientists' great respect for the engineers' technical and environmental knowledge. On many occasions I have wondered at why social scientists (and I do mean those working on environmental topics) are so cautious when it comes to describing environmental problems. It is as if they don't think it will ever be possible for them to understand environmental problems or environmental technology other than in the broadest sense. Thus they usually speak of it only in very general categories (that is, 'environment', 'technology'). The diversity of environmental problems (for example, global warming, eutrophication, biodiversity, and so on) and the understanding that dealing with one environmental problem can have negative effects on other environmental problems are self-evident knowledge among IE engineers, but such relationships seem curiously lost on social scientists, which is something that puzzles the engineers. Similarly, concerning environmental technology, distinctions between end-of-pipe technology and pollution prevention measures are both fundamental and self-evident for IE engineers' analysis of environmental management. When such distinct technical categories are lumped together as 'environmental technology' by social scientists, engineers often start to doubt the relevance or applicability of the work of the social scientists.

Despite social scientists forming such a diverse group in terms of perspectives, there is more unity when it comes to research interests in general. In contrast to engineers, practical problem solving is not their prime ambition. Instead, they are more interested in understanding the 'anatomy' of problems, phenomena or processes. They record their observations and assemble their descriptions through a multitude of methods, too many to mention, but many of them involve the researcher directly as an observer and interpreter. So, in various ways they act as 'seismographs of the social'.

This can also be another reason for their vague renderings of environmental problems and technology – the majority of them are simply not that interested in physical things. Social scientists are more into people and society. It is all about people's attitudes, behaviours, discourses, communication, norms, change, and such things. That the physical world should have so little place when it comes to environmental research is just too strange from an engineering perspective. Fortunately, some environmental social scientists are realizing this too. For example, in 2006, Kallio and Nordberg concluded in a review article that biophysical dimension was missing in environmental management research and the anthropologist Wilk concluded that the phenomenon of bottled water could at the same time be made perfect sense of using logics of the social, but that it does not make any environmental sense.

Just because social scientists have a rich understanding of a problem doesn't mean that they readily will propose a practical solution or recommendation, which is something unfathomable to many engineers. One way I understand it is that social scientists are usually very careful to not mix their research role and their personal political opinion. Through the understanding of a problem they will also see that there are many ways of dealing with it, and to propose one way in particular would mean taking a political stance or playing into the hands of some interest groups. Another way to understand it is that just because they have studied a particular phenomenon a lot does not mean that they know how to manage it practically. They are foremost 'knowledge workers', not managers, politicians, corporate decision makers, public administrators, NGOs activists, and so on. The description made by the social scientist can be seen as an image (of for example a change process in an organization) alternative to the images held by the people in the studied organization. The practical relevance of this alternative image lies in its ability to give the people in the organization new ways of seeing their situation, and since they are the best at doing their own job (not the researcher), they will see what can be done.

The interest in understanding also means that social scientists are more interested in theorizing and in theory development. It is not unusual that they are familiar with the historical development of theories and that they have read texts that are more than 30 years old. Generally I would say that social scientists have a more text-based culture than engineering researchers. Social scientists both read and publish books to a greater extent than do engineers. Also, they cite on an average a greater number of references in their articles than do engineers. Besides pluralism and the urge to understand, such practical differences in publishing patterns also need to be remembered in interdisciplinary endeavours. Engineers who rarely read any article older than five years must rethink their literature search strategies if they are to get in contact with the major works of the social sciences.

Getting Across

Academic research work means quite different things in different disciplines. Anyone in for some interdisciplinary research is bound to end up on some kind of intellectual and cultural journey. As all journeys, it can be bumpy and uncomfortable at times, but there are several ways to prepare for it.

The most useful knowledge for my interdisciplinary ventures has been a solid grounding in philosophy of science. Recognizing different ontologies, epistemologies, axiologies[10] and methodologies has helped me tremendously when figuring out the logics of research in different communities. This 'grammar' of intellectual work was essential for liberating myself intellectually from the implicit thought patterns from my basic training; it is essential now when I evaluate interdisciplinary work with regard to internal consistency; it guides me when I relate the importance of findings from different fields to each other. I simply cannot see how I could identify, nor carry out, good interdisciplinary research without this orientation in different schools of thought.

Equally important is to be able to present one's interdisciplinary work to all kinds of scholars. This is tricky because the presentation needs to be adapted to different audiences. A major part of interdisciplinary communication is to educate one side about the other, and the trick is to understand underlying thought patterns. Otherwise, it will be difficult to get across when schools of thought are different. In collaborations, it might be good to have someone who is not directly involved the empirical work of the project and who can act the role of interdisciplinary facilitator – I certainly wish someone had taken that role at my first meeting with my four supervisors . . . But, all this intellectual knowledge about other communities is facilitated by having some cultural knowledge as well. There are many roads for accessing other research fields. One obvious way is to spend some time in other research groups, not just meet the researchers at conferences. Another is via reading, but not necessarily the research articles – textbooks, book reviews, editorials and review papers can be better ways for learning about debated ideas in other fields.

All this is not easy, but I've never heard anyone regret interdisciplinarity when it comes to research.[11] In spite of this, there exist myths that inter-disciplinary work has little academic value, for example, for tenure and in research assessments. Also, some metaphors used for interdisciplinary research have a negative ring to them: research ends up 'in between' or in disciplinary 'no man's land'. Sometimes I wonder what's behind such statements. Are they not said to discipline researchers to stay within their fold? To me, interdisciplinarity has become an expression for academic freedom – freedom to follow a line of reasoning when exploring a problem. The circumstance that some sociologists speak of the democratization of academic knowledge supports this notion. They ask: why should scholars monopolize their knowledge within disciplines, shouldn't it be free for any scholar to pursue?

Research outside the cultural confines of a discipline also needs quality assessment, but what I've witnessed too often so far in the IE sphere are pretty random affairs. I think this might have to do with a circumstance that quality assessment is much dependent on cultural norms and prac-tices within a disciplinary community, no matter how much we want to believe otherwise. And when we can't rely on our own cultural norms and conventions, we get lost. Here, we do need dialogue! I hope that my cul-tural descriptions and the identification of the importance of knowledge perspectives can do something to advance that dialogue. This book in a way forms a forum for such a dialogue, but it needs to continue, possibly through forums created that culturally support interdisciplinary research, for example, IE awards or IE travel grants.

I also hope by attaching more positive notions to interdisciplinarity, it will encourage daring intellectual crossbreeding and freer intellectual pursuit. Even if a nomadic academic lifestyle is not for everyone, please, don't fence me in . . .

> Oh, give me land, lots of land
> Under starry skies above.
> *Don't Fence Me In.*
> Let me ride through the wide open
> Country that I love.
> *Don't Fence Me In.*
> Let me be by myself in the evening breeze,
> Listen to the murmur of the cottonwood trees.
> Send me off forever,
> but I ask you, please,
> *Don't Fence Me In.*

> (*Words and music by Cole Porter and Robert Fletcher, ©1942,*
> *from the film Hollywood Canteen.*)

NOTES

1. At our department, we prefer to speak of Environmental Systems Analysis. This is a more neutral label than Industrial Ecology, with its loaded metaphor.
2. The article is written by James McEvoy at the Department of Sociology and Division of Environmental Studies, University of California, Davis, California.
3. I have studied and led research on LCA/LCM practices in industry for some 15 years, for example, Baumann (1998), Rex and Baumann (2007). Another research interest concerns socio-material interactions, where I aim to understand how the social shapes material flows and vice versa, for example, Baumann (2008).
4. Formas is a major Swedish research council for environmental research. It has a special committee for evaluating interdisciplinary research proposals. Its guidelines explain what they mean by interdisciplinary research: only collaborations between two departments. A research proposal from a multi-disciplinary department is not accepted.
5. The term 'transdisciplinary' research has several meanings. Transdisciplinarity can be understood as a type of knowing that transgresses the knowing in a single discipline (for example, Nicolescu 2002). In this sense, transdisciplinarity is about intellectual synthesis. Transdisciplinarity can also be understood as a way of working where scientific knowledge and extra-scientific experience come together for practical problem-solving (for example, Mittelstrass 2001). It is in the latter meaning that has gained ground in Industrial Ecology circles. For further reading on transdisciplinarity, see the Swiss academy of sciences' bibliography on www.transdisciplinarity.ch.
6. For example, much research in the LCA community concerns the development of tools, such as tools for ecodesign. This research is to a large extent built upon the researchers' assumption about what should help ecodesign. Research findings about the practice of ecodesigners shows that it is not a lack of tools that hinders ecodesign – this tends to provoke the tool designers.
7. I have field journals from periods when I was a visiting researcher in the UK and in the US; I have recorded seminars on interdisciplinarity; I have done critical incident studies on interdisciplinarity; I have studied the situation for scholarly publishing for interdisciplinary environmental research. Of all this, only the last study is published (Baumann 2002).
8. In contexts of interdisciplinarity, the term 'hybrid disicipline' has come to stand for a new combination of disciplines, often on its way to forming a new disicipline, for example, bioinformatics. However, I prefer the notion of *mongrel* researchers in IE – sturdy and more varied than hybrids. IE then becomes what Østreng (2008) calls a 'multi-disciplinary discipline', rather than a hybrid discipline.
9. This phrase was uttered during a seminar on transdisciplinarity at Chalmers in May 2007 during an exchange between the two research directors of two multidisciplinary centres, one in the UK, the other in Australia. I no longer remember which of the two actually said it.
10. ontology = perspective on reality; epistemology = perspective on knowledge; axiology = overall purpose of research.
11. Interdisciplinarity in a research context should not be mixed up with interdisciplinarity in educational programs. The amount of administration and political diplomacy to coordinate several departments in different faculties can definitely lead to regretting an interdisciplinary initiative.

64   *The social embeddedness of industrial ecology*

REFERENCES

Baumann, Henrikke (1998), *Life Cycle Assessment and Decision Making. Theories and Practices*, PhD dissertation, Göteborg, Sweden: Chalmers University of Technology.
Baumann, Henrikke (2002), 'Publish and perish? The impact of citation indexing on the development of new fields of environmental research', *Journal of Industrial Ecology*, 6(3–4): 13–26.
Baumann, Henrikke (2008), 'Simple material relations handled by complicated organization by or "How many (organizations) does it take to change a lightbulb?"' in proceedings of *What is an Organization? Materiality, Agency and Discourse*, 21–22 May 2008, Montreal, Canada: Université de Montréal.
Guy, Simon and Elizabeth Shove (2000), *The Sociology of Energy, Buildings and the Environment: Constructing Knowledge, Designing Practice*, London, UK: Routledge.
Industrial Ecology blog: 'Industrial Ecology – The Science of Sustainability' industrialecology.blogspot.com (accessed February 2007).
ISO14041 (1998), *Environmental Management – Life Cycle Assessment – Goal and Scope Definition and Inventory Analysis*, International Organization for Standardization, Geneva, Switzerland.
Kallio, Tomi J. and Piia Nordberg (2006), 'The evolution of organizations and natural environment discourse. Some critical remarks', *Organization and Environment*, 19(4): 439–57.
Latour, Bruno (1993), *We Have Never Been Modern*, Cambridge, MA: Harvard University Press.
McEvoy III, James (1972), 'Multi- and interdisciplinary research – Problems of initiation, control, integration and reward', *Policy Sciences*, 3(2): 201–8.
Mittelstrass, Jürgen (2001), 'On transdisciplinarity', *in Proceedings of Science and the Future of Mankind. Science for Man and Man for Science*, Pontificiae Academiae Scientiarvm Scripta Varia 99, Vatican City, 2001.
Nicolescu, Basarab (2002), *Manifesto of Transdisciplinarity* (Translation of La transdisciplinarité – Manifeste, 1996) New York, USA: State University of New York Press, http://nicol.club.fr/ciret/vision.htm.
Østreng, Willy (2008), 'Crossing scientific boundaries by way of disciplines', in W. Østreng (ed.). *Complexity. Interdisciplinary Communications 2006/2007*, Oslo, Norway: Center for Advanced Study.
Rex, Emma and Henrikke Baumann (2007), 'Individual adaptation of industry LCA practice: results from two case studies in the Swedish forest products industry', *International Journal of LCA*, 12(4): 266–71.
SOU (1991), 77. *Life Cycle Analysis of Selected Packaging Materials* (Translation of *Miljön och förpackningarna. Livscykelanalyser av förpackningsmaterial.* Swedish Government Official Report no. 77), Anne-Marie Tillman, Henrikke Baumann, Elin Ericsson and Tomas Rydberg, Göteborg, Sweden: Chalmers Industiteknik.
Wilk, Richard (2006), 'Bottled water. The pure commodity in the age of branding', *Journal of Consumer Culture*, 16(3): 303–25.

First intermezzo Out into the open: the promise of dialogue

Frank Boons

In this book, we intend to address specifically the interdisciplinary nature of the field of industrial ecology. As the book deals with social science perspectives on material and energy streams, it communicates the insights of only one part of the industrial ecology community. Also, personal experiences give me ample reason to suspect that this perspective leads a relatively isolated life within the field. In order to provide openings for connections to the work in other disciplines, simply communicating our perspective will not be enough. For this reason, the book is peppered with a number of intermezzos. In each of these, researchers that come from science, engineering and technology (SET) disciplines comment on a set of chapters. This provides the beginning of a dialogue between the disciplines that feed the industrial ecology community.

The preceding chapter by Henrikke Baumann in a way starts this dialogue. Trained as an engineer, she has been fascinated by social science work, and taken the step to engage herself actively with it, to embody more or less the interdisciplinary nature of our field. My path is different: as a social scientist, I have worked with SET people at different points in my career. Rather than trying to develop myself by acquiring their knowledge, I have reflected many times on these encounters, and tried to distill something out of that. In this first intermezzo, I present some of my experiences in engaging with SET research(ers), and present some of the ideas about dialogue that have inspired Jennifer and me to make this part of the book.

MEETING ENGINEERS

I think my first encounter with what later came to be called the industrial ecology field took place at a Society of Environmental Toxicology and Chemistry (SETAC) conference in Leiden, The Netherlands in 1991. I had just started working with an institute for Environmental Sciences that specialized in social science approaches, and was involved in research that dealt with the ecological impact of products. In the Netherlands, the Dutch government sought to develop a tool that would measure the impact of products more or less unambiguously. The background to this quest included several public discussions about milk packaging and other products, in which the relative ecological impact of alternatives were hotly contested. As an economic sociologist I was interested in these 'battles over the facts' and their consequences for firms and policymakers. To my surprise, the people attending the conference were mainly interested in designing an 'objective tool' called life cycle-analysis (LCA). In a few of the discussions, I tried to express my feeling that maybe they were looking up the wrong alley, but I quickly found that either I was speaking another language (or poor English), or these people just didn't understand the obvious.

Of course, this was a wrong call. I had just been confronted with the peculiarities of interaction between members of different scientific disciplines. In the years that followed, the Institutes projects (which were centered around the introduction of the pollution prevention concept to managers and policymakers) gave me the opportunity to further explore this form of communication. Apart from simple mistakes such as talking about a process for 15 minutes, only to find out later, that we had been talking about quite dissimilar things, I discovered that the engineers brain (or mine) is simply wired in a different way. Whereas I was seeking to develop insight into the context of the way in which a firm was operating, understanding its organizational structure and routines, the beliefs of managers and workers, and the way in which governments tried to influence firm activities, engineers divided up the production process in parts, identified problems, and proposed solutions. Whenever a meeting was held, most of the discussion took place between the consultant with an engineering background and me, rather than involving the firm's representatives.

The major lesson that I learned through this is that the divide that exists between me and anyone coming from the SET-part of the world can only be bridged in a personal contact. I have not found that there are tricks that I can apply that work with engineers in general. Rather, I have to develop, with each new person that I meet, a common understanding. And this is where dialogue comes in.

THE IMPORTANCE OF MAKING YOURSELF KNOWN, AND KNOWING THE OTHER

Some years ago, I got involved in a project concerned with stakeholder dialogue, then a popular item in the sustainability discourse. When I tried to find literature on the topic, I stumbled onto several books that dealt with dialogue in general. Although we use the word dialogue in various ways, to indicate a conversation between two persons in real life or in a movie or theatre play, this literature dealt with something altogether different. It starts from the assumption that whenever one person communicates with another person, her verbal and non-verbal language is based on deep assumptions, thoughts, values and feelings. Most of the time, this deeper layer remains out of sight, and most interaction takes place without providing a connection between the layers of both persons. This results in poor communication. The literature that I started to read provides ways of communication in which these layers are exposed. The purpose is not to arrive at a common understanding, but rather that each person involved develops insight into the other person's assumptions and values. One example of such a dialogue is captured in a book called *The Ending of Time* (Krishnamurti and Bohm 1997). This book presents in written form several dialogues that took place between Krishnamurti, an Eastern philosopher who has lectured and written extensively on the human condition, and David Bohm, the famous physicist. Despite their completely different backgrounds, they uncover their deeper layers and look at them without judgement.

As researchers and practitioners, we are most of the time educated within a discipline, or at least a limited set of disciplinary frameworks. This education is intended to incorporate a specific way of looking at the world. This incorporation helps us in communicating with others who are educated likewise, and makes us select specific problems, approaches and solutions. Incorporation means that after time it becomes almost unconscious. It is a bit like learning how to tie your shoes: at first, you need all the concentration you can muster, but once you've learned it, it is an act that you can do while reading the newspaper, or having a conversation. As soon as we meet with someone from another discipline, this incorporated way of looking (and valuing) the world becomes a barrier. I believe that dialogue is one way of overcoming this barrier: I have to try to place myself into the other person's shoes, and try to experience the way she looks at the world. If the other person is willing to do the same, then it is possible to truly work together.

Yankelovich (1999) defines dialogue as a process of successful relationship building. In his view, dialogue helps to overcome stereotypes, and existing mistrust is taken away. This helps to increase mutual understanding and the sharing of visions, which eventually leads to new perspectives and insights through increased creativity. In my view, the establishment of the field of industrial ecology was possible only as several individuals were able to engage in a dialogue, and in this sense the field is a result of the creativity that flows through dialogue. I like this view, because it shows that dialogue is not about reaching consensus, but rather about discovering each others ideas and assumptions. The diversity that is brought to the table is a basis for creative thought and action.

The institutionalization of the field (Ehrenfeld 2004; Cohen and Howard 2006) in that sense is a mixed blessing: it provides more stability for the members of the community, but at the same time perspectives are in danger of becoming fixed, and assumptions are no longer criticized.

For this reason, it may be good to look at the following principles of a dialogue as identified by Yankelovich:

- *equality among participants*: whenever persons engage in a dialogue, they need to leave behind their respective roles and positions. Otherwise, the attached status and power interfere with the exchange, and dialogue will not take place. Equality (which should not be mistaken for similarity) means the absence of power. We might deceive ourselves in thinking that among scientists, power is not an issue. But the respect of the young PhD student for the successful professor is already a distortion that may inhibit a true exchange;
- *listening with empathy*: 'the ability to think someone else's thoughts and feel someone else's feelings' (Yankelovich 1999: 43). This amounts to stepping into the other persons shoes, trying to think what she thinks, and feel what she feels;
- *bring out assumptions into the open*: the idea is that participants uncover their deeper layers, and the other person listens to them while suspending judgement. So assumptions are not challenged, but empathically considered, with respect. This is not easy; Bohm says: 'This is difficult, because assumptions are linked to our sense of self, and if they are attacked, you react as if you are attacked personally.'

Of course, applying these principles within the format of an edited book is not possible: it requires the actual meeting of persons at a certain time and place. Instead, we provide what could be the starting point for such a dialogue by presenting not only the work of social scientists in the field of industrial ecology, but also reflections on this work by members of the field that originate from other disciplines. This makes it possible to uncover some of the apparent assumptions that underlie the work of our contributors. We hope that in this way, we have created a space in which others can start to explore the beauty of dialogue.

REFERENCES

Cohen, M. and J. Howard (2006), 'Success and its price: the institutionalization and political relevance of industrial ecology', *Journal of Industrial Ecology*, **10**(1–2): 79–88.

Ehrenfeld, J. (2004), 'Industrial ecology: a new field or only a metaphor', *Journal of Cleaner Production*, **12**(8–10): 825–31.

Krishnamurti, J. and D. Bohm (1997), *The Ending of Time*, San Francisco: Harper.

Yankelovich, D. (1999), *The Magic of Dialogue. Transforming Conflict into Cooperation*, London: Nicholas Brealy Publishing.

PART II

Regional approaches

4. Eco-industrial parks and industrial ecology: strategic niche or mainstream development?

David Gibbs

INTRODUCTION

Recent years have seen a growing interest in industrial ecology from both an academic and a policy perspective. Some authors have been quick to claim a leading position for industrial ecology in environmental research – Ashford and Côté (1997) term it a new unifying principle to operationalize sustainable development, while Allenby (1999) calls it the 'science of sustainability'. Similarly, from a policy perspective claims have been made that industrial ecology presents an opportunity to implement sustainable development, combining economic and social benefits with environmental improvements (Korhonen et al. 2004; Opoku 2004). Despite these claims much of the work on industrial ecology remains speculative in nature. Whether they examine theoretical or real-life situations, most authors, whether academics or policymakers, theorize what could be done in potential or existing industrial systems through exploring potential connections and synergies between constituent firms, rather than providing empirical evidence of whether this is happening on the ground. Indeed, a longstanding theme has been what might be termed the 'implementation gap' in industrial ecology, that is, the difference between the theory of industrial ecology and what has been achieved in practice (O'Rourke et al. 1996; and see Boons and Janssen 2005; Chertow 2007 for a more recent evaluation of progress to date). All of this raises questions as to whether an industrial ecology approach has any practical utility and whether industrial ecology can make the leap from the descriptive analysis of materials and energy flows in industrial systems toward a prescriptive framework offering concrete solutions and practical measures for policy-makers and business managers.

The chapter draws upon perspectives developed in science and technology studies that focus upon transition management as a means of

73

investigating how new technologies and ideas become mainstreamed or remain as niche markets. This work has been concerned with the transformation of technological regimes and, within this, has emphasized the role of innovative technological strategic niches in transition management. These technological regimes consist of interconnected systems of artefacts, institutions, rules and norms. The relevance to industrial ecology is that one strand of such work focuses upon innovative experiments in alternative, sustainable technological niches and draws lessons from the challenges they face in the context of a dominant, unsustainable technological regime. The potential value of transition management and strategic niche approaches for a study of industrial ecology is that they stress not just individual actions at the level of the firm or groups of firms, but also the networks and support structures that build up to help these alternative forms of sustainable practice. At the very least it will be necessary to configure new alliances of established and new companies that go beyond the traditional networks of enterprises and supersede traditional competitive relations if industrial ecology is to form the basis for new forms of industrial organization. One attempt to construct such new alliances has come in the form of eco-industrial parks (EIPs) as a planned example of industrial ecology in operation.

Drawing upon the concepts of transition management and strategic niches allows us to explore the future prospects for industrial ecology as theory and policy practice. For example, despite attempts to plan and create eco-industrial parks in the USA, many of these high profile early exemplars in the US have so far failed to evolve beyond the initial planning stage, have subsequently abandoned the industrial ecology theme, or have failed to realize the initial aims of creating synergies between firms. Of particular interest is whether the failure to create synergies is simply a short term problem or whether there are broader structural factors at work inhibiting their development. This raises a set of questions regarding the utility of industrial ecology as policy prescription. Are any attempts to create eco-industrial parks doomed to failure or are they a practicable option, albeit in a limited set of conditions, sectors and locations? Do EIPs act as a strategic niche, demonstrating the potential for industrial ecology to be mainstreamed, or do experiences to date indicate the incompatibility with the extant technological regime. Are there better prospects for both academic and practitioners to discover pre-existing synergies at the local and regional scales and to develop policies that build upon these, as Chertow (2007) has recently suggested? Before addressing these questions, I first outline the literature on transition management and strategic niches. I then provide details of eco-industrial park definitions and developments. In subsequent sections, I draw upon empirical work in 16 EIPs in the USA and Europe, first outlining the methods used for the empirical study and then examining this empirical material in some detail, before returning to a consideration of the potential use of transition management and strategic niches for industrial ecology research in the conclusions.

TRANSITION MANAGEMENT AND STRATEGIC NICHES

Despite claims that industrial ecology represents a new route towards sustainable development, exactly how the transition to new forms of industrial organization based upon industrial ecology principles may come about is not clear in the literature. Here it is useful to draw upon a body of work within social studies of technology which has been concerned with the transformation of technological regimes and, within this, has emphasized the role of innovative technological strategic niches in transition management (Rip and Kemp 1998; Smith 2003; Geels 2005). These technological regimes refer not just to the actual technologies used, but also consist of 'interconnected systems of artefacts, institutions, rules and norms' (Berkhout et al. 2003: 3). Research by Smith (2003, 2004, 2006) is of particular relevance here in that his work focuses upon 'innovative experiments in alternative, sustainable technological niches and draws lessons from the challenges they face in the context of a dominant, unsustainable technological regime' (Smith 2003: 128). These niches are seen as 'nurturing socio-technical configurations, which grow and displace incumbent regime activities' (Berkhout et al. 2003: 9). Taking such an approach allows us to contextualize industrial ecology-based initiatives and to gain a sense of the extent to which they represent a major paradigm shift.

For example, Hayter and Le Heron (2002) draw upon research by Freeman (1992) on techno-economic paradigms (TEP) to develop his suggestion that a 'green paradigm' will form the basis of future economic development. This they suggest will involve both technological and institutional changes. Far from being a technological determinist argument, emphasis is placed on the development of a set of matching institutional forms, including business organization, labour relations, R&D structures and international regulatory forms (similar arguments are developed in Chapters 5 and 6 in this volume). This green techno-economic paradigm will revolve around dematerialization of the economy, the internalization of environmental values by industry, the prioritization of the environment within R&D, as well as take-back strategies and a shift towards selling services rather than products. Thus:

In a green TEP, environmental imperatives become explicit motives for sys-temic change. In a green paradigm, innovation priorities are oriented to radi-cally reducing the use of energy and materials in transportation, construction and manufacturing systems . . . the resource management phase of the ICT [information and communication technology paradigm] is replaced by the phase of eco-development as ecological definitions of productivity recognize the non-industrial values of nature and seek to provide practical definitions for the idea of sustained development. (Hayter and Le Heron 2002: 20)

Industrial ecology approaches could therefore be seen as part of the process of constructing a set of actors and networks that are developing environmentally sustainable niches offering lessons for policy makers in the transition to a new green paradigm. Three types of processes help to construct and develop niches: the evolution of networks to support the niche, learning processes to stimulate the use of new methods and tech-niques and the articulation of expectations and visions to attract attention and enroll more actors (Geels 2005). It is argued that such niches help to transform current technological regimes through their focus on ten-sions within these regimes (Smith 2003). In the work of Freeman outlined above, new techno-economic paradigms arise when the economy is con-fronted by tensions that can not be solved by the existing TEP. These ten-sions are a product of changing circumstances in the wider 'socio-technical landscape', where new trends challenge existing technological regimes. In relation to industrial ecology, we can think of such changes encompass-ing widespread environmental concerns over greenhouse gas emissions, enhanced global warming, the need to reduce waste etc. as constituting an important set of drivers for the development of a new sustainable techno-logical regime. In some accounts, niche activities may break through to the mainstream if they successfully solve bottlenecks in the extant regime (Geels 2005). Conversely, those niches completely at odds with the exist-ing landscape may find it difficult to break through into the mainstream, but some aspects may be more compatible and more easily incorporated (Smith 2003).

If, as Smith (2003: 131) suggests, 'recommendations for radical shifts to sustainable technological regimes entail concomitantly radical changes to the socio-technical landscape of politics, institutions, the economy and social values' they are unlikely to proceed (if at all) without parallel politi-cal actions. However, what is often lacking in the transition management literature is a sense of the politics and power relations involved between the different actors and institutions that may facilitate or hinder the transition. This is an area that requires further study, particularly in relation to the kinds of policy actions that the transition management literature proposes for innovative technological change. Transition is therefore not inevitable, but the outcome (or not) of struggle, agency and power relations, something which may be hidden by strategic niche management approaches that extrapolate from historical studies[1] (Smith 2004; Shove and Walker 2007). Certainly niches are important sources of innovation that may offer solutions for tensions in existing socio-technical regimes, but the 'adaptation process is confined by structures within the existing, mainstream regime' (Smith 2006: 453). Indeed, it may be that existing socio-technical contexts close down spaces for alternative approaches (Shove 1998), except at times of tension when new trajectories are actively being sought, as with the current concerns over climate change, carbon emissions and waste reduction. At these moments certain actors come to the fore, or have their actions legitimated, as in the case of the promoters of industrial ecology. The potential value of transition management and strategic niche approaches for a study of industrial ecology is that they stress not just actions and developments in isolation, but also 'the networks and support structures that have built up to help these alternative forms of sustainable practice' (Smith 2003: 128). This helps us connect industrial ecology practices and activities to wider economic and social structures and indicates the kinds of broader changes that may be necessary. As Keijzers (2002: 356) suggests, 'it will be necessary to configure new alliances of established and new companies that go beyond the traditional networks of enterprises and supersede traditional competitive relations. Transitions towards new systems of technology require new alliances'. Such new alliances may be developed through eco-industrial park initiatives; although by this account such inter-company alliances may be a necessary, but insufficient step. In the longer term, alliances and networks must be developed which connect into the wider techno-economic paradigm if industrial ecology is to become a mainstream development.

THE DEFINITION AND DEVELOPMENT OF ECO-INDUSTRIAL PARKS

Eco-industrial parks are a policy-driven attempt to apply the principles of industrial ecology in specific locations. While defining EIPs has been the subject of some debate (see for example Martin et al. 1998; PCSD 1997; Lowe 1997, 2003), I utilize Cohen-Rosenthal's (2003: 19) definition of an EIP as a:

> community of businesses that co-operate with each other and with the local community to efficiently share resources (information, materials, water, energy, infrastructure and natural habitat) . . . leading to economic gains, gains in

environmental quality and equitable enhancement of human resources for the business and local community.

This definition incorporates a requirement for networking between EIP actors, which is central to the industrial ecology ecosystem analogy. Moreover, while the industrial ecology literature has primarily developed by drawing upon natural science and engineering frameworks, this definition also focuses attention upon the social and policy contexts (Korhonen et al. 2004). While all the aspects of co-operation listed in this definition need not be present at every EIP, I would argue that an EIP should be more than a standard industrial park with a marginal environmental theme, such as environmentally friendly buildings, or a collection of 'green' businesses (for example, environmental technology or recycling businesses) that do not interact with each other.

From the 1990s onwards, a number of local and regional projects were initiated to plan and actively develop EIPs (BCSD 2002). As Heeres et al. (2004: 985) suggest, EIPs were seen as having the potential to overcome the tensions between economic development and environmental protection:

> Attention for eco-industrial park (EIP) development projects has grown enormously among national and regional governments and industries in many countries. It is believed that a well planned, functioning EIP has the potential to both benefit the economy and substantially relieve environmental pressure in and near the location of its development.

Some of the early proposals for EIP development were almost evangelical in their optimism for what could be achieved. Many of these made reference to the much (and perhaps over) cited example of Kalundborg[2] in Denmark where a web of waste and energy exchanges has developed between the local city administration, a power plant, an oil refinery, a pharmaceuticals and enzymes plant and a plasterboard manufacturer, with heat and steam going to municipal heating and a fish farm. This example appeared to offer support for proponents of industrial ecology and eco-industrial parks. For example, Hawken (1993: 63), after citing Kalundborg as an unplanned example of the genre, argues the case for policy intervention to create EIPs – 'imagine what a team of designers were to come up with if they were to start from scratch, locating and specifying industries and factories that had potentially synergistic and symbiotic relationships'. These arguments were particularly influential in the USA. In the late 1990s the US Federal government identified and promoted four EIP demonstration sites through the President's Council for Sustainable Development at Cape Charles, VA, Chattanooga, TN, Brownsville, TX and Baltimore, MD (Cohen-Rosenthal 1996, 2003; Schlarb 2001;

Hendricks and Giannini-Spohn 2003). Although much cited in the industrial ecology literature, support for these demonstration sites was largely symbolic and involved little in the way of Federal resources. The initiative did, however, raise the profile and potential of industrial ecology and led to a number of EIP proposals and developments across the United States. EIPs have also been developed in Europe, particularly in the Netherlands (see Eilering and Vermeulen 2004; Heeres et al. 2004; Mirata 2004). Boons and Janssen (2005) provide an overview of attempts to implement the lessons of Kalundborg in the Netherlands and the difficulties that have arisen in creating such 'top down' planned initiatives. In addition, some parts of Asia, including China, India, the Philippines, Thailand and Sri Lanka (see Chiu and Yong 2004; Erkman and Ramaswamy 2003; Lowe 2003) have also seen EIP proposals and developments.

RESEARCH DETAILS AND METHODS

Despite the growing number of EIP proposals and developments there has been relatively little academic research that attempts a critical evaluation of their operations. Where published work does exist, this has often focused upon isolated examples (for example Roberts 2004; Mirata and Emtairah 2005) or has been written by those heavily involved in their promotion and management (see for example the collection of papers in Cohen-Rosenthal and Musnikow 2003). In order to address this gap I conducted a research project to examine eco-industrial park developments in the USA and Europe. The first stage of the research identified EIPs in these two locations through internet and literature searches. A survey by email, fax and telephone was then conducted between January and March 2002 to collect basic background information on the characteristics of each initiative. The survey produced a total of 19 responses, from both operational (14) and planned (five) EIPs. This survey was used as a basis to choose case studies for further in-depth, semi-structured interviews. This case study work was designed to address a number of key features of industrial ecology identified through a close reading of the literature: the cycling of materials and energy; networking and cluster building; and the contribution to sustainable development outcomes. Table 4.1 shows these key features and the specific research questions used to address these.

The interview survey was conducted at ten sites in the USA and six in Europe (see Table 4.2 for summary details of these EIPs). These 16 case study EIPs were chosen on the basis that they were (or stated that they intended to be) engaged in inter-firm networking, as well as contributing to local economic and social objectives, that is, they sought to incorporate the

Table 4.1   Key features of industrial ecology and research questions

Features of Industrial Ecology	Research Questions
Cycling of materials and energy Minimization of: 　Waste production 　Energy consumption 　Raw material consumption	• Is there evidence for industrial symbiosis at EIPs? • Do EIPs act as closed systems? • Does this lead to lock-in to current processes?
Networking and cluster building	• Do EIPs involve networking behaviour between firms? • What is the role of trust and cooperation in developing EIPs? • At what scale should industrial ecology be implemented?
Sustainable development *('win–win–win' outcomes)* Gains for: 　Economy 　Environment 　Society	• Do EIPs involve local collaboration and partnership? • Can EIPs be promoted by public policy intervention? • Do EIPs lead to improved economic, environmental and social outcomes, compared to locality/region in which located?

key features of industrial ecology listed in Table 4.1. Interviews were conducted with stakeholders at each development and a critical review of secondary material undertaken both via the internet and on-site. At each site, up to eight interviews were carried out with relevant individuals including park managers, project developers, local authority representatives (from planning and/or economic development departments), consultants, participating firms, environmental organizations, community representatives and chambers of commerce. A total of 53 interviews with a total of 63 individuals were conducted. Field work was conducted in the US in July 2002 and December 2003, while the European sites were visited throughout 2003 and 2004. In the following sections the results from the survey are evaluated in relation to the specific research questions outlined in Table 4.1. It should be noted of course that this still remains a fairly limited set of cases and there are other eco-industrial developments, especially in Europe, that are not included here. Care should therefore be taken when interpreting the wider implications from this set of case studies. More details of the study and the results have been published elsewhere (Gibbs et al. 2005; Gibbs and Deutz 2005, 2007). These publications were specifically focused

Table 4.2 Main features of eco-industrial parks in interview survey

Park	Location	Status	Funding	Developer	Objectives	'Greenness'
US Sites						
Devens Planned Community, MA	Former army base, rural area	Opened 1996	Public – incl. Federal	Public agency	Balancing economic development, environmental performance and social values	Eco Star Program, green building incentives
Phillips Eco Enterprise Center, MN	Urban area, deprived neighbourhood	Opened 1999	Public (state, county and city) and private	Community non-profit	Living wage jobs, clean industries	Architecture, some 'green' tenants
Port of Cape Charles Sustainable Technology Park, VA	Rural, remote location in economic decline	Opened 2000	Public (county, federal and state)	Public agency	Creation of living wage jobs	Architecture, covenants, points system
Gulf Coast By-Product Synergy Project, Freeport, TX	Large petrochemicals complex	Phase 1 2003 (internal to Dow Chemicals); Phase 2 2004 (with 10–15 companies)	Private and public (Federal)	Private companies/US BCSD	Reduced wastes and costs	Waste treatment facility, utilities, by-product synergy

Table 4.2 (*continued*)

Park	Location	Status	Funding	Developer	Objectives	'Greenness'
Londonderry Eco-industrial Park, NH	Small community, adjacent to airport and freeway to Boston	Under construction	Private	Private sector	Strengthen local economy, reduce environmental impacts	Covenants, architecture, gas fired power plant as anchor tenant, water treatment
Redhills Ecoplex, MS	Rural location, next to lignite mine and power plant, high job losses	Under construction	Public (State)	Public agency	Job creation	Recruiting for loop closing, power plant as anchor tenant
Dallas Eco-industrial Park, TX	Run down neighbourhood in South Dallas	Under construction	Public (Federal and city)	Local authority	Job creation, improving neighbourhood	Environmental education
Ecolibrium, Computer and Electronic Disposition, Austin, TX	Outskirts of Austin on major landfill site	Planned	Public (Federal)	Public sector consortium	Reduced waste to landfill, job creation	Recycling computers and electronic equipment
Front Royal, Eco Office Park, VA	Washington DC commuter belt	Planned	Public (Federal)	Public agency	Jobs for residents, reduce commuting outside town	Architecture, networking

	Location	Status	Public (city)	Consultants/local authority	Creating labour-intensive businesses	Networking – energy, materials, personnel
Bassett Creek, MN	North of downtown Minneapolis					
European sites ABLE Project	West Yorkshire, former landfill	Moving from trial to operational	Public (Charities, regional health authorities, national redevelopment body, private sector)	Local authority agency	Diversion of cardboard from landfill; creation of work/training experience	Recycling loop (cardboard, to animal bedding, to compost with worms, worms fed to fish, sale of fish and caviar), provision of training/work experience
AvestaPolarit	South Yorkshire, part of steel manufacturing complex	Pre-operational	Public (EU, local authority, private sector)	Local authority agency	Diversion of wool scour and plastic from landfill; creation of jobs for learning disadvantaged	Recycling loop (wool scour composted with green waste, use of compost to reclaim landfill), use of disadvantaged labour
Ecosite du Pays de Thau	Near Montpellier, southern France, coastal location	Operational	Public (local authorities)	Public sector (company owned by LAs)	Pollution prevention and sustainable development	On-site synergies (nutrients from sewage treatment used in production of marine algae, which used on site and sold for various applications)

Table 4.2 (*continued*)

Park	Location	Status	Funding	Developer	Objectives	'Greenness'
Eco Dyfi	Machynlleth, Central Wales, rural location	Operational	Public (EU, Welsh Development Agency)	Community partnership	Community regeneration	Energy efficient buildings, green tourism, planned networking for wood industries, renewable energy projects
Ecotech	Swaffham, Norfolk, rural location	Operational	Public (EU, local authority)	Private company	Improved environmental performance on industrial estates	Energy efficient buildings, wind turbines, planned inter-firm networking
Humber Industrial Symbiosis Project	Based in Scunthorpe, covers the Humber sub-region	Operational	Public		Reducing waste	Inter-firm industrial symbiosis across the sub-region

upon addressing the set of questions listed in Table 4.1 and upon evaluating the empirical material from the research project. A key early concern was to try and evaluate eco-industrial developments from perspectives in local and regional development research on trust and networking (Gibbs 2003). This proved problematic given the limited networking activities taking place. More recent work has focused on evaluating eco-industrial initiatives as a specific type of 'cluster development' prevalent in regional development strategies (see Deutz and Gibbs 2008). In this chapter I draw upon this earlier empirical work, but my main concern here is to interpret this from the theoretical perspective of transition management and strategic niches outlined in the previous section. The next section of the chapter provides a summary of findings from the empirical material, before turning to this reinterpretation in a subsequent section.

ECO-INDUSTRIAL PARKS: IMPLEMENTING INDUSTRIAL ECOLOGY?

EIPs as Industrial Symbiosis

The survey of EIPs had as a main concern the extent to which industrial symbiosis is being implemented i.e., whether firms in the case study locations were networked through materials interchange and energy flows. However, whereas the initial survey of the secondary literature and website material indicated that networking activities were present in the case study EIPs, the study found few inter-firm exchanges and interactions, particularly of the types proposed in the industrial ecology literature i.e., materials and energy interchanges. The case study that came closest to meeting EIP ideals was the Ecosite du Pays de Thau in Southern France, where a number of spin-out companies have been formed to exploit synergies enabled by technologies developed on-site. Here, marine micro-algae feed on nutrients from the sewage treatment process and are subsequently processed for use in a variety of applications including pharmaceutical, cosmetic and food products. Onsite companies are encouraged to network through the provision of shared functions including administration, research and recycling, as well as through facilities for education and conferences. In most of the other cases, industrial symbiosis synergies were frequently in the very early planning stages. At both Londonderry[3] and Redhills Ecoplex, for example, power plants had been developed as anchor tenants (that is, the largest, and often first, tenant intended to encourage other tenants to locate there) to facilitate resource and raw material sharing – for example through the supply of steam and low cost power to local businesses, such as aquaculture and horticulture.[4] However, as elsewhere, in neither case were such synergies currently operational. Some other examples of positive environmental impacts were found at the EIPs. Londonderry EcoPark, for example, planned to use waste water for cooling at its associated power plant, saving some four million gallons of water extraction from the nearby Merrimack River. However, the survey revealed that very few sites had any plans to either monitor or develop targets for waste, emissions or energy use, calling into question the extent to which any environmental improvement can be either monitored or measured.[5]

Closed Systems, Dynamism and Scale

In the widespread absence of substantive interchange and networking activities, none of the case study locations were operating as a closed system. Thus the questions of 'lock in' and path dependence leading to a lack of innovation and adaptability, much debated in the industrial ecology literature (see for example Boons and Berends 2001), were not barriers to implementation at the time of the survey. On the question of scale, the difficulty of establishing interchange and networking at specific bounded locations may suggest that a more fruitful eco-industrial strategy might be to build upon existing waste and energy interchanges (which may not consciously identify themselves as eco-industrial developments or industrial ecology) at a wider spatial scale, to form some kind of 'local–regional industrial ecosystem'.[6]

With respect to dynamism, there was certainly evidence that EIP developments have had to respond to changes in economic circumstances, although not in the ways that the industrial ecology literature envisages. Within the latter, concerns are expressed that change in any one component of the EIP (such as firm closure, firm relocation or elimination of a specific waste stream) could have major adverse consequences for the system as a whole (Schlarb 2001). However, due to the early stages of EIP development in the case studies, the issues that arose were not those of particular locations becoming locked in to specific development paths based upon a limited number of participants and processes and the presence of an anchor tenant. Rather, dynamic economic conditions have inhibited tenant recruitment or led to the abandonment of the eco-industrial theme in favour of more conventional economic development aims and activities. This was particularly evident at some of the US EIPs. Some of these introduced covenants at the early stages of park development in order to restrict entry to those firms meeting the environmental, economic and social aims of park development. For example these covered issues such as grey water use, landscaping requirements, recycling and employment practices, with potential park tenants being 'scored' on how well they met these requirements. Those EIPs with such covenants had frequently abandoned these when it became evident that recruiting *any* tenants was difficult; let alone placing any restrictions on who could be recruited. At other locations, rather than impose these norms upon tenants pre-entry, attempts were being made to incorporate dynamism by recruiting tenants to a site-wide environmental management system responsive to firms' needs.

The Role of Trust and Co-Operation Between Participants

Much of the industrial ecology literature emphasizes trust and co-operation as key factors influencing networking and interchange activity (see Gibbs 2003 for a summary). Given the absence of the latter, this proved difficult to investigate amongst those firms located at the case study EIPs. Certainly interactions between businesses other than in the form of materials or energy exchanges did exist, including discussions aimed at setting up such interchanges, as well as other forms of cooperative behavior (e.g. interchange of personnel, cooperative purchasing, travel-to-work arrangements etc.). In essence this represented the initial stages of building a sense of community within the EIP as suggested by Schlarb (2001). Devens in the USA has perhaps gone furthest in implementing this type of activity through introducing its 'Ecostar' program to encourage environmentally favourable behaviour (including interchanges) among onsite and other local firms. This was believed to have produced positive results in terms of what one respondent called 'reducing the mental distance between the companies' as a possible precursor to more material firm interchanges. Thus, while EIP promoters and policy makers may not be able to force improved environmental performance, they can at least provide guidance and put frameworks in place to encourage interaction (Mirata 2004). As one respondent stated 'what you can do is create opportunities for . . . cross-filtration of ideas and getting firms to meet each other and develop trust between them'. If this can be nurtured over time, then EIP development may foster interaction and co-working, whereby firms and other actors learn about appropriate behaviour and alter their own behaviours and actions. A similar proactive role is played by the UK's National Industrial Symbiosis Programme (NISP) outlined in Chapter 5 with NISP acting as a broker to encourage and foster network emergence and development. Eco-industrial development may therefore comprise one method to develop the types of institutional learning processes and cultural change associated with a transition to a more sustainable regime.

Despite the lack of networking activities, issues of trust and co-operation were of key importance for the initial development and subsequent implementation of many of the projects. Issues of trust often arose in the early stages of EIP development, where these new and potentially risky projects needed support from key individuals such as policymakers and financiers. Here, pre-existing links and trust in the ability of EIP promoters to deliver on their proposals was often the crucial deciding factor as to whether the project received political and/or financial support (see Chertow and Ashton, this volume for similar conclusions drawn from the rather different setting of Puerto Rico). In addition, good personal relationships between those involved in establishing the EIP, as well as the key role of certain individuals taking a lead role in driving the project forward, were also of central importance to EIP development, echoing Andrews (2001) suggestion that industrial ecology studies need to pay attention to microscale activity (for example, the behaviour and motivation of individuals). However, while trust and respect for the individuals involved is evidently important, over and above the personal qualities of the individuals, both parties to an agreement needed to gain something. For example at two of the UK EIPs, the landowners were providing land and/or buildings in return for a nominal rent, but the projects also addressed their own waste disposal problems. While in both cases the EIP promoters had built up a good relationship with the project developer, neither projects would have gone ahead if there had not been clear financial or environmental benefits for the landowners themselves.

Local Collaboration and Partnership in the Formation of EIPs

Mirata (2004: 970) argues that 'having the right institutional setting in a region is among the most important elements for IS [industrial symbiosis] programs and is an area where coordination bodies can make a contribution'. Certainly in the case study examples local collaboration and partnership were found to be of key importance in setting up EIPs. Strong interest has come from local governments in the USA, although it may be that the burden of expectation above and beyond environmental improvement (for example, job creation, economic regeneration) has hindered their development (Schlarb and Musnikow 2003; Hendricks and Giannini-Spohn 2003). Local institutional capacity was in large part based upon a history of collaborative working on past projects within a locality and the capacity this engendered for future projects, such as EIPs. A good example of this was at the Eco Dyfi project in Wales, where close relationships between individuals and the local community through the catalytic role of the Centre for Alternative Technology had led to a community-controlled development agency for the area, including a number of potential eco-industrial developments. In several of the US EIPs, community involvement was also high. In some cases this had arisen through sites having a legacy of pollution from past uses and a general community desire to support any initiative that sought to remediate this pollution and to create a better physical environment. Certainly this had helped to foster both public and political support for EIP developments, as these were perceived to be both environmentally benign and to have a potentially positive economic benefit for economically and environmentally disadvantaged communities. The management of EIPs was frequently in the hands of proactive institutions that were attempting to encourage links to form between tenants. These included various forms of incentives (for example rent reduction), encouragement (for example through an intranet, newsletter) or some forms of on-site compulsion (for example a requirement to participate in a variety of shared functions). In two of the UK projects, an institution set up to encourage green business activity had played a key role in identifying potential partners for synergistic relationships through its activities across the wider region, and was able to draw upon a large store of tacit knowledge about industrial activities. Some form of coordinating body or organization would therefore seem to be important for eco-industrial development, whether this is to catalyse new interactions or to help sustain existing relationships (Mirata 2004). The importance of capacity building and the key role of a proactive coordinating body are also highlighted in Chapter 5 in this volume.

Public Policy Intervention

The research revealed that there was substantial public sector involvement in EIP development and EIPs were largely the outcome of public policy intervention. Indeed, the majority of case study EIPs were being developed as part of a broader local economic development strategy. All 19 respondents to the initial survey had local authority involvement in park development, 17 of the 19 were predominantly publicly funded and 15 included job creation and/or protection as one of the major aims of the development. EIPs are seen not just as a means of increasing the eco-efficiency of participant firms, but also as a basis for a new form of local and regional development. EIP locations were frequently in areas eligible for public sector assistance and/or in areas of need of economic and social regeneration. At the time of the survey, EIP development appeared to be promoted by a small group of policy makers in these areas who were attempting to use industrial ecology as a strategic niche to influence local economic development strategies. Their ability to break through into the mainstream of policy, however, appeared to be limited by other local policymakers who were more comfortable with conventional development strategies, even if these were environmentally and socially destructive. Once again this illustrates the need to take into account the power relations at work and to evaluate who has the power to make and set the local development policy agenda. As Paquin and Howard-Grenville (this volume, Chapter 5: p. 103) point out industrial symbiosis remains a new approach often "unknown to others on whom the success of the programme may depend (for example local environmental authorities, regional development agencies and so on.)'.

In both the US and the UK case studies company respondents argued that existing regulations act as a deterrent to the establishment of symbiotic relationships between firms. For example, it was believed that the current definition of a substance as hazardous waste under the US Resource Conservation and Recovery Act effectively prohibited recycling and reuse of waste streams. Similarly in the UK, current waste management regulations were felt to inhibit symbiotic relationships building up due to restrictions on storage of wastes. In the US, pressure groups such as the Business Council for Sustainable Development were lobbying national policymakers for a change in the law to encourage and allow industrial ecology projects. Of equal importance in both cases, however, would appear to be lack of motivation on the part of private sector firms to become involved with networking and materials interchange activities.

EIPs as Sustainable Development

Industrial ecology is often seen as a key means by which sustainable development can be advanced combining economic and social development with environmental protection. On the evidence from the case study EIPs, their contribution to environmental aims is limited by the lack of success at establishing industrial symbiosis. Some examples of environmental benefits did exist, with several of the case studies targeting reduced carbon emissions as a key contribution to sustainable development. These included reduced fossil fuel use and dependence through utilizing a ground heat pump at the Phillips Eco Enterprise Center in Minnesota, photovoltaic cell arrays at Cape Charles and the Eco Dyfi site, and a wind turbine at Ecotech. However, in two cases (Redhills Ecoplex and Londonderry) the synergies planned are centred on fossil fuel-fired power stations with their attendant contribution to carbon emissions.

In some cases EIPs recorded improved economic performance. Thus, at several of the US EIPs, developers were strongly of the opinion that designation as an EIP had helped to speed up the development process because of its benefits as a marketing device and a means to create a 'unique selling point'. However, there are limitations in using eco-industrial development as a marketing tool, as opposed to a sign of a more deeply held commitment to sustainable development, in that lack of initial success could result in the abandonment of any pretence of industrial ecology in favour of an alternate strategy. Moreover, even developments with an apparently deep-seated commitment to sustainable development can be forced to bow to economic realities. In cases such as Cape Charles, designation as an EIP has not helped to aid economic competitiveness and the site has been sold off for housing development, with no prospective buyer prepared to operate the park under the system of restrictive covenants that were intended to encourage eco-industrial behaviour. Much also depended upon the local economic context, where attracting tenants to remote, rural locations had, not surprisingly, proved more difficult than in more successful areas located close to major conurbations. Hence, the broader economic context plays an overriding role in deciding the relative success of EIP operations – not surprisingly those located in more successful economic contexts were also likely to be more successful in terms of tenant recruitment. EIP development is therefore not a straightforward means of overcoming the economic constraints of particular locations. The social expectations around EIPs are typically focused on the creation of jobs, perhaps paying slightly more in cleaner industries than typical for the area. The lack of economic success also clearly limits the potential contribution of EIPs to social goals.

ECO-INDUSTRIAL DEVELOPMENT: AN EARLY STAGE NICHE?

It is evident from the research findings that making industrial ecology operational through EIP development is at an early stage of development. Despite the best efforts of planners and developers, a 'planned Kalundborg' had yet to develop at any of these case study sites, with a substantial gulf between the expectations created by this example and the probability of recreating it elsewhere. This is despite the fact that many of the case study locations are amongst the most cited examples of industrial symbiosis in action, indicating the value of primary research over making assumptions from secondary (and often promotional) literature. While all of the case study sites initially claimed to be engaged in, or planning for, materials and energy interchanges (all did so in response to the initial telephone/fax/email survey, hence their choice as case studies), the in-depth interviews and site visits revealed the problematic nature of developing this into reality (see Chertow and Ashton this volume, for similar results from their empirical work in Puerto Rico). The evidence from these case studies indicates that EIP development to date had been concerned principally with infrastructural provision and tenant recruitment with an expectation that relational assets will (or should) emerge with time. Many of the respondents had emerged from the process of EIP promotion and development as both older and wiser. For them, EIP development and its proposed benefits were initially attractive as they sought new forms of development that would not only bring economic benefits, but also social and environmental gains for their localities. However, moving beyond the conceptual stage through to company recruitment and establishing firm interchanges had proved much more problematic than their initial optimism for the concept had suggested.

In part this may be a product of promoting and developing specific eco-industrial *parks*, focused on a particular bounded site. Although this is rarely mentioned in the industrial ecology literature, a geographical perspective is important within industrial ecology given that it is explicitly concerned with connections between firms across space (Seuring 2004). As Cohen-Rosenthal (2003: 15) states 'eco-industrial development provides an alternative that celebrates the possibility of place'. One question that this raises is the appropriate scale for eco-industrial initiatives – should these be park-based or at some wider local or regional scale (Sterr and Orr 2004)? With regard to interpreting industrial ecology as a strategic niche, this also raises the question of whether developing EIPs is the best strategy to break through into the mainstream of economic development. EIPs may offer opportunities for the learning processes associated with new approaches and to articulate the vision of industrial ecology to enroll more actors as outlined in the transition management literature, but the long term nature of these EIP developments and their seemingly problematic nature may mean that other approaches at a wider spatial scale may be more successful (see for example the work of the UK's NISP operating at the regional scale, outlined in Chapter 5).

Part of the problem with EIP recruitment is that expecting firms to relocate to a site specifically to procure secondary materials is perhaps unrealistic when the 'minor importance of waste costs and relatively low costs of attaining secondary materials' (Sterr and Orr 2004: 949) means that these will play a small part in most firms' location decisions. By-product flows will only be crucial to location decisions if they are the most important inputs for a firm (Desrochers 2004). Even in such rare cases, decisions as to the source of inputs and supplies may not be within the decision making powers of local managers, but subject to corporate decision making and their fit with broader corporate strategies and sourcing policies (Boons and Janssen 2005). As Randles (2007) points out, there may well be a spatial mismatch between the scales at which eco-industrial parks and companies operate. This had rarely been considered by EIP developers, more frequently there appeared to be an implicit assumption that tenants would be self-contained autonomous firms able to make their own decisions on external links. At some of the US case study sites, the potential for materials interchange had been investigated and subsequently rejected on the grounds of incompatible inputs and outputs. As one US respondent pointed out 'what we are trying to do is mandate co-operation and you really can't do that'. In some cases (notably Cape Charles), the difficulties involved had led to the abandonment of any attempt at EIP activities.

Indeed, the development of symbiotic exchange relations has been a problematic element of EIPs that has been noted by others. For example, Heeres et al. (2004) suggest there are a variety of barriers to the establishment of exchanges. These may be: technical, where an exchange is technically not feasible; economic, where exchanges are economically unsound or risky; informational, where the appropriate people do not have the relevant information at the right time; organizational, where exchanges may not fit with corporate structures; and regulatory or legal, where exchanges are not allowed to occur. Heeres et al. (2004) found particular problems for their US EIP examples,[7] where the projects were focused on developing physical energy, water and material waste interchanges. They contrast the lack of success here with their Dutch cases, where initial development was focused on setting up pollution prevention projects related to utility sharing, such as combined treatment of waste water or combined cogeneration of heat and power. Involvement in what were perceived by firms as low risk and both economically and environmentally beneficial projects had encouraged participation in further EIP developments with greater risk.[8] They suggest that this may be a good entry point into industrial ecology, where EIP development 'is a long-term process [and] in order to stimulate development, it is important to focus on the establishment of low cost, high benefit utility sharing projects and "simple" exchanges' (Heeres et al. 2004: 994). This is not to suggest that Dutch developments are unproblematic. Research by Eilering and Vermeulen (2004) indicates that despite encouragement in the form of national policy and funding from the Dutch Ministry of Economic Affairs, out of over 200 projects funded they could only identify 85 completed projects and only eight of these where attempts were being made at utility sharing and symbiosis.[9] Boons and Janssen (2005) make similar observations on the Dutch experience and conclude that EIPs are no longer a national policy priority.

94   *The social embeddedness of industrial ecology*

Overall, then, the evidence presented here and in other studies concur with O'Rourke et al.'s (1996: 94) comment that 'a large gulf separates descriptions of what industrial ecology can be, and specific examples and strategies for implementing industrial ecology'. Hence although EIPs appear to be growing in number, the policy lessons to be drawn are that their development to fruition is likely to be a long process and that immediate positive results are unlikely to be forthcoming. Certainly, developing symbiotic relationships between firms and encouraging networking activity is difficult to achieve. Where it does have potential, time is then needed to gain the confidence of firms and other participants. From a policy perspective, there is an issue as to whether the park element of EIPs is an essential feature, or whether an emphasis on co-location is actually a hindrance to achieving industrial symbiosis except in a limited number of cases. As stated, there may be more potential benefits to be gained by identifying and building upon existing networking activities involving the exchange of waste and energy at a wider spatial scale to develop a 'local-regional industrial ecosystem' (Chapter 5 provides a similar argument based on the work of NISP and terms this a process of 'facilitated emergence' where NISP is an active player shaping both the path of the network and the content of inter-firm exchanges). Indeed, combining the two issues of appropriate scale and degree of intervention provides us with a fourfold typology of eco-industrial developments (see Figure 4.1). In recognition of these difficulties, an academic critique (albeit sympathetic) has developed more recently suggesting that the EIP approach may not represent the best means to implement industrial ecology (see O'Rourke et al. 1996; Andrews 2001; Thomas et al. 2003; Chertow 2004).

This is not to suggest that the EIP developments examined in this chapter possess no merits. Despite the problems they had experienced, respondents claimed that eco-industrial development had contributed to local economic development at the case study sites, albeit that it proved difficult to quantify the exact benefits. At one US EIP, the available lots had been sold within four years, instead of the expected ten years for a comparable 'non-eco-industrial' park. In such cases, eco-industrial development was seen as a means to speed up the development process and as a means of differentiating the development. Respondents argued that developing an EIP effectively creates a 'unique selling point' for the local area, or at least offers a niche market for particular types of company. There is a broader set of questions here relating to industrial ecology and the potential placed upon it for economic development and job creation. Schlarb (2001) argues that industrial ecology has moved from a technologically-driven approach, focusing upon resource exchanges, to a broader look

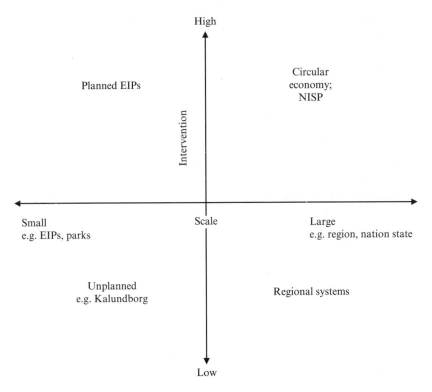

Figure 4.1   A typology of eco-industrial developments

at systems and networks, involving non-material exchanges, to a third stage involving community-based interactions. If this is so (and actual evidence for this is lacking) then it raises questions about how we define industrial ecology. In Schlarb's approach, industrial ecology becomes a social construct, such that it encompasses virtually any form of networking and interconnection between businesses, the community and the public sector, not just materials recovery and interchange. While this may be an appropriate form of local development activity in some localities, it is substantially different to original conceptions of industrial ecology. Indeed, using the industrial ecology concept for these purposes seems to place a substantial additional burden on such developments, raising high expectations of creating another Kalundborg and extending the idea substantially beyond the more modest aims of its original proponents. Conversely, in the absence of any networking and firm interconnection EIP promoters are really just engaged in fairly conventional property development activities, albeit with a green tinge.

INDUSTRIAL ECOLOGY, SUSTAINABLE NICHES AND TRANSITION MANAGEMENT

What then are the prospects for future EIP and industrial ecology-based projects? The evidence presented here suggests that the former are problematic as they have developed to date. Returning to the transition management literature, we can certainly see that tensions within the existing technological regime has helped to create the space within which EIPs or industrial ecology initiatives can be established. Growing societal concerns over carbon emissions and enhanced global warming have engendered a search for new approaches to industrial and economic development. Indeed, many of those promoting the case study EIPs saw these as contributing towards such new approaches and as a model that could inform changes to development strategies in their localities. However, as with other transitions, the dominant regime is likely to be slow to change. If not yet a new techno-economic paradigm, industrial ecology (at least in theory) holds out the prospect of a substantially different way of organizing economic development that could help mitigate environmental impacts. Certainly industrial ecology represents a shift away from a focus on individual firms (such as through eco-efficiency measures and clean technologies) towards a focus on the wider socio-technological regime in the manner suggested in transition management accounts (Smith 2003). In part this helps to explain the appeal of industrial ecology and its attempted implementation through eco-industrial parks. From this perspective industrial ecology comprises a radical paradigm shift in a shift from a 'throughput' to a 'roundput economy' (Korhonen 2001). The extent though to which the development of some of the case study EIPs represents a radical shift in industrial organization is debateable. Thus, the examples of Red Hills, Londonderry and the Gulf Coast complex all involve dependence on fossil fuel development either in power stations or petrochemicals.

To date it could be argued that the case study EIP initiatives have helped to develop the process of constructing and developing a strategic niche: they have articulated expectations and visions that may help to enrol more participants; constitute a learning experience to stimulate further developments; and have developed networks to support the niche. Certainly many of those involved with the development of the case study EIPs began with pre-defined goals and visions of an economy based upon industrial ecology. This much is apparent from interviews with participants and in much of the promotional literature produced by the case study EIPs. For example, promotional material for the Red Hills Ecoplex in Mississippi states: 'still think of "industrial park" as synonymous with "smoke stack",

"pollution" and "expensive eyesore"? Fortunately it's time to think again
. . . the EcoPlex mimics a natural, efficient ecosystem'.

One shortcoming evident from those engaged in developing the case study EIPs has been in an area where work on transition management is also weak – the concentration upon technological/technical solutions as opposed to recognizing the importance of institutional changes, both formal (as in laws on waste composition) and the more informal rules and norms that actors abide by. The initial emphasis on developing infrastructure in some of the case study examples has been to the detriment of devoting energies to facilitating corporate and individual interaction. This was particularly the case at many of the US EIPs, where building the park had come before an appraisal of potential recruitment. A regime shift is likely to require changes in regulatory systems, technologies, attitudes and practices (Berkhout et al. 2003). More formal sets of rules such as waste regulations have also been relatively neglected until recently, where lobbying work in the USA is attempting to try and change Federal definitions so as to encourage industrial symbiosis. An important related development here may be the creation of institutional forms and networks to support, promote and lobby for industrial ecology. In the USA an attempt to establish a National Center for Eco-industrial Development[10] to support and train practitioners and to conduct research met with limited success and the Center appears to be moribund, although there is a growing body of researchers and organizations established to support work on industrial ecology. In the UK, the National Industrial Symbiosis Programme is supported by central government funding to encourage and develop a number of regional symbiosis projects (see Chapter 5).

Even where success has been limited, the transition management literature suggests that 'niche experiments that fail to grow and branch nevertheless succeed in generating useful experience' (Smith 2004: 223). Lessons learned can include both lessons internal to the niche, such as improved knowledge of how EIPs might be encouraged and operationalized, and lessons external to the niche, such as the types of institutional reforms that might assist EIP development. Those actors engaged with industrial ecology developments may therefore be amongst: 'the "idealists" (producers and supportive users) who initiate a sustainable niche [and] are later joined by entrepreneurial "system builders" (who open the niche out to a wider set of users) and, eventually, by serious amounts of capital seeking to profit from the proto-regime' (Smith 2003: 130). One lesson that seems to have been learned is the difficulty of developing eco-industrial parks *de novo* and the limits placed upon these parks by their small scale focus. Instead, both policy makers and academic commentators have begun to think more in terms of 'uncovering' existing symbiosis and broadening the spatial scale to a wider regional focus. Thus, Chertow (2007), in an analysis of 15 'planned' and 12 'self-organized' industrial symbiosis projects suggests that planned projects have rarely been successful. By contrast, pre-existing self-organizing systems are more successful in generating symbiotic exchanges although they are 'never mapped and described using ecological metaphors' (Chertow 2007: 20). Chertow goes on to argue that 'uncovering' such pre-existing industrial ecosystems and then building on these through public policy intervention is a more fruitful task than establishing new eco-industrial parks (see also Chertow and Ashton, this volume). In this manner, industrial ecology activists are undertaking the kinds of re-envisioning of the original ideals as suggested by Berkhout et al. (2003) as they learn from experience. Indeed, it has recently been argued that one of the benefits of a transition management approach is that it is able to build in such reflexivity and thus review possible goals or end-states (Walker and Shove 2007). While to date progress may appear to be slow, recent examples from the UK where the Government has established and sponsored a National Industrial Symbiosis Programme (Mirata 2004; www.nisp.org.uk) and from China, where a more far reaching programme of developing a 'circular economy' is planned to mitigate the environmental consequences of China's rapid industrial and economic growth (Fang et al. 2007), indicate that industrial ecology initiatives will continue to develop. Specific eco-industrial parks perhaps have less of an assured future except in a limited set of particular circumstances. Indeed, the case study EIPs illustrate the problems of developing industrial ecology projects in isolation from the rest of the mainstream economy around them. Those that were least successful were those located in local economies where *any* form of economic development was already problematic.

As yet, industrial ecology offers only a partial solution to the kinds of tensions and bottlenecks that transition management accounts suggest are important in engendering regime change. Part of the problem may be that the tensions are not yet perceived to be crucial enough to warrant radical action. For example, the barriers imposed by regulations on waste management and the early attempts to change such regulation evident from the case study material indicate that the broader techno-economic paradigm is slow to change. In the future, moves towards carbon pricing and climate change mitigation strategies may help to provide the increased tensions that will engender such a shift. For those engaged in work on industrial ecology, drawing upon the transition management and strategic niche literatures may prove helpful in both conceptualization and policy formation. Certainly an approach that emphasises 'the complex and dynamic co-evolution of the social and the technical' (Walker and Shove 2007: 214) would help to avoid the focus on potential technical solutions evident in some work on industrial ecology. Future research work needs to focus much more on positioning industrial ecology initiatives within their broader political, regulatory and economic contexts and to analyse the power relations at work as networks form, develop and shift over time (see Chapter 5 for similar arguments).

ACKNOWLEDGEMENTS

This chapter is based upon research funded by the Economic and Social Research Council (Grant number R000239428). My thanks to Pauline Deutz and Amy Proctor for their important contributions to the empirical work and to the conceptual development of the research. I am grateful to all those who gave up their time to be interviewed during the course of the study. All errors and omissions remain the responsibility of the author.

NOTES

1. Smith (2004) makes this same point through a comparison with the Alternative Technology movement in the UK. This movement had a keen awareness of the need to consider political and economic power structures.
2. Korhonen (2004b) points out that despite the large number of papers citing Kalundborg as the prime example of industrial symbiosis in action, it relies upon non-renewable fossil resources and produces CO_2 emissions, neither of which is compatible with his concept of roundput.
3. The introduction of a power plant as an anchor tenant was particularly controversial at Londonderry, see Wasserman (2001). Due to a failure to secure long term contracts, the plant became insolvent and was taken over. The demand for steam remains unproven.
4. Again, there is a question as to whether dependence upon power plants utilizing gas (Londonderry) and lignite (Redhills) can be defined as industrial ecology.
5. See Eilering and Vermeulen (2004) for similar findings in The Netherlands.
6. See similar arguments in Sterr and Orr (2004).
7. Heeres et al. (2004) looked at three US EIPs, including Cape Charles.
8. Even so, it is worth noting that this has not led to a particularly well developed set of eco-industrial parks in The Netherlands, as the papers by Heeres et al. (2004), Eilering and Vermeulen (2004) and Boons and Janssen (2005) indicate.
9. Of the eight, only four were discovered to have achieved symbiosis and/or utility sharing.
10. See http://www.usc.edu/schools/sppd/research/NCEID/Menu.html (Accessed 14 December 2007). The latest news item on the site is for 2003.

REFERENCES

Allenby, B.R. (1999), *Industrial Ecology: Policy Framework and Implementation*, Englewood Cliffs, NJ: Prentice Hall.

Andrews, C. (2001), 'Building a micro foundation for industrial ecology', *Journal of Industrial Ecology*, **4**(3), 35–51.

Ashford, N.A. and R.P. Côté (1997), 'An overview of the special issues' (on industrial ecology), *Journal of Cleaner Production*, **5**(1/2), i–iv.

Berkout, F., A. Smith and A. Stirling (2003), 'Socio-technological regimes and transition contexts', SPRU Electronic working paper series no. 106, SPRU, University of Sussex.

Boons, F. and M. Berends (2001), 'Stretching the boundary: the possibilities of flexibility as an organisational capability in industrial ecology', *Business Strategy and the Environment*, **10**(2), 115–24.

Boons, F. and M.A. Janssen (2005), The myth of Kalundborg: social dilemmas in stimulating eco-industrial parks', in J. van der Bergh and M. Janssen (eds), *Economics of Industrial Ecology: Materials, Structural Change and Spatial Scales*, Cambridge, MA: MIT Press, pp. 337–55.

Business Council for Sustainable Development (2002), National Industrial Symbiosis Programme, Business Delivery of Political Strategy on Resource Productivity, BCSD North Sea Region.

Chertow, M.R. (2004), 'Industrial symbiosis', *Encyclopedia of Energy*, **3**, 1–9.

Chertow, M. (2007), '"Uncovering" industrial symbiosis', *Journal of Industrial Ecology*, **11**(1), 11–30.

Chiu, A.S.F. and G. Yong (2004), 'On the industrial ecology potential in Asian developing countries', *Journal of Cleaner Production*, **12**, 1037–45.

Cohen-Rosenthal, E. (1996), 'Designing eco-industrial parks: the US experience', UNEP *Industry and Environment*, October–December, 14–18.

Cohen-Rosenthal, E. (2003), 'What is eco-industrial development?' in E. Cohen-Rosenthal and J. Musnikow (eds), *Eco-Industrial Strategies: Unleashing Synergy between Economic Development and the Environment*, Sheffield: Greenleaf, 14–29.

Cohen-Rosenthal, E. and J. Musnikow (2003), *Eco-Industrial Strategies: Unleashing Synergy between Economic Development and the Environment*, Sheffield: Greenleaf.

Desrochers, P. (2004), 'Industrial symbiosis: the case for market coordination', *Journal of Cleaner Production*, **12**, 1099–110.

Deutz, P. and D. Gibbs (2008), 'Industrial ecology and regional development: eco-industrial development as cluster policy', *Regional Studies*, **42**(10): 1313–28.

Eilering, J.A.M. and W.J.V. Vermeulen (2004), 'Eco-industrial parks: toward industrial symbiosis and utility sharing in practice', *Progress in Industrial Ecology*, **1**(1/2/3), 245–70.

Erkman, S. and R. Ramaswamy (2003), *Applied Industrial Ecology: A New Platform for Planning Sustainable Societies*, Bangalore: Aicra.

Fang, Y., R.P. Côté and R. Qin (2007), 'Industrial sustainability in China: practice and prospects for eco-industrial development', *Journal of Environmental Management*, **83**, 315–28.

Freeman, C. (1992), *The Economics of Hope*, London: Pinter.

Geels, F.W. (2005), *Technological Transitions and System Innovations: A Co-Evolutionary and Socio-Technical Analysis*, Cheltenham, UK and Northampton, MA, USA: Edward Elgar.

Gibbs, D. (2003), 'Trust and networking in inter-firm relations: the case of eco-industrial development', *Local Economy*, (18), 222–36.

Gibbs, D. and P. Deutz (2005), 'Implementing industrial ecology? Planning for eco-industrial parks in the USA', *Geoforum*, **36**, 452–64.

Gibbs, D. and P. Deutz (2007), 'Reflections on implementing industrial ecology through eco-industrial park development', *Journal of Cleaner Production*, **15**(17).

Gibbs, D., P. Deutz and A. Proctor (2005), 'Industrial ecology and eco-industrial development: a new paradigm for local and regional development?' *Regional Studies*, **39**, 171–83.

Hawken, P. (1993), *The Ecology of Commerce*, New York: Harper Business.

Hayter, R. and R. Le Heron (2002), 'Conclusion: institutions and innovation in territorial perspective', in R. Hayter and R. Le Heron (eds), *Knowledge, Industry and Environment*, Aldershot: Ashgate, pp. 399–409.

Heeres, R.R., W.J.V. Vermeulen and F.B. de Walle (2004), 'Eco-industrial park initiatives in the USA and The Netherlands: first lessons', *Journal of Cleaner Production*, **12**, 985–95.

Hendricks, B. and S. Giannini-Spohn (2003), 'The role of government in eco-industrial development', in E. Cohen-Rosenthal and J. Musnikow (eds), *Eco-Industrial Strategies: Unleashing Synergy between Economic Development and the Environment*, Sheffield: Greenleaf, pp. 68–88.

Keijzers, G. (2002), 'The transition to the sustainable enterprise', *Journal of Cleaner Production*, **10**, 349–59.

Korhonen, J. (2001), 'Co-production of heat and power: an anchor tenant of a regional industrial ecosystem', *Journal of Cleaner Production*, **9**, 509–17.

Korhonen, J., F. von Malmborg, P.A. Strachan and J.R. Ehrenfeld (2004), 'Management and policy aspects of industrial ecology: an emerging research agenda', *Business Strategy and the Environment*, **13**, 289–305.

Lowe, E.A. (1997), 'Creating by-product resource exchanges: strategies for eco-industrial parks', *Journal of Cleaner Production*, **5**(1–2), 57–65.

Lowe, E. (2003), 'Eco-industrial development in Asian developing countries', in E. Cohen-Rosenthal and J. Musnikow (eds), *Eco-Industrial Strategies: Unleashing Synergy between Economic Development and the Environment*, Sheffield: Greenleaf, pp. 341–52.

Martin, S.A., R.A. Cushman, K.A. Wetz, A. Sharma and R.C. Lindrooth (1998), 'Applying industrial ecology to industrial parks: an economic and environmental analysis', *Economic Development Quarterly*, **12**(3), 218–37.

Mirata, M. (2004), 'Experiences from early stages of a national industrial symbiosis program in the UK: determinants and coordination challenges', *Journal of Cleaner Production*, **12**, 967–83.

Mirata, M. and T. Emtairah (2005), 'Industrial symbiosis networks and the contribution to environmental innovation: the case of the Landskrona industrial symbiosis program', *Journal of Cleaner Production*, **13**, 993–1002.

O'Rourke, D., L. Connelly and C.P. Koshland (1996), 'Industrial ecology: a critical review', *International Journal of Environment and Pollution*, **6**(2/3), 89–112.

Opoku, H.N. (2004), 'Policy implications of industrial ecology conceptions', *Business Strategy and the Environment*, **13**, 320–33

President's Council for Sustainable Development (1997), Eco-Industrial Park Workshop Proceedings, 17–18 October 1996, Cape Charles, Virginia. Accessed 10 May 2002 at http://clinton2.nara.gov/PCSD/Publications/Eco_Workshop.html.

Randles, S. (2007), 'Multiscalar landscapes and industrial ecology', *Progress in Industrial Ecology*, **4**(3/4), 164–83.

Rip, A. and R. Kemp (1998), 'Technological change', in S. Rayner and E. Malone (eds), *Human Choices and Climate Change*, vol. 2, Columbus, OH: Batelle, pp. 327–99.

Roberts, B.H. (2004), 'The application of industrial ecology principles and planning guidelines for the development of eco-industrial parks: an Australian case study', *Journal of Cleaner Production*, **12**, 997–1010.

Schlarb, M. (2001), *Eco-industrial Development: A Strategy for Building Sustainable Communities*, Cornell University, Washington, DC: United States Economic Development Administration.

Schlarb, M. and J. Musnikow (2003), 'Community engagement in eco-industrial development', in E. Cohen-Rosenthal and J. Musnikow (eds), *Eco-Industrial Strategies: Unleashing Synergy between Economic Development and the Environment*, Sheffield: Greenleaf, pp. 100–111.

Seuring, S. (2004), 'Industrial ecology, life cycles, supply chains: differences and interrelations', *Business Strategy and the Environment*, **13**, 306–19.

Sterr, T. and T. Orr (2004), 'The industrial region as a promising unit for eco-industrial development – reflections, practical experience and establishment of innovative instruments to support industrial ecology', *Journal of Cleaner Production*, **12**, 947–65.

Shove, E. (1998), 'Gaps, barriers and conceptual chasms: theories of technology transfer and energy in buildings', *Energy Policy*, **26**(15), 1105–12.

Shove, E. and G. Walker (2007), 'Caution! Transitions ahead: politics, practice, and sustainable transition management', *Environment and Planning A*, **39**, 763–70.

Smith, A. (2003), 'Transforming technological regimes for sustainable development: a role for alternative technology niches?' *Science and Public Policy*, **30**(2), 127–35.

Smith, A. (2004), 'Alternative technology niches and sustainable development', *Innovation: Management, Policy and Practice*, **6**, 220–35.

Smith, A. (2006), 'Green niches in sustainable development: the case of organic food in the United Kingdom', *Environment and Planning C*, **24**, 439–58.

Thomas, V., T. Theis, R. Lifset, D. Grasso, B. Kim, C. Koshland and R. Pfahl (2003), 'Industrial ecology: policy potential and research need', *Environmental Engineering Science*, **20**(1), 1–9.

Walker, G. and E. Shove (2007), 'Ambivalence, sustainability and the governance of socio-technical transitions', *Journal of Environmental Policy and Planning*, **9**(3), 213–25.

5. Facilitating regional industrial symbiosis: network growth in the UK's national industrial symbiosis programme

**Raymond Paquin and
Jennifer Howard-Grenville**

INTRODUCTION

In the years since the discovery of Kalundborg's long-lived network of resource exchanges, industrial symbiosis, and its potential for reducing the environmental impact of industrial activity on a local or regional scale, has been the subject of intense interest. Industrial symbiosis is defined as the enlistment of geographically proximate facilities in the 'physical exchange of materials, energy, water, and by-products' (Chertow 2000: 314). While some industrial symbiosis occurs between firms that are closely co-located, such as those in the same industrial park (see Chapters 4 and 6), other efforts to develop industrial symbiosis are undertaken on regional geographic scales. This chapter considers regional-scale industrial symbiosis, and, in particular, the development of a network of industrial symbiosis facilitated by a single brokering organization.

It is now well documented that instances of self-emerging industrial symbiosis, similar to Kalundborg but often more modest in scale, are infrequently observed (see Chapter 6). On the other hand, efforts to create viable industrial symbiosis through the establishment of eco-industrial parks and other activities, have largely failed (See Chapter 4). In this chapter, we explore a 'third way' of establishing industrial symbiosis, the facilitation of a regional-scale industrial symbiosis network. We track the development of industrial symbiosis in the West Midlands region of the UK, and its facilitation by the National Industrial Symbiosis Programme (NISP). NISP was established, in the words of its founder, to 'work with the willing', engaging with companies who wanted to participate in potential resource exchanges. It also recognized the inherent limitations in working with established companies operating over a relatively large geographic region – thus, potential exchanges had to be logistically feasible and economically attractive to the companies involved. Through a variety of activities ranging from holding workshops to introduce the idea of industrial symbiosis, through making specific introductions between firms, to in-depth, joint innovation projects, NISP was able to facilitate a large number of resource exchanges over a relatively short period of time. From NISP's inception as a regional pilot program in 2001, industrial symbiosis activity in the West Midlands increased dramatically. By 2007, 243 participating members (companies and a few non-profit organizations) had engaged in 307 industrial symbiosis projects.

What led to this rapid growth in industrial symbiosis activity? What kind of network formed between firms engaged in industrial symbiosis, and how did that network grow? We consider these questions in this chapter by drawing on archival data on all initiated, attempted, and completed resource exchanges in the West Midlands between 2005 and 2007. Data from interviews with NISP staff and participating company members enhanced our understanding of observed changes in the network. While the emergence and growth of a network of organizations can be regarded as indicative of structural embeddedness – all firms in the network are in some (direct or indirect) way connected to all others, potentially altering how information flows and power is exercised – our analysis suggests that network itself must be understood in relation to other dimensions of embeddedness. For example, we find that the trajectory of network growth can best be understood by considering the political, economic and cultural embeddedness of key actors in the network. This finding accords with the observation made by network scholars that networks 'are already embedded in their broader "network" of economic and social relations' (Provan et al. 2007: 481). It also supports the approach taken by some industrial ecology scholars who have attended to the broad social conditions surrounding industrial symbiosis arrangements, drawing attention to the historical, cultural and political conditions in which they emerge (Tomescu 2005; Cohen 2006; Gibbs et al. 2002; Ashton 2008; Howard-Grenville and Paquin 2008), and enabling infrastructure and institutions (Burstrom and Korhonen 2001; Korhonen and Snakin 2001; Jacobsen and Anderberg 2004). By probing specifically how a network of industrial symbiosis evolves over time, we also explicitly attend to the temporal embeddedness of such arrangements.

INDUSTRIAL SYMBIOSIS, NETWORK STRUCTURES, AND TEMPORAL DYNAMICS

Network approaches have become increasingly important in the social sciences as sociologists and others have sought to understand organizations and individuals in relationship to each other, rather than as distinct entities subject to a sea of external forces (Emirbayer 1997). A network describes the web of relationships existing between a set of individual or organizational actors. More formally, 'a network is a metaphor to characterize a form of economic organization in which organizations have . . . permeable boundaries, and numerous connections to other organizations' (Smith-Doerr and Powell 2005: 380). Social network theory and the analytic techniques of social network analysis (SNA) offer powerful ways of visualizing, analysing and comparing network structures and relationships. Network 'ties' are the formal or informal connections between 'nodes' (typically organizations or individuals, depending on the network being studied). Social network analysis offers ways of measuring not only the relative importance of ties between actors (nodes) in a network but also enables researchers to probe characteristics of the whole network, comprised of the aggregate of all ties. The whole network may be sparse or dense, centralized around one or a few focal actors, or more balanced. Each structural configuration of the network has implications for how information flows, how power is concentrated (or not) and how the network evolves (Kilduff and Tsai 2003; Smith-Doerr and Powell 2005).

The literature on the emergence and development of industrial symbiosis has tended to mirror findings from the literature on networks more generally. Social network analysis is starting to be used in studies of industrial symbiosis to probe these relationships more fully (Ashton 2008; Jacobsen and Anderberg 2004; Howard-Grenville and Paquin 2008). On the one hand, a few instances of viable, self-emerging industrial symbiosis have been documented, or 'uncovered' (Chertow 2007; Gertler and Ehrenfeld 1996). Perhaps the best known and longest-lived example of this is Kalundborg, where, over a period of more than 35 years, 20 physical resource exchanges have developed between six key organizations, and a handful of peripheral ones, within the Kalundborg industrial park (Ehrenfeld and Chertow 2002). While the exchanges have had to overcome some significant technical challenges, the success of this system is frequently attributed to the 'short mental distance' between managers in the close-knit community (ibid.). Indeed, while each exchange was developed bilaterally as a business opportunity and had to meet economic and environmental criteria, managers of many of the early participating organizations knew each other through prior social interactions.

Kalundborg represents what network scholars have called a 'serendipitous' network, or one that forms through random social processes and is not necessarily oriented around a particular goal nor administered by a governing body (Kilduff and Tsai 2003). Trajectories of such networks tend to involve slow, decentralized growth, the development and flourishing of many sub-networks, and the inclusion of relatively heterogeneous actors. Serendipitous networks may be resilient and enduring because they build upon pre-existing social ties and trusting relationships (Gulati and Gargiulo 1999; Uzzi, 1996). Indeed, many studies find that structural stability within these networks flows from the social embeddedness of actors (Kilduff et al. 2006). The robust and long-lived nature of Kalundborg's industrial symbiosis certainly supports this general observation.

On the other hand, numerous efforts have been made to initiate or accelerate the development of industrial symbiosis. While some of these have been successful (for example, in Australia and China; Van Beers et al. 2007; Zhu et al. 2007), a great many have not. Challenges to the actual development of industrial symbiosis relationships are well documented in this volume (see Chapters 4 and 6) and elsewhere (Chertow 2007; Gibbs et al. 2005). These include technical and regulatory challenges (Ehrenfeld et al. 2002; Gertler and Ehrenfeld 1996), the difficulty of establishing trusting relationships between firms previously unknown to each other (Burström and Korhonen 2001), and the fact that the environmental and economic benefits – if immediately present at all – are typically unequally distributed among parties (Chertow and Lombardi 2005).

These results echo the expected trajectories of 'constructed' or 'goal-driven' networks identified by network scholars (Kilduff et al. 2003). Goal-driven networks are characterized by the presence of an administrative member who 'acts as a broker to plan and coordinate the activities of the network as a whole' (Kilduff and Tsai 2003: 89). Members are assumed to share a common goal that they seek to attain through their participation in the network. As a result, a goal-directed network may have relatively clear boundaries, experience little sub-network formation, and may be comprised of relatively homogenous actors (Kilduff and Tsai 2003). Furthermore, in such a network, the trajectory and robustness of the network is particularly sensitive to the activities and internal legitimacy of this administrative body (Human and Provan 2000).

The 'third way' that we explore in this chapter, the development of industrial symbiosis networks through 'facilitated emergence', relies on the presence of a brokering organization to bring firms together. Brokerage is defined as the process 'by which intermediary actors facilitate transactions between other actors lacking access to or trust in one another' (Marsden 1982: 202). In the case of facilitated industrial symbiosis, the broker engages individual firms interested in such collaborations but who otherwise lack some combination of experience, knowledge, or contacts with other interested firms. By making introductions, the brokering organization may 'stand in' as an alternative to pre-existing social ties and thus speed the development of a trusting relationship between previously unknown firms. Additionally, the active hand of the broker can strategically shape the development of a broader-based regional exchange network. Each of these slightly different activities relies on two different forms of legitimacy. The former (connecting individual firms to each other) depends on the legitimacy of the network as a form of interaction, the latter (establishing industrial symbiosis regionally) depends on the legitimacy of the network as an entity (Human and Provan 2000).

This facilitated emergence approach also raises questions about the dynamics of an industrial symbiosis network as it forms and grows. Early network forms may 'lock in' certain structures and norms of interaction. Some research suggests that initial actors in emerging networks tend to remain dominant over time because they have a disproportionately large impact in shaping the early rules or norms of interaction (Baum et al. 2003). Our first research question probes these network dynamics: how does the initial configuration of the industrial symbiosis network shape its growth or evolution?

Our second research question looks specifically at the role of brokerage in facilitating network emergence and development. In organizational research, brokerage has largely been considered a 'structural' concern focused on the positioning of actors within a network. For example, Burt's work argues that powerful brokers are those who fill 'structural holes' within the network (Burt 1992). Others argue that 'brokerage is inherently and inextricably tied to structural position in transaction networks' (Gould and Fernandez 1989: 94). More recent work, however, has begun to integrate action with structure, exploring not just the 'positioning' of brokers but how they engage in the brokering process, and its outcomes (Hargadon and Sutton 1997; Hargadon and Douglas 2001; Obstfeld 2005). Industrial symbiosis research views brokers as possessing more than simply a valued structural position. Institutional 'anchor tenants' (Burström et al. 2001) such as local authorities (von Malmborg 2004), key manufacturing facilities (Chertow 2000; Chertow and Lombardi 2005), or professional associations (Baas and Boons 2004), can be critical to the development of exchanges. Such entities are valuable to the extent that they are regarded as trustworthy and hence possibly enhance the legitimacy of the emerging network and the network as a form of interaction (von Malmborg 2004).

Also, our second research question explicitly probes the effect of a broker on the developing network of exchanges. We ask: how does the presence of a brokering organization shape the growth or evolution of the network? How do the actions and interests of the brokering organization shape the network evolution?

METHODS

Research Setting

The focus of this study is on the activities of the National Industrial Symbiosis Programme (NISP) in the West Midlands region of the United Kingdom. Formed in April 2005, NISP's goal is to 'encourage government and industry of the benefit of industrial symbiosis (IS) as a key policy tool in helping the UK to achieve a sustainable economy, further supporting the integration of an industrial symbiosis approach into the nation's resource management strategy' (NISP 2006). NISP operates on a regional level to facilitate industrial symbiosis projects and, while national in scope, operates semi-autonomously in each of the UK's 12 economic regions. Within each region one or more NISP employees or 'practitioners' work with companies to identify possible industrial symbiosis projects. They engage in a range of brokering activities – from hosting networking events and workshops for firms, to facilitating direct introductions between interested firms, and coordinating in-depth consulting projects with individual firms.

NISP grew out of a regional pilot project, WISP (West Midlands Industrial Symbiosis Programme) which began informally in 2001 and formally launched in 2003. The national program continues to be headquartered in the West Midlands region. Our analysis begins to track the network in 2005 because this was the time that the program was secure enough to move beyond its pilot phase, and when it formalized its own project tracking process to enable data collection. Both of these events were related to the receipt of national-level funding and a mandate to increase the scope of the program into other UK economic regions.

As of 2007, the great majority of NISP's funding came from the UK government, originating indirectly through the collection of the UK landfill tax. Passed into law in 1996, the landfill tax set an escalating tax on industrial landfill which in 2008 was 32 GBP/tonne and expected to rise to 48 GBP/tonne by 2010. Part of these tax revenues were set aside specifically to competitively fund regional and national organizations, such as NISP, to assist UK firms in finding novel ways to remain economically competitive under increasingly stringent UK and EU environmental regulations. NISP's funding is tied not to specific industrial symbiosis projects but to its ability to create aggregate reductions in landfill, carbon dioxide and other environmental metrics in economically beneficial ways. Due to its funding structure, NISP's services are free to interested businesses.

NISP's activities in the West Midlands offer a good setting in which to explore the trajectory of facilitated industrial symbiosis because this relatively mature region displays elements of both goal-directedness and serendipity. It involves an administrative body (NISP) that has explicit goals for (and whose success is measured against) reducing net environmental impact. On the other hand, industrial symbiosis remains a relatively new environmental activity for UK firms, unknown to the great majority of businesses in the region, and also unknown to others on whom the success of the program may depend (for example, local environmental authorities, regional development agencies, and so on). As a result, efforts to build and gain legitimacy for the network were expected to involve building on prior relationships and connecting previously unconnected firms. The evolutionary paths of such networks are poorly understood, and the practical challenges to developing and maintaining them are equally poorly understood.

Data

We collected quantitative and qualitative data to enable us to represent and analyse the network structure in the West Midlands, and to understand some of the processes behind its emergence and change.

Quantitative data: archival records of interfirm resource exchanges
We collected quantitative data on all initiated, attempted, in-progress and completed industrial symbiosis projects facilitated by NISP in the West Midlands from 2005 (earliest period at which this data was formalized) to 2007. These data included facility name, location, industry, size, prior experience in the exchange network; and project information such as the materials involved, the quantity and quality of material, which facility was the intended receiver of the material, when the project was initiated, when and if it ended (failed) and changes over time. Projects were tracked on a 1 to 5 scale with: 1 = introduction made between relevant firms; 2 = firms discussing project past introduction; 3 = firms negotiating details of projects (costs, logistics, etc.); 4 = firms beginning project; 5 = project is ongoing or complete. We used NISP's own internal tracking scale as our basis for capturing the progress of individual projects.

Qualitative data: interviews

Between December 2005 and November 2007, we conducted open ended and semi-structured interviews with 11 NISP staff directly or indirectly involved in NISP's work in the West Midlands. In these interviews, we probed individual histories and roles within NISP, how interviewees perceived NISP as an organization and a broker, and how they engaged with firms in their particular roles within NISP. We also held dozens of informal interviews and conversations with NISP staff during our visits to NISP offices and when attending other events. These gave us more insight into some of the nuances of NISP's operations. We also conducted 23 interviews with members of companies who participated in NISP in either the West Midlands or East Midlands region. Some of these companies had initiated or completed industrial symbiosis projects through NISP; others had not but had attended workshops and/or expressed interest in engaging in potential projects. The company interviews gave us a sense of how NISP's activities were viewed more broadly, and helped us understand different ways that companies engaged with NISP.

Analysis

We analysed the archival resource exchange data using standard social network analysis software UCINET version 6 (Borgatti et al. 2002). This software allowed us to analyse characteristics of individual nodes within a network, as well as characteristics of the overall network. In our case, the network nodes were individual companies engaged in industrial symbiosis projects and the ties represented the actual projects. It is important to note that not all ties represented completed projects. As mentioned above, we used NISP's own scale (1 through 5) to capture the status of individual projects from '1' representing the fact that two firms had been introduced to each other around a specific project idea, to '5' representing a fully completed (or ongoing) symbiosis project. Thus, we consider the status of individual projects as a measure of tie strength between the firms involved.

We analysed the emerging resource exchange network quarterly from 2005 to 2007 (nine periods total), with each quarter providing a 'snapshot' of the evolving network. Each successive quarterly 'snapshot' provided a cumulative view of all exchanges in the network up until that point in time. For our first time period (2005), a number of firms and projects are already active in the network. Of course, these firms did not all immediately jump into action during this time period, rather these projects were already under development but it was in this period that NISP first formally captured data on these projects. As discussed above, NISP's precursor organization (WISP) began in the region in 2001, but formal project data was not tracked until 2005. Thus, the data listed as '2005' is an aggregated baseline of the network roughly from its beginning through the end of 2005.

Once we had obtained numerical and graphical data of the industrial symbiosis network across these time periods, we assessed how the network changed over time. This was done by relying both on our social network analysis and by drawing on our interviews to add texture to the quantitative findings.

FINDINGS

The Growing Network

By several measures, the network of industrial symbiosis projects in the West Midlands, and hence the firms connected through such a network, grew considerably between 2005, and 2007. The number of industrial symbiosis projects grew from 175 in 2005, to 307 in 2007. The number of firms involved in these projects also grew substantially from 162 firms in 2005, to 243 in 2007. During this period, the number of new industrial symbiosis projects outpaced new firms engaging in the resource exchange network. Another way to view this is through the mean number of projects a firm was involved in during this time. This measure grew from 2.20 in 2005, to 2.53 in 2007.[1] This implies that the network grew by engaging new firms in industrial symbiosis and, importantly, by re-engaging firms already in the network in new projects. Table 5.1 provides a number of descriptive measures for the network for each quarter from 2005 to 2007 and includes the mean number of projects (exchanges) per firm.

The rate of network growth increased somewhat later in the time period studied. This is most easily seen by the change in the graphs shown in Figure 5.1, where a marked increase in slope occurs in early 2007. Figure 5.1 also discerns between the core component or 'main' network (meaning the larger group of firms who are cohesively connected to each other) and other unconnected components that are not connected to the main network. In social network analysis, the 'network' per se is often not a completely connected network, but rather a collection of unconnected or sparsely connected subgroups of actors. For ease of discussion, we will refer to the largest subgroup or core component as the 'main' network; and the smaller unconnected subgroups collectively as 'components' (Scott 2000). Figure 5.2 shows graphical portrayals of the overall network

The social embeddedness of industrial ecology

Table 5.1   *Descriptive measures of the growing industrial symbiosis network*

Time periods	T0 2005	T1	T2	T3	T4 2006	T5	T6	T7	T8 2007
Number of firms in network									
'Main' network	**111**	111	120	128	**136**	153	153	177	**203**
'Components'	**51**	53	49	46	**44**	32	39	42	**40**
Total	*162*	*164*	*169*	*174*	*180*	*185*	*192*	*219*	*243*
Number of exchanges in network									
'Main' network	**146**	145	154	165	**183**	203	211	252	**287**
'Components'	**29**	31	28	27	**25**	21	21	23	**20**
Total	*175*	*176*	*182*	*192*	*208*	*224*	*232*	*275*	*307*
Network measures									
Mean exchanges per firm – *entire network*	**2.20**	2.17	2.19	2.26	**2.39**	2.47	2.45	2.52	**2.53**
Eigenvector centrality (SD) – *main network only*	**4.66** **(12.59)**	4.69 (12.58)	4.53 (12.09)	4.31 (11.73)	**3.76** **(11.53)**	3.50 (11.17)	3.40 (10.92)	3.94 (9.87)	**4.66** **(8.76)**
Network centralization index (%) – *main network only*	**102.8**	103.1	100.9	100.7	**94.9**	98.6	98.2	94.3	**91.5**

Note: 2005, 2006 and 2007 are in bold since they are used in comparison later in the chapter.

at three time periods (2005, 2006 and 2007) with the 'main' network and 'components' differentiated by shape and colour. Each dot depicts a firm, and each line is an industrial symbiosis project initiated, underway, or completed between the connected firms.

By discerning the main and component portions of the network, another trend is clear in the overall network growth. Both the proportion and actual numbers of firms and projects unconnected to the main portion of the overall network decrease over time. In other words, industrial symbiosis activity becomes concentrated within the 'main' network, comprised of more fully interconnected firms. Two dynamics contribute

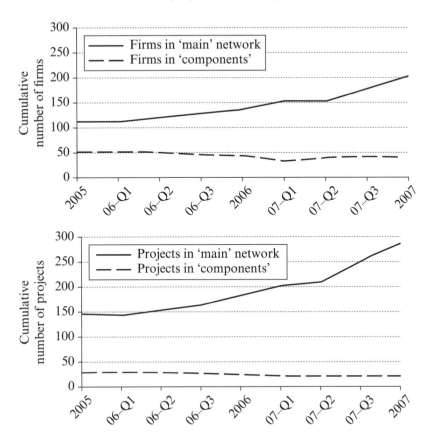

Figure 5.1 *Number of firms and industrial symbiosis projects in the exchange network over time*

to this. First, as can be seen in the network snapshots in Figure 5.2, firms in the components tend to develop new projects with firms in the main network, in effect, bringing all the firms from a given component into the main network. An example of this is seen in the circled set of firms in the lower part of these network diagrams. Second, and less obvious from the network diagrams, is that most new industrial symbiosis projects involve new firms (previously not in the network at all) engaging with existing firms in the main network; of the 81 firms who enter this network after 2005, the large majority engage with firms already in the main network (as opposed to firms in the components). Thus, network growth results primarily from increasing activity within the main network, and only secondarily from activity in the components.

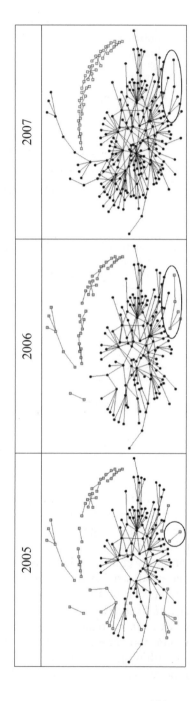

Notes and Legend:
Main network = black circles
Unconnected components = grey squares
Each snapshot shows active firms (those engaged in industrial symbiosis projects) during that time period. As the network is cumulative, each time period has more firms and exchanges than the previous.
The expanding oval shows the growth of one particular component in the network from 2005 to 2006, and its subsequent connection to the main network as a firm from the component and a firm from the main network engage in a new industrial symbiosis project during 2007.

Figure 5.2 Snapshots of the growing exchange network in 2005, 2006 and 2007

Qualitatively, our interviews with NISP staff and company participants supported the findings of rapid network growth and offered reasons for it. One oft-cited reason for companies engaging with NISP was that it expanded their access to information and opened them up to potential new opportunities and contacts. For example, one interviewee remarked that NISP offered them 'really an added opportunity to network and find out about [additional] opportunities'. Another noted that 'They [NISP] have the time and energy to get around and talk to a huge cross section of companies within the region that they are operating in. It's quite easy for them, from the outside looking in, to recognize that a company might have a waste product that another company could use'. This interviewee went on to add, 'the benefits to us of NISP, [are that] they are able to come up with ideas that we wouldn't have thought of, and then they introduce us to other companies that we might never have crossed swords with'.

From NISP's point of view, generating contacts and engaging more firms was essential to growth and success, and took up a considerable amount of time and effort, especially in the early days. One NISP practitioner said 'the challenge for us was to try and engage businesses, but why will they come if every other business group in the country is knocking on their door? So we tried to establish events and workshops around themes'. As interest in the programme grew, NISP staff could become more selective and 'hands on' in their work with firms because recruitment to the programme required less time. One NISP regional coordinator put it this way:

> When you start off the programme you generate the membership. . . . After that level, [when] there are about 80 members within a region, you find that the companies are making referrals through their supply chain, saying 'this programme is good we got such and such out of it, you might get involved with it as well'. We are finding that whereas in the first few months we were making all the phone calls to get people to come in now we are getting calls to the office from people who heard of us, now it's about 50–50 calls in to calls out.

As this change occurred, NISP staff were able to potentially add more value and engage existing firms in projects that might have required more innovation and facilitation. This may be one of the reasons that the number of projects per firm increases over time, as sheer recruitment is gradually replaced by more strategic development of industrial symbiosis projects. The latter type of activity is valued and sought after by both participating firms and NISP itself. For example, one company member noted that 'what I need NISP to do is actively facilitate between people'. Another observed that NISP would add value to their business by 'analyz[ing] the information they have and go[ing] back to companies and say[ing] there is an option *here* for you'.

While our data do not show it explicitly, there is a potential tension between the need to recruit firms and show rapid growth in the network – an early indicator of 'success' – and the need to develop complex, knowledge-intensive projects that may require significant investments of time, expertise, and technology. We turn next to analysing in more detail where and how the growth in the network occurred, and to further probing the incentives of participating companies and NISP itself.

'Churn' in the Network

As discussed above (and shown in Table 5.1), both the number of firms and number of projects increases over time with new projects in the network out-pacing new firms engaging the network. On its own, this is fairly consistent with prior work on social networks which suggests that those already in the network (especially those central in the network) continue to reengage and profit from their position in the network over time (Baum et al. 2003). In other words, the 'rich get richer' (para, Provan et al. 2007). As we look more closely at firm-level activity, however, this does not bear out exactly in the industrial symbiosis network.

In the 'rich get richer scenario', network analyses would show an increasing stratification within the network between more central and less central actors. One measure of this is the network centralization index. This index provides a network-level measure of range of centralities of individual firms in the network, with centrality representing how connected each firm is to all others. A high centralization index indicates a network where a few key actors are highly connected to all others, and less central actors tend to be connected only to those central actors. In the 'rich get richer' scenario of network growth, we would expect to see the network centralization index increase over time, suggesting increased network stratification. As shown in Table 5.1, the West Midlands industrial symbiosis network does the opposite, with its network centralization index decreasing from 102.8 per cent in 2005, to 95.3 per cent in 2007. This decreasing stratification among firms in the network suggests that firms are not necessarily engaging in industrial symbiosis projects with the most centrally connected (and by implication, experienced) firms but with other, less connected, firms. This network growth path in itself might be regarded as a healthy one, for it reduces the tendency for power and information to be concentrated among a few highly connected actors, and enables the potential infusion of new ideas and relationships throughout the network. We now consider possible explanations for this path.

First, an analysis of the connectedness of individual firms shows considerable 'churn' among the highly connected firms over time, elaborating

Table 5.2   Rank ordering of firms by centrality at 2005 and 2007

	Top 20 Most Central Firms in 2005			Top 20 Most Central Firms in 2007, plus Firm A	
Firm	2005 Ranking	2007 Ranking	Firm	2005 Ranking	2007 Ranking
A	1	44	BX	76	1
B	2	81	DH	n/a	2
C	3	134	CD	82	3
D	4	135	CG	85	4
E	5	136	DI	n/a	5
F	6	60	DJ	n/a	6
G	7	137	AJ	36	7
H	8	138	J	10	8
I	9	144	AT	46	9
J	10	8	CE	83	10
K	11	69	DK	n/a	11
L	12	121	DL	n/a	12
M	13	86	AR	44	13
N	14	139	V	22	14
O	15	140	AH	34	15
P	16	141	DM	n/a	16
Q	17	50	DN	n/a	17
R	18	113	DO	n/a	18
S	19	131	CA	79	19
T	20	20	T	20	20
			. . .	. . .	. . .
			A	1	44

Notes: Only firms J and T, ranked 10th and 20th respectively in 2005 were among the top 20 most central firms in 2007. Firm A, the most central firm in 2005, was ranked 44th in 2007.

on the trend in the network level centralization index. Table 5.2 shows this descriptively with a rank ordering of the 20 most central firms in 2005, against their centrality ranking in 2007; and vice versa with the 20 most central firms in 2007 – eight of which were not even in the network in 2005. Even when taking a comparable percentage of 'top' firms in 2007 as in 2005 (in this case the top 30 most central firms in 2007 to the top 20 in 2005), only two top firms in 2005 are in the top 30 firms in 2007 (these are shaded in grey). That so many firms who join the network 'late' become so central suggests something unusual in the network's growth. Understanding this requires a more in-depth exploration of NISP's activities and goals as a regional industrial symbiosis broker.

NISP's regional brokering activities

From our interviews, we learned that NISP engages in a number of distinct activities to facilitate industrial symbiosis projects. First, NISP sponsors regular workshops in each region for firms interested in learning more about or getting involved in industrial symbiosis projects. NISP staff and workshop attendees independently referred to these events colloquially as 'speed dating', and formally as 'Quick Wins' workshops. At such events, NISP staff introduced the idea and demonstrated, through examples, the value of industrial symbiosis. They then facilitated the sharing of waste and by-product information between firms. These networking sessions were valuable in several ways. First, they quickly gave attendees an idea of what types of projects their firms might get involved in. As one attendee noted, she was intrigued and surprised by the opportunities that came up during the workshop. She said, 'I've been to one networking session where we all sat down and did a grid, [of] what [resources] we want and what we have; which I found absolutely fascinating. . . . [At the beginning] we were sitting there and thinking "God this is hard" and then at the end of it there were 132 synergies.' Synergy is the term used by NISP to refer to potential or actual resource exchange or industrial symbiosis projects.

The workshops also provided NISP with each firms' contact information and details of its resource needs and capabilities which it may later use to facilitate introductions between firms with matching resource needs and capacities. NISP staff often followed up on the information gathered from networking events with visits to individual facilities to learn more about their environmental and waste management activities. These visits also enabled NISP staff to develop relationships with representatives from individual facilities – increasing NISP's perceived value in facilitating future industrial symbiosis projects between unconnected firms (Uzzi 1997).

This information helped NISP staff gain an increasingly 'transparent' view of the potential industrial symbiosis field or network in the region (Dorado 2005; Hargadon et al. 1997). In our interviews, we found that firms both (a) felt that their firms lacked this broader inter-firm perspective and (b) looked to NISP (and other business support organizations) to help provide them with that more strategic perspective. One company participant noted that 'more importantly you meet people on the cutting edge of technology – new systems, new methods – and you can start working with them. You say, ok, let's see what you've got. Let's see if it's applicable to our industry.'

These activities, combined with NISP's internal decision to hire staff with greater industry-specific experience, increased NISP's aggregate level of expertise. This expertise was of value in both establishing the industrial symbiosis network as a legitimate form in the region, and in developing specific industrial symbiosis projects between interested firms. This change

allowed NISP staff to move beyond simply making introductions to providing guidance and expertise around particular industrial symbiosis projects
as needed. Lastly, NISP staff began engaging with individual facilities in
more traditional consulting relationships – assisting with business and
strategy development, funding, R&D support, and so on – around new
types of industrial symbiosis projects or expanding capacity for prominent
resource streams in the region. For example, one NISP practitioner shared
an experience of hearing from a farmer who wanted to use his farm waste
to generate energy through anaerobic digestion, and sell the excess energy
to a new industrial facility on an abutting site. The NISP practitioner liked
the idea, but felt that the farmer was 'thinking too small'. Accordingly,
working with the farmer, the industrial facility next door, and the local
authority, he helped generate a plan to pull in additional waste streams
and to build an energy facility five to ten times larger than the farmer had
originally envisioned. This kind of activity not only expanded the scope of
potential projects, but was seen as generating regional capacity and having
a number of 'spillover' benefits.

NISP's Impact on the Network

Our understanding of NISP's activities from the interview data is reflected
in some quite significant changes in the actual resources exchanged over
time. Figure 5.3 shows, by major resource type, the cumulative number
of industrial symbiosis projects over time. Two types of exchanges are
particularly worth noting for their increased prominence later in the time
periods studied: (a) expertise – when one firm or organization provides
technical, production, or some other specialized expertise to help develop
a new project; and (b) infrastructure – when one firm or organization
engages in a consultative approach to help another develop or expand
its capacity for engaging in industrial symbiosis. Given that one-third
of industrial symbiosis projects in the network by 2007 are 'expertise'
projects, we focus solely on those projects here.

NISP's engagement as an expert in projects – or rather in 'expertise'
projects – increases from 9 to 27 projects or from 18.8 per cent to 32.1 per
cent of the total number of expertise projects from 2005 to 2007. By 2007,
8.8 per cent of the total projects in the network are due to NISP's role as
expert in these 27 'expertise' projects. This suggests that NISP's influence
on the network is more than merely a 'broker' passing information or
making introductions (Marsden 1982), rather it is an active player fundamentally shaping the network's path and the content of the exchanges, as
suggested by some of the interview data.

To examine the influence of NISP activity on the network, we removed

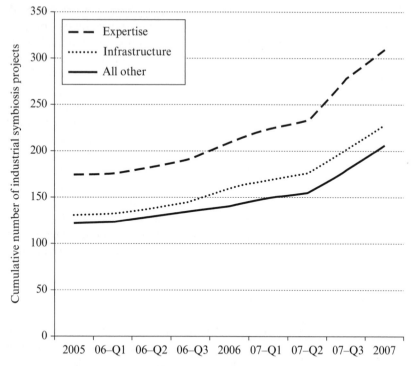

*Figure 5.3   Types of resources exchanged in the industrial symbiosis
network over time*

NISP's expertise projects from the overall network. We compared this
second network to our original network as a way to evaluate the influence
of NISP's expertise activities on the network over time. Table 5.3 provides
some comparative descriptive data on these two networks at three points
in time – 2005, 2006 and 2007. In Table 5.3, we see that for 2005, the
networks look very similar by these measures, but with a quite marked
divergence in these measures by 2007.

   Statistical comparison of the networks in 2005 and 2007 shows that remov-
ing NISP's expertise activities significantly changed the network structure
and its pattern of evolution. Most importantly, when NISP's expertise activities are removed from the network, the 'churn' in the top firms observed
earlier is less pronounced and no longer statistically significant. Thus, if
NISP's expertise projects are ignored (but its typical brokering activities
remain), it seems that the 'rich may in fact be getting richer'. In other words,
the most connected firms tend to gain proportionally more of the new
industrial symbiosis partners and projects over time, when looking at non-

Table 5.3   Comparison at three points (2005, 2006, 2007) of networks with and without NISP's expertise projects

	With NISP's expertise projects			Without NISP's expertise projects		
	2005	2006	2007	2005	2006	2007
No. of Firms – *Whole Network*	162	180	243	159	177	235
No. of Firms – *'Main' Network only*	111	136	203	106	133	194
No. of Industrial symbiosis projects	175	208	307	167	200	281
Eigenvector Centrality (SD) – *'Main' network only*	4.66 (12.59)	3.76 (11.53)	4.66 (8.76)	4.88 (12.84)	3.51 (11.75)	2.82 (9.76)
Network Centralization Index – *'Main' network only*	102.8%	94.9%	91.5%	102.9%	90.0%	95.3%

expertise exchanges. Furthermore, this suggests that NISP's own activities are differentially influencing the network's growth path. The heavy increase in NISP's engagement in expertise activities in 2007 may reflect either the fact that opportunities to pick 'low hanging fruit' (achieve relatively simple industrial symbiosis exchanges) have decreased, or that a strategic decision was made to pursue these more innovative, potentially higher valued-added activities. Our interviews suggest the latter, but more research is needed to determine the contribution of each of these possible explanations.

Challenges to growth of the network
The growth of the industrial symbiosis network was not without some challenges. Among these were working out how NISP would work with companies and find a balance between advocating for particular projects and respecting the need for companies to make these decisions for themselves. One NISP practitioner observed, 'every [company] meeting that we go to we try to make the decision as informed as possible, whether it be legislation or supply, etc. You can give advice there but it is really down to the companies concerned if they want to move forward.' He added, 'you can sit behind a company and act as a sounding board for them, [but] obviously we don't want to push it too far because we don't want to be interfering with the business process.'

Some companies appeared to want more hands-on involvement from NISP. One interviewee noted that reviewing their waste streams on their own was 'a bit resource intensive from our point of view.' He added that he would have liked NISP to be more proactive, reviewing his waste and that of others and saying 'we see that you have this, well we have a match here with this other company, how about hooking it up?' Others, especially larger companies, felt that they had a good handle on many of their waste streams and, while they supported NISP's overall activities, had no need to engage in particular industrial symbiosis projects. One company member observed 'unfortunately by the time NISP came along we had really sorted out all of our waste streams. Had it been ten years earlier I think we would have been more enthusiastic about using it. We are very supportive of it but we aren't actually using it.'

For many other companies, NISP was of valuable assistance but it took time and effort to build trust and learn about opportunities. Part of this involved sorting out how NISP was distinguished from a number of other organizations who offered similar services. For example, one company interviewee noted:

> There's also another organization that's also funded by the government that's called WRAP – Waste Resources Action Programme. That's been going since, must be 2001 . . . To a certain extent, they've been doing what NISP is now set up to do. But, they're [WRAP] now concentrating on finding the actual methodology of reuse, recycling in the end market. So they're concentrating on end markets now, whereas NISP is doing more of the facilitation role.

A NISP practitioner added that building relationships with companies was essential to aid their understanding of opportunities and willingness to pursue them. 'We try to understand the business benefit that might be accruing from a particular opportunity, [but] it's also a trust issue,' he noted. He went on to say that 'if you rely on the database [NISP's internal knowledge management database of potential waste exchanges], you lose the trust from the businesses; you become a passive waste exchange. So the networks and trust are the key here.' It is perhaps not surprising, given the importance of trust in developing other industrial symbiosis arrangements (Burström et al. 2001), that it is seen as so central even in a rapidly-growing, facilitated industrial symbiosis network.

DISCUSSION

Our analysis of the evolution of industrial symbiosis in the West Midlands demonstrates the effects of an active broker on the structure of the network itself as well as the level and nature of activity within it. Our findings show that the industrial symbiosis network grew significantly over a period of only three years, and that growth occurred primarily by new firms entering the network and becoming engaged in projects with firms already involved in other industrial symbiosis projects within the network. This in itself suggests that it may be possible to build a goal-directed network for industrial symbiosis. This path differs substantially from the self-emergence of Kalundborg's industrial symbiosis in the absence of any facilitating body (until late in its existence). It also contrasts the planned approaches to setting up eco-industrial parks which have often failed to develop any significant industrial symbiosis activity at all (see Chapter 4 in this volume).

By exploring where and how growth occurred in the regional industrial symbiosis network, we revealed that the facilitating organization – NISP – had a disproportionately large impact on the network changes, particularly in the latter stages of our study. There are several possible explanations for this, all of which bear further study. First, NISP was acting not merely as a traditional broker occupying a position within the network that enabled it to make introductions between firms, but it was also acting as a network participant in its own right. In other words, it had its own agenda for seeding and developing certain types of industrial symbiosis projects and the increase in 'expertise' projects may have reflected this. Whether this was the result of regional staff gaining experience and expertise and becoming more inclined to work on more complex projects, or the result of the growth in staff and the addition of their individual networks and interests to the brokering activity, it suggests that brokering such a network needs to be understood not merely as a structural activity of making introductions. Indeed, which introductions are made and which projects are pursued aggressively is a reflection of individual interests and experience.

A second, and somewhat related explanation for the structural shifts in the network development, is found in understanding NISP's funding model and the metrics used to track its performance as an organization. As a primarily government-funded program, NISP's success is tracked by a number of specific environmental metrics, such as tons of material diverted from landfill, and reductions in carbon emissions, potable water use, and so on. As the 'low hanging fruit' associated with the diversion of some high tonnages (for example, construction aggregate or glass recycling) is achieved in a region, other projects may require more sophisticated technological development, investment in capacity, and multi-party collaborations. The additional inclusion of economic metrics to track NISP's success (for example, money saved, jobs created) as well as more detailed environmental metrics will inevitably further shape NISP's incentives for pursuing certain projects over others.

It is not possible with the data at hand to tease out these various influences, but the overall shift in the network development supports the general observation that structural network changes must always be understood in relation to the economic and other interests of the participants and brokers. In other words, structural embeddedness is in part a reflection of other forms of embeddedness, including temporal embeddedness which captures the trajectory of network growth. Indeed, networks are themselves embedded in broader relational contexts (Provan et al. 2007). In this case, the rapidly changing political, regulatory and economic contexts surrounding resource provision, use, and disposal produce shifting incentives for brokers and other actors engaged in industrial symbiosis. This results in more pronounced network dynamics than those typically ascribed to social networks. Indeed, our finding that the network 'churns', and becomes less stratified rather than more so, contradicts prior work on network development that suggest an increasingly centralization of key actors as the 'rich get richer' over time (Baum et al. 2003).

Our research suggests that the presence and nature of involvement of the brokering organization may be critical to the evolution of regional-scale industrial symbiosis, but also raises a number of questions for further study. These include a number of questions around brokerage itself: how does the value of a broker as perceived by other firms in the network change over time, how robust is the network under various degrees of intervention by a broker, and what characteristics must a broker possess to be effective in developing a network? The existing literature on industrial symbiosis provides some clues as to the importance of these questions. For example, issues of trust become even more pronounced when public entities – who might otherwise be in a regulatory role – begin to try to operate as collaborating partners (Burström et al. 2001).

Another critical set of questions to pursue address the nature of industrial symbiosis projects generated through a facilitated network model. Some have suggested that industrial symbiosis is more complex than simply a resource exchange between two firms, akin to traditional recycling. For example, Chertow has proposed a 'three-two' heuristic for what comprises industrial symbiosis: at least three firms must be involved in the exchange or sharing of at least two resource streams (Chertow 2007). Using this heuristic, relatively few of the resource exchanges captured in the West Midlands network would qualify. However, several of the 'expertise' projects that targeted more complex schemes (for example, the anaerobic digester that would pull in additional waste streams and operate as a larger facility) may well qualify. Perhaps the shift towards these types of projects, as observed earlier, marks the development of a more robust and longer-lived set of network ties than those that might be developed only around simple two-firm recycling or reuse arrangements. On the other hand, even 'simple' exchanges are likely critical to the establishment of relationships that lead to further and grander projects. The advantage of facilitating introductions in a network is that it at least gets companies into contact with each other. Whether they go on to develop a specific project or not, their thinking about the issues may have changed, or their openness to pursuing a project when the time and partnership is right may have been primed. Indeed, in the absence of any communication between firms, one finds very little industrial symbiosis activity (see Chapter 6 of this volume), whether of a simple or more complex nature. As one company interviewee observed:

> It could be that NISP would be just as valuable in putting us in contact with like-minded people rather than just the raw data and the waste materials, because I can learn just as much by talking to people. For instance, [I had] conversations with [a company] and they are coming in this afternoon. If it wasn't for NISP perhaps we would never have heard about them.

CONCLUSION

While the success of Kalundborg is indisputable, many observe that improvement of resource consumption on a regional scale cannot wait three decades to develop in other parts of the world. The evidence from this study that facilitated industrial symbiosis networks can grow significantly, achieve demonstrable net environmental gains, and do so in such a short period of time offers an alternative to the oft-debunked 'constructed' approach of developing dedicated eco-industrial parks. Our findings, however, also suggest just how sensitive facilitated industrial symbiosis can be to the activities, goals and incentives of a brokering organization, and the other firms involved. Whether a 'facilitated emergence' approach as shown here can offer a robust 'third way' model of facilitated inter-organizational environmental collaboration depends to a great degree on the nature of the broker, the dynamics of the network and the robustness of the system that evolves as a result.

NOTE

1. Because industrial symbiosis projects are interfirm collaborations, the project/firm ratio is not computed as #projects / #firms. Rather, since industrial symbiosis projects require at least two (and in our data, sometimes more) firms collaborating, the project/firm ratio equals the averaged sum of the number of projects each firm is engaged in.

REFERENCES

Ashton, W. (2008), 'Understanding the organization of industrial ecosystems: A social network approach'. *Journal of Industrial Ecology*, **12**: 34–51.

Baas, L.W. and F.A. Boons (2004), 'An industrial ecology project in practice: exploring the boundaries of decision-making levels in regional industrial systems', *Journal of Cleaner Production*, **12**(8–10): 1073–85.

Baum, J.A.C., A.V. Shipilov and T.J. Rowley (2003), 'Where do small worlds come from?' *Industrial and Corporate Change*, **12**(4): 697–725.

Borgatti, S.P., M.G. Everett and L.C. Freeman (2002), *Ucinet for Windows: Software for Social Network Analysis*, Cambridge, MA: Analytic Technologies.

Burström, F. and J. Korhonen (2001), 'Municipalities and industrial ecology: reconsidering municipal environmental management', *Sustainable Development*, **9**(1): 36–46.

Burt, R.S. (1992), *Structural Holes: The Social Structure of Competition*, Cambridge, MA: Harvard University Press.

Chertow, M.R. (2000), 'Industrial symbiosis: Literature and taxonomy', *Annual Review of Energy and the Environment*, **25**: 313–37.

Chertow, M.R. (2007), '"Uncovering" industrial symbiosis', *Journal of Industrial Ecology*, **11**(1).

Chertow, M.R. and D.R. Lombardi (2005), 'Quantifying economic and environmental benefits of co-located firms', *Environmental Science and Technology*, **39**(17): 6535–41.

Cohen, B. (2006), 'Sustainable valley entrepreneurial ecosystems', *Business Strategy and the Environment*, **15**(1): 1–14.

Dorado, S. (2005), 'Institutional entrepreneurship, partaking, and convening', *Organization Studies*, **26**(3): 383–414.

Ehrenfeld, J.R. and M.R. Chertow (2002), 'Industrial symbiosis: the legacy of Kalundborg', in R.U. Ayres and L.W. Ayres (eds), *Handbook of Industrial Ecology*, Cheltenham, UK and Northampton, MA, USA: Edward Elgar.

Ehrenfeld, J.R. and N. Gertler (1997), 'Industrial ecology in practice: the evolution of interdependence at Kalundborg', *Journal of Industrial Ecology*, **1**(1): 67–79.

Emirbayer, M. (1997), 'Manifesto for a relational sociology', *The American Journal of Sociology*, **103**(2): 281.

Gertler, N. and J.R. Ehrenfeld (1996), 'A down-to-earth approach to clean production', *Technology Review*, **99**(2): 7.

Gibbs, D., P. Deutz and A. Proctor (2005), 'Industrial ecology and eco-industrial development: a potential paradigm for local and regional development?', *Regional Studies*, **39**(2): 171–83.

Gould, R.V. and R.M. Fernandez (1989), 'Structures of mediation: a formal approach to brokerage in transaction networks', *Sociological Methodology*, **19**: 89–126.

Gulati, R. and M. Gargiulo (1999), 'Where do interorganizational networks come from?', *American Journal of Sociology*, **104**(5): 1439–93.

Hargadon, A.B. and Y. Douglas (2001), 'When innovations meet institutions: Edison and the design of the electric light', *Administrative Science Quarterly*, **46**(3): 476–501.

Hargadon, A. and R.I. Sutton (1997), 'Technology brokering and innovation in a product development firm', *Administrative Science Quarterly*, **42**(4): 716–49.

Howard-Grenville, J. and R. Paquin (2008), 'Organizational dynamics in industrial ecosystems: Insights from organizational behavior theory', in M. Ruth and B. Davidsdottir (eds), *Dynamics of Industrial Ecosystems*, Cheltenham, UK and Northampton, MA, USA: Edward Elgar.

Human, S.E. and K.G. Provan (2000), 'Legitimacy building in the evolution of small-firm multilateral networks: a comparative study of success and demise', *Administrative Science Quarterly*, **45**(2): 327–65.

Jacobsen, N. and S. Anderberg (2005), 'Understanding the evolution of industrial symbiotic networks: the case of Kalundborg', in J. Van Den Bergh and M. Janssen (eds), *Economics of Industrial Ecology: Materials, Structural Change, and Spatial Scales*, Cambridge, MA: MIT Press, pp. 313–35.

Kilduff, M. and W. Tsai (2003), *Social Networks and Organizations*, Thousand Oaks, CA: Sage.

Kilduff, M., W. Tsai and R. Hanke (2006), 'A paradigm too far? A dynamic stability reconsideration of the social network research program', *Academy of Management Review*, **31**(4): 1031–48.

Korhonen, J. and J.-P. Snäkin (2005), 'Analysing the evolution of industrial eco-systems: concepts and application', *Ecological Economics*, **52**(2): 169–86.

Marsden, P.V. (1982), 'Brokerage behavior in restricted exchange networks', in P.V. Marsden and N. Lin (eds), *Social Structure in Network Analysis*, Beverly Hills, CA: Sage, pp. 201–18.

NISP (2006), National Industrial Symbiosis Programme. NISP website: http://www.nisp.org.uk/, accessed 1 May 2006.

Obstfeld, D. (2005), 'Social networks, the tertius iungens orientation, and involvement in innovation', *Administrative Science Quarterly*, **50**(1): 100–130.

Provan, K.G., A. Fish and J. Sydow (2007), 'Interorganizational networks at the network level: a review of the empirical literature on whole networks', *Journal of Management*, **33**(3): 479–516.

Scott, J. (2000), *Social Network Analysis: A Handbook* (2nd edn), Thousand Oaks, CA: Sage.

Smith-Doerr, L. and W.W. Powell (2005), 'Networks and economic life', in N.J. Smelser and R. Swedberg (eds), *The Handbook of Economic Sociology*, (2nd edn), Princeton, NJ: Sage/Princeton University Press.

Tomescu, M. (2005), *Innovative Bioenergy Systems in Action. The Mureck Bio-Energy Cycle: Synergistic Effects and Socio-Economic, Political and Sociocultural Aspects of Rural Bioenergy Systems*, Lund: Lund University for Industrial Environmental Economics.

Uzzi, B. (1996), 'The sources and consequences of embeddedness for the economic performance of organizations: the network effect', *American Sociological Review*, **61**: 674–98.

Uzzi, B. (1997), 'Social structure and competition in interfirm networks: the paradox of embeddedness', *Administrative Science Quarterly*, **42**(1): 37–69.

Van Beers, D., G. Corder, A. Bossilkov and R. Van Berkel (2007), 'Industrial symbiosis in the Australian minerals industry', *Journal of Industrial Ecology*, **11**(1): 55–72.

von Malmborg, F. (2004), 'Networking for knowledge transfer: towards an understanding of local authority roles in regional industrial ecosystem management', *Business Strategy and the Environment*, **13**(5): 334.

Zhu, Q., E.A. Lowe, Y. Wei, and D. Barnes (2007), 'Industrial symbiosis in China: a case study of the guitang group', *Journal of Industrial Ecology*, **11**(1): 31–42.

6. The social embeddedness of industrial symbiosis linkages in Puerto Rican industrial regions

Marian R. Chertow and Weslynne S. Ashton

INTRODUCTION

Industrial symbiosis occurs among firms in geographic proximity that engage in 'a collective approach to competitive advantage involving physical exchange of materials, energy, water, and by-products' (Chertow 2000). Communication, trust and willingness to cooperate have been found to play important roles in the development of these collaborative relationships, but have not been as well-studied as more technical aspects until recently. Several authors, most notably Hoffman (2003), have challenged industrial ecology researchers to tie in social science disciplines as environmental issues merge technical and social dimensions. Perhaps more than other industrial ecology concepts, industrial symbiosis clearly necessitates an understanding of the social dimensions that would facilitate inter-firm collaboration. As with business clusters studied by Michael Porter and others, industrial symbiosis has been found to be more successful in those locations where 'pre-existing locational advantages exist' (Chertow 2007). Part of this phenomenon is explained through the recognition, often overlooked by industrial ecologists, that existing firms are already embedded within a region's organizational structures.

For the past decade, research at Yale University's Center for Industrial Ecology has explored the existence of industrial symbiosis and further potential for developing it in locations across the US and the world. Most notably, over seven years (2001–2008), these studies were conducted under the 'Puerto Rico: An Island of Sustainability' project, examining different industrialized regions of this Caribbean island. Initial studies focused on technical factors – industry identification and material flow analysis. Through the course of the research, we uncovered several 'kernels' of industrial symbiosis and two nascent industrial ecosystems – Barceloneta and Guayama. Our findings in these systems suggested the need to increase focus on the nature of relationships among firms and the social embeddedness of the industrial symbiosis ties.

This chapter presents the insights gained by explicitly examining the social embeddedness of inter-firm relations alongside technical material flow aspects. It is based on a descriptive examination of four Puerto Rican industrial areas studied with a common methodology primarily in 2005, as well as the two industrial ecosystems in Barceloneta and Guayama. The next section presents background information on industrial symbiosis, a review of how social embeddedness is treated in our work and initial findings from Puerto Rico that indicated greater attention was needed to social dimensions in this research area. A description of the methodology employed in the research follows. Results and a comparison of the role of social embeddedness in different industrial regions where industrial symbiosis has and has not developed conclude the chapter.

BACKGROUND

Industrial symbiosis (IS), a sub-field of industrial ecology (IE), borrows from biology the notion of symbiotic relationships where unrelated organisms can find mutual benefit through the exchange of resources. By means of symbiotic inter-firm links, businesses strive for a collective benefit greater than the sum of individual benefits that could be achieved by acting alone (Lowe et al. 1995). Under idealized conditions, IS can provide a general framework for moving towards regional sustainability (Boons and Baas 1997). The 'keys to industrial symbiosis are collaboration and the synergistic possibilities offered by geographic proximity' (Chertow 2000). Although sometimes used interchangeably with the term 'eco-industrial parks' (EIPs), industrial symbiosis is not limited to the proximate real estate of an industrial park, but also pertains to broader and narrower spatial geographic levels. Three types of synergies are regarded as industrial symbiosis as follows (Chertow et al. 2008):

- Byproduct exchanges – use of traditionally discarded materials or wastes as substitutes for commercial products or raw materials;
- Utility sharing – pooled use and shared management of commonly used resources such as steam, electricity, water, and wastewater; and
- Shared services – collective provision of services by a third party to satisfy ancillary needs, such as waste management or fire suppression.

Brought to light in the early 1990s, Kalundborg, Denmark, provided the first example of a mature, self-organized industrial ecosystem in the world. Since the symbiosis and its many benefits both to individual companies and to the region were uncovered, there have been many initiatives to search for and replicate Kalundborg's success in other parts of the world through planned eco-industrial parks. This approach has been less successful than initially perceived because of the complex nature of business siting decisions, as well as economic, technical, organizational and motivational barriers that face exchanges (Brand and de Bruijn 1999; Gibbs 2003; Gibbs et al. 2005). Despite these failures, once we remove the neat packaging of the EIP label, we have found a wide range of inter-firm exchanges. According to the patterns we have seen, inter-firm links organized for business reasons such as byproduct exchanges, cogeneration and wastewater reuse, can act as 'kernels' or 'precursors' to more complex exchanges as they help to establish the benefits of collaboration (Chertow 2007).

Social Embeddedness

Frequent and open communication and inter-personal trust are thought to be important components of ongoing interactions in industrial ecosystems. Kalundborg, for example, is small enough that managers (and other staff) from different companies know each other and regularly interact through forums such as the Rotary Club. There, inter-firm relationships embedded in social relations were key enablers of ongoing industrial symbiosis (Jacobsen 2005).

There are several layers of social embeddedness (see Figure 6.1) among firms in a given business network – (a) one-to-one relations between firms in the same core industry; (b) relations between firms in a core industry with those in complementary industries; (c) direct or indirect relations through shared membership in local economic or social institutions; and (d) shared norms through the overarching culture governing institutional and business relations (Johannisson et al. 2002). Firm relations can be embedded at each of these levels, from very simple dyadic relations between a pair of firms, to complex ones that occur on multiple layers (for example, firm-to-firm and shared membership in more than one local institution). Firms with more complex relations are expected to be more embedded within the system than those with only simple ones.

In addition, Boons and Howard-Grenville (Chapter 1) describe six mechanisms through which the social context enables and constrains choices and activities within networks. Within self-organized and facilitated networks engaged in industrial symbiosis, a further refinement of the six mechanisms of embeddedness follows:

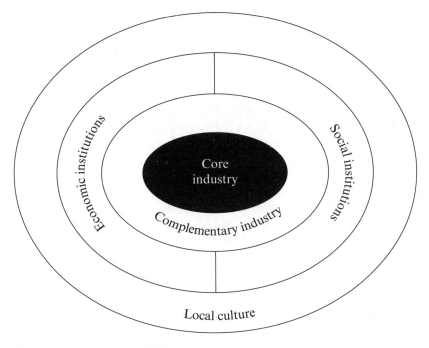

Source: Johannisson et al. (2002)

Figure 6.1   Layers of embeddedness surrounding inter-firm relations

1. Cognitive: mental distance between firm managers to perceive opportunities for collaboration and material reuse/exchange.
2. Cultural: norms regarding what is waste and willingness to cooperate beyond firm boundaries.
3. Structural: the nature and extent of social relations, including actor and sub-group interaction.
4. Political: power relations among different actors; policy and regulatory environment that govern waste management practices.
5. Spatial: proximity of firms and availability of resources.
6. Temporal: the change in quality and quantity of synergies over time.

Embedded business networks are expected to have high levels of social capital, meaning that they avail resources and opportunities to member firms and that the interactions of members are motivated not only by immediate economic returns but also by their relationships with others (Uzzi 1996). High levels of cooperation, resource sharing and adaptive learning are also more commonplace in embedded networks,

132   The social embeddedness of industrial ecology

which provides benefits that arms-length market transactions do not. The importance of network effects are thought to differ across different types of actors, types of relationships, resources exchanged, institutional environments and time (Mizruchi et al. 2006).

PUERTO RICO: RESEARCH ON INDUSTRIAL SYMBIOSIS AND SOCIAL EMBEDDEDNESS

The Yale Center for Industrial Ecology has been conducting industrial symbiosis research over the last decade. For the first few years, this research involved small-scale initiatives modelled after Kalundborg. Early studies approached this research at locations throughout the world, by focusing primarily on technical factors using material flow analysis, a key tool of industrial ecology. Firm-level material flow analyses (MFAs) were used to identify water, energy and material streams that could be traded within the location/system of interest, determine any pre-existing synergies, and evaluate the potential for IS through proposed inter-firm material linkages (Chertow and Portlock 2002).

From 2001 to 2008, 30 studies were conducted with graduate students and faculty in different industrialized regions of Puerto Rico as part of the 'Puerto Rico: An Island of Sustainability' (PRIOS) project (see Figure 6.2). Puerto Rico was chosen as the site for this research for several reasons. First, as an island, boundary questions become clear and tracking of material flows on and off the island is simpler than in other geographic settings (Deschenes and Chertow 2004). Second, Puerto Rico is very industrialized, which makes it of interest to industrial ecologists. Third, it falls under US federal jurisdiction, making information availability better than most of its Caribbean island neighbours as well as many other countries.

The island's 'ecology' (including beaches and mountains that have made it an attractive tourist destination) is much better known than its extensive 'industrial' side. Puerto Rico boasted of producing 16 of the top 20 best selling drugs in the United States in 2004 (PRIDCO 2007). Historically, the island transformed itself from an agricultural to an industrial society by promoting a program of 'industrialization by invitation' that began in the 1940s (PRIDCO 1995). Under this strategy US-based and foreign firms were invited to locate to the island with generous packages of benefits including tax holidays, streamlined business establishment procedures, and ready building and infrastructure. The Puerto Rico Industrial Development Company (PRIDCO) has been the lead agency for industrial promotion charged with attracting companies to the island, assisting in their set-up, and managing properties to house them. A core component

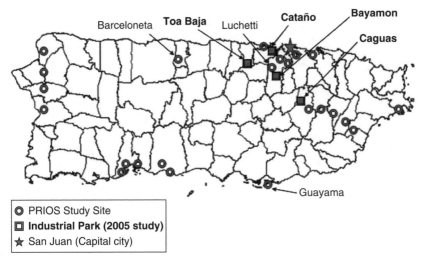

Figure 6.2   *Study sites in the 'Puerto Rico: An Island of Sustainability'*
                project, 2001–2008 (this chapter's case study sites are
                highlighted in bold)

of PRIDCO's real estate portfolio has been 139 industrial parks, which
are located all across the island and vary in area, number of industries,
industry origin (local or multinational), and industry type (some have
firms from different industries and others are in related industries). The
rationale behind their creation was to provide building space and basic
infrastructure that would be readily available for companies of various
sizes and specialties interested in settling on the island (PRIDCO 1995).

The 'Puerto Rico: An Island of Sustainability' project took place
in two phases. May 2001 to May 2004 was the wide-ranging 'natural
history phase' that explored the island and its industries to gain an
expansive sense of the breadth and depth of the industrial experience
on the island. The study sites varied in organizational and geographic
scope. Some were focused on a single company such as the Bacardi
rum distillery and its supply chain, while other sites ranged from small
industrial parks, to landfills, to a Navy base, to large industrial areas
encompassing several neighbouring municipalities organized as 'techno-
economic' corridors (Yale Center for Industrial Ecology 2004). By the
summer of 2004 we began to recognize key patterns and from 2004 to
2008 applied more directed methodologies with increased focus on the
role that human relationships play in the development of symbiotic
links. We were also able to compare single industry as well as multiple

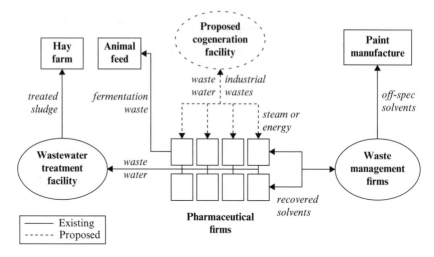

Figure 6.3   Industrial symbiosis linkages in Barceloneta, Puerto Rico

industry clusters, especially the pharmaceutical cluster in Barceloneta and the mixed-industry cluster in Guayama. As the island's best examples of symbiotic clusters, these are described in turn emphasizing organizational aspects.

Barceloneta is home to a cluster of pharmaceutical manufacturers spanning three municipalities off the same road west of San Juan. The cluster sits above the island's most abundant north coast aquifer system. At the end of the 1970s, two sharing agreements among the firms were launched. One involved shared financing and management of the Barceloneta Regional Wastewater Treatment Plant (BRWTP) by the water utility and a group of eight private companies. The eight companies formed an industry Advisory Council for this arrangement. It provided a forum for frequent discussion about issues of common concern among managers of the member facilities. The council served an important function of institutionalizing a 'culture of cooperation' among members, such that members evaluated and promoted numerous proposals for IS-type projects, such as shared cogeneration (Ashton 2008). The other arrangement involved shared services for hazardous waste treatment and solvent recycling with a single supplier (Safety-Kleen). Some companies later developed byproduct exchanges to reuse fermentation residues, recovered solvents and treated sludge from the BRWTP (see Figure 6.3).

Guayama is located on the very dry southern coastal plain of the island. It is the site of a mixed industry area with a petrochemical

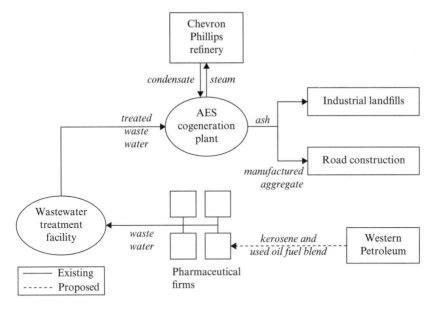

Figure 6.4   Industrial symbiosis linkages in Guayama, Puerto Rico

refinery, pharmaceutical manufacturers and a coal-fired power plant (see Figure 6.4). The AES power plant began operating in 2002. Its siting in Guayama was conditional on its ability to use treated wastewater from the Guayama Regional Wastewater Treatment Plant as its primary water supply because of regional water scarcity. It was also required to provide cogenerated steam to the Chevron-Phillips petrochemical facility (Chertow and Lombardi 2005). AES recently launched a business unit to market its ash byproducts to industrial landfills to stabilize liquid waste and to road and other construction sites as aggregate material (Siberon 2007). AES is the anchor in the Guayama exchanges and has adopted a position in which they are continuously looking for IS opportunities with others on the island. Their presence has also raised consciousness about IS in this region, and a few neighbouring firms are also pursuing IS-type synergies. Prior to AES' siting in Guayama, there were many instances of communication and exchange among managers of regional firms. Managers of the larger industrial facilities met on a semi-regular basis to coordinate emergency management and other related activities (Marquez 2005). In some instances, managers moved between companies for professional advancement taking tacit knowledge and social networks from their previous employers with them.

The Need for Understanding the Social Context

During the course of the spring 2003 fieldwork, the need for consideration of social dimensions became especially acute. Graduate student researchers were assigned to investigate the potential for symbiosis at the Luchetti Industrial Park but were faced with a dilemma on their first day in the field. They had arranged with one of the facility managers to host a lunch to which other managers in the park were invited. Unfortunately, the research team was unable to find the facility after driving around for more than an hour despite frequent calls to the company and stops to ask directions from people on the streets of the industrial park. Even the roadside food vendors were unable to locate the company. Eventually the group spotted one of the company's trucks and followed it into the facility, where only two managers of the more than two dozen invited companies turned up. This raised our suspicion that neighbouring companies, which we thought could be expected at least to be familiar with each other, did not, in fact, share communication. Subsequent research revealed that even regarding the important issue of seasonal flooding which all the firms in the park faced on a regular basis and which limited access to facilities for as much as several weeks per year, the companies did not systematically cooperate (Johnson et al. 2003).

At the same time, our research in the Barceloneta cluster suggested that firms were actively pursuing symbiotic activities and that most managers in this system had regular communication through forums such as the BRWTP Advisory Council and the Community Awareness and Emergency Response committee (Ashton 2003). In 2004 we conducted a social network analysis of the industrial ecosystem in Barceloneta to explore how different types of inter-firm relations as well as personal relationships among managers were related to the observed IS linkages there (Ashton 2008). This study revealed that industrial symbiosis ties between firms were much less frequent than supply chain ties (buying and selling products). It also found that IS-ties among firms (but not supply chain ties) were significantly correlated with trust among managers of those firms. The Advisory Council played an important role in facilitating communication and building trust among the pharmaceutical managers. It was also the venue through which these managers were able to discuss problems of common concern such as high energy prices and to develop solutions to them. Professional associations on the island, particularly the Puerto Rico Manufacturer's Association, was also noted to have played an important role in establishing communication among managers across different industries (Ashton 2008).

Finding strong social networks in Barceloneta and the lack of any social cohesion in Luchetti suggested that an examination of social relationships in a given location would be insightful for understanding the inter-firm relationships that developed there. Thus, we decided to incorporate a social dimension into the technical analysis for the 2005 field projects.

RESEARCH METHODS

Four industrial parks in the metropolitan San Juan region (see Table 6.1) with diverse manufacturing industries were selected to determine what additional insights into industrial symbiosis could be revealed by adding a social dimension. The parks were chosen based on the number and diversity of manufacturing industries present and proximity to San Juan. Given our prior experience at the Luchetti industrial park, we expected that there would be poor communication overall among firms in a given park, but wanted to find if there were instances of social connections leading to or furthering the development of IS at the study sites.

The field teams were assigned in January 2005. The teams were assigned six specific tasks to gather data from firms in the four selected industrial parks as outlined in a 17-page project memo (Yale Center for Industrial Ecology 2005). They were given copies of the island's manufacturers directory (PRIDCO 2002) and were asked to contact the companies listed for their respective parks and conduct background research on them. They then spent one week in Puerto Rico in March 2005 visiting the four industrial parks, interviewing personnel from selected companies within their parks, and other government, academic and private sector officials. They performed semi-structured interviews with 10–20 facilities in each park, attempting to get a good representation of the different industrial sectors present.

The investigation was conducted at two different levels of analysis – the firm level and the industrial park level. At the firm level, it concentrated on characterizing material flow analyses for firms within the industrial park. At the industrial park level, it focused on the description of existing inter-firm synergies. The aggregation of these two led to the construction of an inventory of firm-based material and energy flows and inter-firm synergies. In addition, the social component of industrial symbiosis was explored at the firm level where managers were asked if and how they knew their peers in the park, paying attention to relevant social and organizational networks in the industrial parks. Relations between individual companies and charitable organizations benefiting the greater community, such as a company sponsoring a school, were not evaluated in the research. The explicit research goal was stated as 'identifying social and organizational relationships within the industrial parks that might foster inter-firm symbiotic linkages' (Yale Center for Industrial Ecology 2005).

Table 6.1   Interviewed firms by type and industrial park location

Industrial Park	No. of Firms	No. of Manufac- turing Firms	No. of firms interviewed	Industrial representation of the 66 firms interviewed
Bayamon	59	35	17	Electronics (1), fabricated metals (5), food processing (5), services (1), wood products (5)
Caguas	19	18	17	Electronics (3), fabricated metals (2), food processing (2), medical devices (3), textiles (1), wood products (2), recycling (2), services (2)
Cataño	32	24	21	Building/infrastructure materials (1), chemicals (3), fabricated metals (2), food processing (8), power generation (1), textiles (1), recycling (1), services (4)
Toa Baja	19	16	11	Building/infrastructure materials (4), fabricated metals (3), food processing (3), services (1)

QUANTIFYING MATERIAL AND ENERGY FLOWS

The material flow analysis for each firm encompassed: a description of the material inputs and outputs, including both products and non-product flows. Where time or information was limited, teams were asked to focus on the five most significant materials in terms of throughput per unit of finished product. Energy and water requirements, sources and in-facility usage were to be included in the collected data. A basic material flow diagram was to be constructed for each firm, quantifying its input and output materials by weight and/or value, water and energy use, and major production processes.

Inter-Firm Synergies

The groups attempted to find built-in synergies originally devised as part of the park's physical or administrative design. These could include shared utilities or infrastructure and any joint services originally included in the park's administrative scheme. They also constructed a detailed 'inventory' of any existing inter-firm synergies, especially by-product exchanges, including the material throughput, participants in the initiatives, background on how each synergy emerged, and examination of the costs and benefits obtained as a result of the synergy.

SOCIAL AND ORGANIZATIONAL NETWORKS

Groups were asked to identify the institutional arrangements for administration and on-going management of the industrial park, as well as any existing associations, organizations, formal networks and working groups within the boundaries of the park. Managers were asked to identify to which, if any, of the island-level industry/professional organizations they belonged, as well as questions to evaluate their environmental awareness. They were asked to identify informal (not contract or supply chain-related) relationships they had with others within the park, the frequency and forums of interaction among tenants in the park, and the extent to which managers knew about the production and activities of their neighbours. Finally they were asked to identify any existing leaders among the park tenants or administration, and whether such persons championed particular initiatives in the past.

RESULTS

In all, 70 firms were interviewed by the student teams, 66 within the four parks (listed in Table 6.1), with varying levels of detail provided in terms of material and energy use by the firms. In general, firms were less willing to provide detailed information on the quantities of material used, but could readily identify a large number of their material inputs and outputs. In addition to firms within the park, a few groups reached out to other firms that were either located just beyond the park boundaries or with whom material linkages were revealed by interviewees. One of the parks, Toa Baja, turned out not to be an industrial park per se, but rather was a neighbourhood (barrio) with a large number of manufacturing facilities co-located along a single road.

MATERIAL FLOW ANALYSIS

Each group performed an MFA. Some were more focused at the facility level, identifying the main input and output materials used by the interviewed firms, while others identified and quantified the major material

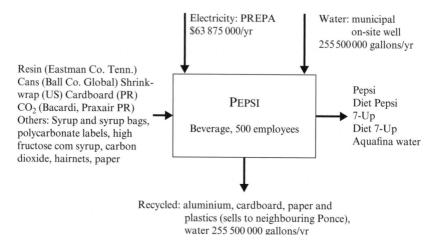

Source: Chi et al. (2005)

Figure 6.5   Material flows at Pepsi in Toa Baja

flows for each industrial sector in the park as well as the entire park. An example of the material flow results for a single facility – Pepsi – is shown in Figure 6.5.

Inter-Firm Synergies

Results indicated that in all four cases, there were no utility or service sharing agreements, a few informal resource sharing arrangements, a small number of by-product exchanges, and many examples of recycling with waste management companies. None of the groups reported any built-in synergies in the industrial parks – neither energy nor water/wastewater utility sharing nor joint service provision infrastructure was found. There were a few examples of resource sharing between companies, such as of raw materials and equipment sharing during emergencies. There was one example of water sharing during occasional shortages in Toa Baja, where Master Products, a concrete producer, provides potable water to Holsum Bakers (Chi et al. 2005). By-product exchanges typically paired companies within the parks with buyers/sellers outside the park. In a few examples, there were by-product exchanges between companies located in two different regions in the study. For example, Bacardi, which is located in Cataño, just outside the industrial park there, sells carbon dioxide (a fermentation

Table 6.2   Inter-firm synergies uncovered in industrial parks

Facility	Facility location	Material by-product	Use	Recipient	Recipient location
Pan Pepin	Bayamon	Bad batches of bread and dough scraps	Animal feed	Pig farmers	On island
Barma	Bayamon	Pallets	Reuse	B&B	Within park
DOE, Productos Tu Gusto	Bayamon	Pallets and drums	Material storage	Professional Ironworks	Within park
Industrial Roofing	Cataño	Wood Pallets	Fuel wood	Local community	Within municipality
Molinos	Cataño	Grain residue from flour	Animal feed	Nutrimix	On island
Bacardi	Cataño	CO_2 from fermentation	Drink carbonation	Pepsi	Neighbouring municipality (Toa Baja)
Ochoa Group	Cataño	Various materials	Acts as waste broker	Various	On and off island
Holsum	Toa Baja	Used oil and grease	Alternative fuel	San Juan Cement	Neighbouring municipality (Dorado)
Various	On island	Used oil	Alternative fuel	Master Products	On island (Toa Baja)
Master Products	Toa Baja	Water	Share water during shortages	Holsum	Within park (Toa Baja)

by-product) to Pepsi, which is located in Toa Baja (Aristizabal et al. 2005). Many examples were also found of wastes being collected and aggregated by dedicated waste management companies for further recycling or sale to third parties as raw materials. None of the companies in Caguas had by-product exchanges (Delgado et al. 2005). Selected by-product synergies are listed in Table 6.2.

The groups encountered several business relationships (for example, supply chain) among neighbours in the parks. C-Axis, a manufacturer of metal rings and springs used in heart valves, located itself inside the Caguas Industrial Park to be close to St Jude Medical, its largest client. CNC-2000 and Veolia Water also provided goods to St Jude, but did not co-locate as they are not solely dependent on St Jude's business (Delgado et al. 2005). Several companies in Cataño share goods or services providers, such as the Ochoa Group which supplies chemicals to many firms and

Arrowpac, which provides shipping and distribution services to others (Aristizabal et al. 2005). Three food manufacturers in Bayamon, Pacheco, Barma and Estrella, reported sharing ingredients in situations where one company had run out before a new supply had been delivered. Two paper and printing manufacturers in this park, Oles and Labels Unlimited, also occasionally share supplies and sell to Carla's Sweets as does Flexible Packaging (Berv et al. 2005).

SOCIAL TIES

Communication among firms in all four parks was minimal. There were a number of bilateral relationships among firms in many of the parks. Some informal social ties were present and some have resulted in synergies across firms. No formal social networks were found, such as through industrial park associations. Several firms belonged to industry associations that were sectoral or national in scope. Of special mention is the Puerto Rico Manufacturers' Association (PRMA), which facilitates interaction among managers at various levels of manufacturing firms throughout the island. Firms in the study tended to be small to medium sized enterprises that were locally owned and operated, which suggests that they operate within the same cultural and political context. The larger enterprises, some of which were not locally owned, were nonetheless run by Puerto Rican managers. The social ties in each of the parks are discussed separately and then compared with the layers of embeddedness in Table 6.3.

Bayamon – Despite the apparent lack of a strong park-wide community in Bayamon, interviews revealed many solid business connections among neighbours in the park. There was one notable previous attempt at cooperation through a park association that had disbanded in the mid-1990s. Oles, an envelope producer, and Labels Unlimited, a producer of labels and similar office supplies, have had multiple opportunities to work together because of the complementary nature of their products. Curiously, this business relationship developed only after the managers of the two companies met through a shared interest in the Ford Mustang cars that each owned. In another example of personal relationships leading to business synergies, familial ties between the owner of Carla's Sweets and one of the managers at Flexible Packaging enabled close cooperation between the two. Flexible Packaging worked with Carla's Sweets to design and produce specialty packaging (Berv et al. 2005).

Caguas – PRIDCO was mentioned as a major force in forming inter-personal relationships among the firms in the Caguas Industrial Park

Table 6.3   Layers of embeddedness present in each of the industrial parks

Embeddedness layer	Bayamon	Caguas	Cataño	Toa Baja
One-to-one core industry relations	No core industry, firms in mixed industrial setting			
One-to-one complementary business relations	Few dyads between pairs of firms in which managers had previously established relationships	Several informal relations among employees in neighbouring firms but no firm-level relations	Few dyads between pairs of firms	Little or no interaction between pairs of firms, except for two larger firms
Direct and indirect relations through local institutions	One park-level association defunct for almost a decade; PRIDCO was not seen as bridging relationships among park tenants	No local institutions exist; PRIDCO was seen as important for linking firms	Shared membership in business-community groups; strong role of Mayor in brokering relations	No local institutions exist
Shared culture governing norms and relations	Mostly locally-owned firms in same cultural-political context			

as it held functions in which park tenants participated. Some informal relationships have developed, for example carpooling among employees from different companies, attending neighbours' Christmas parties and borrowing machinery from neighbours during emergencies (Delgado et al. 2005).

Cataño – Relationships in Cataño were set in the context of a town plagued by environmental problems since the 1950s. Both community activist and neighbourhood associations exist to create public demand for pollution reduction and have had regular interaction with companies in the town. The municipal government also plays a role in Cataño's social fabric as the

Mayor holds periodic meetings with companies (once or twice a month), to address common issues, which, in turn, has created positive sentiments among the business community. Through this process, companies are encouraged to interact with each other (Aristizabal et al. 2005).

Toa Baja – Informal social ties were found to be weak and networks nonexistent in Toa Baja, despite a few examples of resource sharing. Companies within this neighbourhood (which was not a formal industrial park) tended neither to interact with their neighbours nor to engage in business with them. Some companies were knowledgeable about their neighbour's business, but belonged to unrelated sectors. Others could barely identify the company next door. No one unifier existed to connect the companies (Chi et al. 2005).

PROPOSED SYNERGIES

After examining the existing material and social relationships within the parks, the groups also proposed partnerships for material exchanges in each of the parks to utilize materials and meet the needs of firms in their respective parks. In the Toa Baja park, for example, unrealized opportunities were found in the area of utility sharing, where joint power generation capacity could be installed either for back-up or as an alternative source. In addition, the existence of landfill gas capture infrastructure could be coupled with methane capture from Holsum's wastewater treatment plant to provide energy for local companies. The team also proposed a water cascade from Pepsi or Holsum, which both use potable water in food/beverage manufacture, to Master Products, which does not need potable water for concrete production. Waste oil from various industries, including Holsum (which currently sends its used oil to San Juan Cement), could be used by Master Products (Chi et al. 2005).

DISCUSSION

The four industrial parks were found to have a low level of synergies of any type, which raises the question of whether there is a serious under-utilization of beneficial opportunities for agglomeration economies and coordinated resource management or whether the poor communication and basic level of relationships observed inhibits symbiosis. Indeed, numerous opportunities for symbiosis were imaginable in line with the examples of by-product exchanges and small industrial ecosystems previously identified on the island. This section addresses the reasons that could account for the low level of synergies at the case study sites through comparison with the Barceloneta and Guayama sites where symbiosis was better developed.

The types of industrial symbiosis activities can differ in industrial settings based on industry composition (Chertow et al. 2008). In single-industry dominated clusters, utility and service sharing are more likely to be observed as firms tend to have similar resource requirements and material flows. Byproduct exchanges are more common in mixed industrial regions because of the diversity, and potential for matching diverse inputs and outputs. Previous work under the PRIOS project found that service and distribution firms, which are very common in Puerto Rican industrial parks, are more suited to service sharing especially around waste aggregation and management (Chumfong et al. 2004). It would be expected that the four industrial parks studied, as they are all mixed-industry parks, would have greater potential for byproduct exchanges than utility or service sharing, and indeed more of the former and barely any of the latter were observed.

Technical barriers identified elsewhere in the literature were also found in Puerto Rico, related to low volumes of waste materials and incompatible materials between different industries. In addition, many environmental resources, such as water availability and landfill capacity, were under-priced creating economic disincentives to reuse secondary materials. We also found that some companies feared communicating about waste disposal because of the possibility that they might be held liable for their current or past practices, and this also can work against by-product exchange.

The Puerto Rico Industrial Development Company (PRIDCO), as the main administrator of industrial parks on the island, provided occupants with all of their basic infrastructural needs and coordinated a suite of economic incentives. The rationale behind the creation of industrial parks was to provide basic amenities that would be readily available for companies of various sizes and specialties interested in settling on the island (PRIDCO 1995). After dynamic growth in manufacturing in the1960s through the 1980s, today's industrial parks are shells of their former selves – with unoccupied and derelict buildings, aging power and water infrastructure and inadequate transportation and communications networks. They were developed more as a strategy to attract new industries to the island rather than as a means to build a competitive advantage for firms through agglomeration economies. Thus, there was little or no effort on the part of the government to establish communication and build supply chain or other types of synergies among park tenants.

The lack of communication among park tenants has stood out as an underlying problem that inhibits community building and the expansion of synergies found in the parks. There were only a few instances where inter-personal ties formed among firm managers, and in some instances, these later led to business partnerships. This presents a striking comparison with the Barceloneta pharmaceutical cluster where managers in this cluster regularly interact through a variety of forums, notably the BRWTP Advisory Council and various sub-groups within the Puerto Rico Manufacturers' Association. These inter-personal interactions coupled with a long history of inter-firm collaboration beginning in the late-1970s has created a culture of cooperation within the sector, such that new initiatives for shared resource management have been continuously evaluated (Ashton 2008). Similarly, companies in Guayama had a history of interaction even though the firms all belong to different industrial sectors, including staff movement between firms, long before the industrial symbiosis initiatives in the region were pursued (Chertow et al. 2008). The difference in these cases presents a strong point regarding social embeddedness – the firms in Barceloneta and Guayama are socially embedded through a history of communication, whereas those in the industrial parks are not as the companies have little awareness of each other.

The mechanisms of embeddedness are contrasted in Barceloneta, Guayama and the four industrial parks in Table 6.4. The minimal amount of communication among firms presents a critical cognitive barrier, as few interviewees were aware of their neighbours' businesses, material usage and potential for synergies with them. As many of the companies interviewed were small and medium enterprises, their attention to environmental issues had to compete with other, often more pressing demands including maintaining daily operations. In addition, high-tech companies are often secretive and guard proprietary information for patent protection and manufacturing purposes. Even where there were existing relationships (for example Master Products sending water to Holsum during shortages), this did not necessarily lead to systematic examination of all synergistic possibilities such as Holsum providing treated wastewater to Master as it did not require potable water.

Motivational barriers may take the form of unwillingness to work with neighbours because of pre-constituted allegiances and preferences for maintaining existing supply chain relations and are thus more tied to cultural and social structural embeddedness. Many firms expressed their pursuit of pollution prevention and eco-efficiency strategies, to effectively manage resource usage within their facilities rather than exploring opportunities for sharing *across* firms. Finally, numerous managers expressed that Puerto Ricans do not have a sensibility for this sort of sharing, or for considering by-products as a potential revenue stream.

With little embeddedness through either firm-to-firm and shared institutional relations (Johannisson et al. 2002), it is hard to imagine that any

Table 6.4   Mechanisms of embeddedness in Barceloneta, Guayama and the industrial parks

Mechanism	Barceloneta	Guayama	Industrial Parks
Cognitive	Short mental distance developed through ongoing forums	Short mental distance developed through ongoing forums	No shortening of mental distance, even among firms that interact
Cultural	Few firms actively consider byproducts for reuse most focused on traditional waste management	AES leadership has led to greater willingness to reuse by-products in region	Few firms actively consider byproducts for reuse; most focused on traditional waste management
Structural	Collaboration within pharmaceutical industry firms, less so with other industries	Collaboration across mixed industries, in local and island-wide networks	Weak to non-existent social networks do not facilitate interaction
Political	Pharmaceutical firms have political power to adopt collective practices in industry's interest	Public and government 'social licence to operate' influenced adoption of synergies	Small firms with lower level of political power concentrate on firm-level environmental compliance
Spatial	Abundant water supply supported location of pharmaceutical industry; synergies mostly concentrated among firms in one neighbourhood	Scarcity of water resources required synergistic reuse of wastewater; synergies mostly concentrated among firms in one neighbourhood, but increasingly with partners across island	Few relationships built even among immediate neighbours in parks
Temporal	IS activities ongoing, but do not show an acceleration	IS activities have grown tremendously in short period	Few IS activities have started or built up over time

kind of collaboration would be possible, even around the most pressing issues. A preliminary step to address this would involve increasing familiarity among neighbouring firms before they would even contemplate possible areas for inter-firm collaboration on bilateral and multilateral bases. As many firms in all of the industrial parks studied belonged to the Puerto Rico Manufacturers' Association, this organization could serve an important role to bridge familiarity among neighbours in the respective parks, much like the role of the National Industrial Symbiosis Program in the United Kingdom (see Howard-Grenville and Paquin in Chapter 5). In mixed industry parks, such as those in the study, IS depends on relationships between firms in complementary industries more than core industry relationships. Thus, the layers of embeddedness of Figure 6.1 can be re-defined to place core and complementary industries within the same first-order layer. It also suggests that in settings with a single dominant industry (such as pharmaceuticals in Barceloneta), relationships with complementary industries outside of the core should be pursued owing to the limited material exchange opportunities among members of the same industry.

One of the limitations of this study design was setting boundaries at the industrial park-level as the teams found many synergies with others outside the parks and even more across the island. Sterr and Ott (2004) faced a similar spatial challenge in Pfaffengrund, Germany, where the industrial site 'proved to be much too small for almost every kind of material cycle, and due to a lack of redundancy, the stability of output-input connections was potentially endangered by even the smallest fluctuations'. The Puerto Rico industrial parks are spatially embedded in an island that is heavily industrialized, which allows for larger players with more substantial flows to take part in materials cycling. Broadening the regional scope could lead 'to a relatively high probability of finding fitting partners for output-input relations, not only between producers and waste disposers, but even among the industrial producers' (Sterr and Ott 2004). When the scope is enlarged, more inter-firm linkages are observed, but the problem remains of embedding these practices within communities rather than how they currently occur as random occasional bilateral exchanges.

CONCLUSION

For many years, a technical approach was used to understand and promote industrial symbiosis linkages among groups of firms. This approach led to the uncovering of numerous kernels of industrial symbiosis as well as nascent industrial ecosystems with well developed local networks of collaboration. The technical approach focused on inter-firm linkages that increased the reliability of manufacturing operations by lowering the environmental and economic cost of water and energy supplies and by using excess materials as inputs to other facilities. The addition of a social dimension to the technical analysis has highlighted how personal relationships underlie business relations, as well as identified critical barriers to the development and implementation of inter-firms synergies such as industrial symbiosis.

A comparison of the development of industrial ecosystems in Barceloneta and Guayama with the much lower level of symbiotic exchanges in the four industrial park case examples, suggests that social embeddedness plays as vital a role as the resource needs of the companies. The Barceloneta and Guayama industrial symbiosis relationships were embedded on several levels through: (a) firm-to-firm relations among core and complementary industries; (b) shared membership in local organizations such as emergency management committees; and (c) shared political and cultural environments. The firms in the industrial parks lacked regular channels for communication, and thus inter-firm collaboration appeared only sporadically where firm managers had had the opportunity to meet and discuss their business needs. There were several occasional examples of buying and selling products, sharing materials and machinery, by-product exchanges and even service sharing, which were preceded by some sort of personal familiarity among those in the distinct firms. Many opportunities for collaboration were overlooked, however, as there was no systematic means to identify and evaluate them.

Several reported barriers to the development of industrial symbiosis, particularly informational and motivational ones, are essentially issues of social embeddedness related to cognitive and social structural mechanisms. Without communication, there can be no information flows, and without repeated interaction and the build-up of trust, there is little motivation for firms to engage in collective action. By understanding how firms communicate in a given setting, there is an opportunity to build upon the existing embeddedness rather than trying to implement synergies that have no local buy-in.

REFERENCES

Aristizabal, A., M. Gerst, K. Hamilton and A. Voynov (2005). 'Industrial Symbiosis in Cataño, Puerto Rico', Research Paper for the Spring 2005 Industrial Ecology Course, New Haven, CT: Yale School of Forestry & Environmental Studies.

Ashton, W. (2003), 'Inter-firm collaboration in eco-industrial networks with a case study of Puerto Rico's pharmaceutical manufacturing cluster', *School of Forestry & Environmental Studies*, New Haven, CT: Yale University.

Ashton, W. (2008), 'Understanding the organization of industrial ecosystems: a social network approach', *Journal of Industrial Ecology*, **12**(1): 34–51.

Berv, D., O. Cowley, J. Howland and S. Smiley Smith (2005), 'Minillas Industrial Park Bayamon, Puerto Rico', Research Paper for the Spring 2005 Industrial Ecology Course, New Haven, CT: Yale School of Forestry & Environmental Studies.

Boons, F.A.A. and L.W. Baas (1997), 'Types of industrial ecology: the problem of coordination', *Journal of Cleaner Production*, **5**(1&2): 79–86.

Brand, E. and T. de Bruijn (1999), 'Shared responsibility at the regional level: the building of sustainable industrial estates', *European Environment*, **9**: 221–31.

Chertow, M.R. (2000), 'Industrial symbiosis: literature and taxonomy', *Annual Review of Energy & Environment*, **25**: 313–37.

Chertow, M.R. (2007), '"Uncovering" industrial symbiosis', *Journal of Industrial Ecology*, **11**(1): 11–30.

Chertow, M.R., W.S. Ashton and J.C. Espinosa (2008), 'Industrial symbiosis in Puerto Rico: environmentally-related agglomeration economies', *Regional Studies*, **42**(10): 1299–312.

Chertow, M.R. and D.R. Lombardi (2005), 'Quantifying economic and environmental benefits of co-located firms', *Environmental Science & Technology*, **39**(17): 6535–41.

Chertow, M.R. and M. Portlock (2002), 'Developing industrial ecosystems: approaches, cases and tools', bulletin no. 106, New Haven, CT: Yale School of Forestry & Environmental Studies.

Chi, Y., G. Griebenow, J. Rauch and B. Scherzer (2005), 'Industrial symbiosis in Puerto Rico: Toa Baja industrial park case study', Research Paper for the Spring 2005 Industrial Ecology Course, New Haven, CT: Yale School of Forestry & Environmental Studies.

Chumfong, I., M. Kumar, W.K. Liew and C. Mahendra (2004), 'Port of the Americas and Value-Added Zone, Ponce, Puerto Rico', Research Paper for the Spring 2004 Industrial Ecology Course, New Haven, CT: Yale School of Forestry & Environmental Studies.

Delgado, T., K. Drakonakis, B. Feingold and C. Howe (2005), 'Industrial Symbiotic Potential of the Caguas Oeste Industrial Park, Caguas, Puerto Rico', Research Paper for the Spring 2005 Industrial Ecology Course, New Haven, CT: Yale School of Forestry & Environmental Studies.

Deschenes, P.J. and M.R. Chertow (2004), 'An island approach to industrial ecology: toward sustainability in the island context', *Journal of Environmental Planning and Management*, **47**(2): 201–17.

Gibbs, D. (2003), 'Trust and networking in inter-firm relations: the case of eco-industrial development', *Local Economy*, **18**(3): 222–36.

Gibbs, D., P. Deutz and A. Proctor (2005), 'Industrial ecology and eco-industrial development: a new paradigm for local and regional development?', *Regional Studies*, **39**: 171–83.

Hoffman, A. (2003), 'Linking social systems analysis to the industrial ecology framework', *Organization & Environment*, **16**(1): 66–86.

Jacobsen, N. (2005), 'Industrial symbiosis in the making: bridging social and technical explanations – The case of Kalundborg, Denmark', *11th*

Annual International Sustainable Development Research Conference, Helsinki, Finland.

Johannisson, B., M. Ramirez-Pasillas and G. Karlsson (2002), 'The institutional embeddedness of local inter-firm networks: a leverage for business creation', *Entrepreneurship & Regional Development*, **14**(4): 297–315.

Johnson, J., S. Quinn, E. Shelton and Z. Zhang (2003), 'Luchetti Industrial Park: retrofitting an industrial park for symbiosis', Research paper for the Industrial Ecology Spring 2003 Course. New Haven, CT: Yale School of Forestry & Environmental Studies.

Lowe, E.A., S.R. Moran and D.B. Holmes (1995), 'A fieldbook for the development of eco-industrial parks', Report for the US Environmental Protection Agency, Oakland, CA: Indigo Development International.

Marquez, N., Loss Prevention Manager, Chevron-Phillips Core, 27 October. Personal communication.

Mizruchi, M., L.B. Stearns and C. Marquis (2006), 'The conditional nature of embeddedness: a study of borrowing by large US firms, 1973–1994', *American Sociological Review*, **71**: 310–33.

PRIDCO (1995), *La Importancia de Industrialización en Puerto Rico*, San Juan, PR: Puerto Rico Industrial Development Company.

PRIDCO (2002), *Puerto Rico Directory of Manufacturers*, San Juan, PR: Puerto Rico Industrial Development Company – Economic Analysis & Strategy Planning Area.

PRIDCO. (2007), 'Puerto Rico Industrial Development Company Homepage', available at: http://www.pridco.com.

Siberon, G., Environmental Manager, AES Puerto Rico, 20 May 2007. Personal communication.

Sterr, T. and T. Ott (2004), 'The industrial region as a promising unit for eco-industrial development – reflections, practical experience and establishment of innovative instruments to support industrial ecology', *Journal of Cleaner Production*, **12**(8–10): 947–65.

Uzzi, B. (1996), 'The sources and consequences of embeddedness for the economic performance of organizations: the network effect', *American Sociological Review*, **61**(4): 674–98.

Yale Center for Industrial Ecology (2004), *Sustainable Industrial Development Model for Puerto Rico*, EDA Project No.: 01-79-07795 Final Report, New Haven, CT: Yale University and the Fundación Luis Muñoz Marín, 54.

Yale Center for Industrial Ecology (2005), *Industrial Ecology Class Projects: Industrial Symbiosis in Puerto Rican Industrial Parks*, New Haven, CT: Yale School of Forestry and Environmental Studies, 17.

Second intermezzo A transdisciplinary perspective on industrial ecology research

Cynthia Mitchell

INTRODUCTION

In this 'dialogue' chapter, my intention is to contribute to the exchange of ideas between social science perspectives and SET (science, engineering, technology) perspectives in industrial ecology research. My brief from the editors is to reflect on the chapters exploring regional approaches. Specifically, I am tasked with reflecting on the elements of the work that resonate with my experience, that are different, and that raise questions, and to do so by connecting my responses to my experiences. This I found an intriguing brief, not least because it leaves me feeling somewhat exposed – this intermezzo is a public and enduring account of something akin to the process of review as well as an exploration of the development of my own epistemological stance.

Having a dialogue between disciplines who share an interest in exploring and implementing industrial ecology concepts is essential for it to reach its potential. And the mode we have chosen for doing so here is something of a compromise, since it is just one iteration, rather than an ongoing dialogue. That said, I think it is a worthwhile step in a useful direction, so here goes . . .

To respond, I firstly give a brief account of my perspective, such as it is now – that of an engineering- and science-trained transdisciplinary researcher engaged with making a difference. I have synthesized the reflections into three sections: resonant concepts, differences, and clarifying questions.

MY PERSPECTIVE

In the spirit of this being a narrative, I'll begin by telling my story. My qualifications are in engineering and science. My passions are around learning and change for sustainability for all. My experience is based in the higher education sector, in conventional engineering faculties for eight years, and for a further eight years, in the rather less conventional Institute for Sustainable Futures (ISF) at the University of Technology Sydney, where I've directed our inter- and transdisciplinary postgraduate programme, whilst supervising graduate students, and leading contract research projects on urban infrastructure in which we develop, adapt and/or apply theoretical frameworks, methodologies, and analytical approaches drawn from the disciplines of engineering, systems, economics, business, learning and social sciences.

ISF occupies an intriguing space: the gap between university and industry. More than 80 per cent of our funds come from our research contracts. Our potential academic collaborators wonder if we might be too industry-focused, doing consulting rather than research,[1] whilst our potential clients wonder if we might be too academic. Surviving and thriving in such a challenging space is a wonderful driver for reflection and construction of conceptual frameworks to characterize what it is that we do. I'll explain the core of these here because they are the backdrop for the role I've been asked to take in this intermezzo. They have been developed collaboratively with my colleagues and students at the Institute, so I'll switch to 'we' for this description.

We conceive of our inter- and transdisciplinary research in line with ISF's mission, which is to create change towards sustainable futures. We've come to the view that life is far too messy to throw up 'problems' that can be 'solved'. So rather than seeking problem solutions, we wonder if we might be seeking 'problem re-solutions'? Certainly, we seek to make a recognizable improvement in some perceived real world situation. We have one foot firmly planted in 'the situation' (for example, drafting a plan for government to meet Sydney's water demand at the lowest societal and environmental cost), with the other foot firmly planted in the academy (for example, ensuring our doctoral students graduate). That leads us to specify three distinct outcome spaces:

1. The situation: there should be some recognizable improvement in the situation as a result of our work – a change in vision (for example from local best practice in new urban design to an integrated urban metabolic system), a change in strategy (for example revised company objectives that embed a shift from harm minimization to a restorative intent), or the uptake of a new tool (for example a model that treats water demand and supply options equally);
2. The stock of knowledge: because we begin with what is already known, we have a responsibility to contribute to the stock of knowledge of

theory and practice in our disciplines and sectors, through scholarly, industry, community and other outlets;

3. The practitioners involved: first, because we want to maximize the change we contribute to, we want our collaborators to do things differently as a result of working with us, and second, because we inhabit the cutting edge, the way we work should contribute to and/ or facilitate a transformational learning experience (Taylor 1998) for ourselves and for those we engage with in our projects.

This leads us to operate in something of a composite fashion with respect to the types of cross-disciplinary research noted in the literature (for example, Boix Mansilla 2006). Our epistemic value propositions are concerned with finding the balance between contextual specificity and generalizability, and between the rigour of quantitative modelling and the richness of qualitative processes, and between finding out and acting, whilst ensuring validity by finding a balance between the trandisciplinary intent of our work and retaining the integrity of its disciplinary origins.

RESONANT CONCEPTS

The concept from the preceding chapters that resonates most is the overarching interest in seeing change on the ground, and wanting to explore that change in order to work out where and how to intervene to enable its growth and development (that is, in Meadows et al. (1993) terms, improvements in both quantity and quality). Linked to this is the explicit connection to and exploration of other fields. Paquin and Howard-Grenville (Chapter 5) are deeply embedded in network analysis, and do a wonderful job of situating their work in that field, as does Gibbs for the field of socio-technical transitions.

In Chapter 5, recognizing and working with the political and cultural embeddedness of key actors resonates strongly with AtKisson's (1999) change agent and transformer roles, which are core to our praxis. For example, one water authority we have worked with over the life span of ISF has continually strengthened its commitment to sustainability as a core value for its operations. For the last three years, we have been collaborating on implementing environmental costing within their business operations as a means of tracking their expenditure on and movement towards their goals. That involves working across the organization, getting buy-in from the senior executives so they can argue for it at their board, and to the government pricing regulator, collaborating with local managers to extract relevant data, setting up the analysis in a way that can be readily handed over to staff in the future, interpreting and presenting the results in ways that can be communicated publicly in an annual report, and so on. This year, they did it themselves.

In the chapter by Chertow and Ashton, the resonant concept is in understanding the world in terms of two interacting spheres – the biophysical sphere and the socio-institutional sphere – the what and the how, for want of more sophisticated descriptors. Over the course of two years, I co-led a group of experienced and early career academics from design, history, economics, learning, ecology, engineering, futures and systems to develop a transdisciplinary framework to guide catchment management interventions. The framework has three dimensions: the what and how, perspectives (role-based, personal and specialized experience), and ways of finding out and acting. In co-developing the framework, we discovered together that the 'ah-hah' moments only arise after sitting with the discomfort and deep frustrations that come when attempting to communicate across epistemic, value and disciplinary divides. And that arriving at the ah-hahs requires commitment and trust, and trust takes time to develop across these divides, especially where no previous relationships exist (Palmer et al. 2007).

In the chapter by Gibbs, the notion of paradigmatic change being driven by tension in the explanatory system as it stands resonates with Kuhn's (1970) structure of scientific revolutions. Because our interest is in enabling both evolutionary and revolutionary change, we use Kuhn's insight explicitly and implicitly. For example, we have found it a powerful explanatory tool for arguing the need to move to new models for sanitation in developing and developed countries.

Also in Gibbs' chapter, I find resonance with the experience of the power of rating tools to shift behaviour. We have been working in the Australian building sector for a decade, and the advent of rating tools in the last few years has been a major factor in the transformation that has taken place. However, I wonder whether rating tools' role should be viewed as transitory? They are essential in creating awareness of what is preferable, and they lead to a focus on 'counting' green, rather than 'thinking' green. That is, finding the right balance between prescriptive and performance based approaches is difficult, and sadly it seems easy to get prescriptive tools wrong, and end up being inconsistent with preferred long term outcomes.

DIFFERENCES

The standout difference between my experience and the work reported in the chapters is in the approach to and analysis of interviews as a source of empirical data.

Each chapter includes interviews as part of their data. All three provide a short general description of their method. However, in none, were the details of the qualitative methodology, method and analysis revealed – there is no information about how interviews were conducted, how interviewees were recruited, what prompts were used, how the ethical implications were managed for either 'formal' or 'informal' interviews, what the stance of the interviewer was, for example, on the participant/ observer spectrum, what collection methods were used for example, notes, recorded, transcribed, what analysis was undertaken for example, coding, interpretation, or about what assumptions the researchers held about the validity of their interpretations. Interestingly, none make reference to qualitative methods texts.

I found I had a strong response to this omission. I think this response stems from the particular 'strawberry runner'[2] path I have taken to arrive at transdisciplinary work, and the values I have developed along the way. Let me explore this a little.

For about a dozen years, I have been working with qualitative methods with my postgraduate students and in contract research. I learned qualitative methodologies through having a go at applying them and reflecting on what went right and wrong and why, through reading about them, and through some formal training – short courses, seminars, and the like. And still, I see myself as something of a neophyte[3] in qualitative methodologies.

The experience of doing qualitative work fundamentally challenged the ideas of 'repeatability' and 'representativeness' so deeply ingrained from my engineering training. I came to know it wasn't physically possible to do, transcribe and exhaustively analyse huge numbers of in-depth interviews. And yet I had a hunch there was at least utility (and hopefully, validity) in reporting on the wonderful diversity arising from this kind of work.

My first attempt to publish this kind of research was salutary. Our paper describing what engineering academics mean by environmental, economic, and social sustainability was discarded out of hand by the editor of an international engineering education journal, and warmly praised by the editor of a high-profile international education journal. I came to describe the work as 'indicative, rather than exhaustive or comprehensive'.

But still, I found qualitative work confusing. In quantitative work, I knew the rules – significant figures, rough statistics, model variables that matter, and so on. But in the qualitative work I read, both research outcomes and methodological texts, the variability vexed me. Then I went to an intensive qualitative methods course, where the facilitator talked us through examples of readings across a spectrum of epistemological values, and the scales fell off. For years, I had felt like I had all the pieces of a giant jigsaw, but not the box with the picture on the front. I could put a few pieces together here and there, but not the whole picture. All of a sudden, with the epistemological spectrum, I had the picture on the front of my jigsaw box! I had a means for structuring and positioning the contributions and perspectives relative to each other. Now, I draw this spectrum in various ways, for example with something like positivism on one end, and something like post-modernism on the other, with empiricist, constructivist and critical approaches in between. The spectrum allows me to articulate what it is that is valued and gives meaning within each epistemological domain. I find this device adds a significant dimension to the discussion about working across disciplines, since some span many epistemological domains.

My take accords with Nicolescu (2002): there are always rules and norms, and they are essential for ordering the world and our interactions, and they have both disciplinary and epistemological foundations. If anything, I find as I move away from my epistemological roots, I feel a stronger need to be explicit about these rules, norms and epistemological foundations. I am aware that this felt need may be precisely because I am on less familiar ground. It may also be in part a response to the lack of anything vaguely epistemological in my engineering and science training. I think it is also because I feel a certain responsibility to be able to be explicit about what constitutes quality in our inter- and transdisciplinary research efforts. I see this question of quality as far from resolved, either in the literature or in practice, and it is an active area of research for me[4] – a kind of meta-reflection on the goals of our Institute's work and how we might know their calibre. I frequently have cause to wonder about where is a good place for us to publish our work, and what practices would help our staff ensure good quality outcomes, and who could examine a transdisciplinary PhD thesis, and how would we know if our collaborators experienced transformational learning through our projects, etc.

Certainly, in our graduate students' programme, we emphasize the need for them to be aware of and explicit about their epistemological stance and to reflect on how that influences their choice of theoretical framework, methodology, method, data capture, analysis, and its interpretation and positioning in both the academic and practice worlds. Part of my motivation in doing this is my belief that it is easy for those of us from a positivist background to do poor quality qualitative research, albeit unintentionally, and I have seen too much evidence of this. Explicit consideration of positionality and its implications reduces the likelihood of that happening. Whether implicit or explicit, there should be enough in any paper for me to be able to discern the nature of those foundations, and judge the work according to the appropriate rules. I suspect this is the basis for my jarred response to a lack of description of qualitative approaches in all three chapters.

There is a second standout difference between the three chapters I've been asked to reflect on and our practice, and that is about how the interviews are reported in the papers. In the final version of their chapter, Paquin and Howard-Grenville do a wonderful job of enriching their quantitative network analysis with quotes from wide-ranging interviews – it is these stories that answer the question: what led to changes in network structure? In the other two chapters, they are absent. The text lacks the richness associated with quotes, stories, vignettes . . . the intent seems to be to seek generality, and to do so whilst inadvertently obscuring some potentially significant data and its analysis.

I see myself as epistemologically plural. In any particular project, I endeavour to make space for a range of perspectives and exhort my collaborators to do the same. Where there are numbers, those numbers should be meaningful in the local context – accurate, reliable, repeatable, and so on. And for qualitative data, my exposure to social scientists, and my experience of using social science theories, methodologies, methods, and approaches, has given me the opportunity to develop beyond epistemological naivety (Ison 2008). My preference now is to give voice to those who have contributed to the research in this way, and to do so explicitly by including significant quotes and narratives, and providing research participants the opportunity to comment on and exercise control over my interpretation of their story. An example is a recent scoping paper on creating successful management entities in the decentralized wastewater industry in the USA, where every page has at least one quote or narrative story (Willetts et al. 2008).

This approach accords strongly with a recent paper (Morgan 2007) advocating a pragmatic approach to qualitative research, foregrounding the need to acknowledge personal history and its influence on our decisions and actions. Morgan advocates abduction (moving back and forth between induction/data and deduction/theory), intersubjectivity (for example, simultaneously holding the views that there is a single 'real world' and that each individual has a unique perspective on what constitutes that world), and transferability (a focus on the factors that enable or disable the transfer of knowledge gained in one context to a different context).

So, I see the absence of quotes and narratives as not so much wrong, but more as such an opportunity missed – somewhere, there is a wonderfully rich data source that could deepen our understanding of what is happening, and give us more effective insights into where else and how else we might intervene to broaden the uptake of industrial ecology regionally, and we are denying ourselves the chance to engage with it and learn from it.

CLARIFYING QUESTIONS

In the penultimate draft of Paquin and Howard-Grenville's chapter, I sought clarification of the modelling process as someone unfamiliar with the model, its outputs, and their meaning, and I wondered about the opportunity to enrich and enliven their interpretation of its outputs through the inclusion of qualitative data and analysis. Their final draft deals elegantly with those questions, so here, all that is left for me to wonder about is how the changes in the network uncovered by this analysis connect to changes in actual impacts (environmental, social and economic) associated with the operations of the network members.

In the chapter by Chertow and Ashton, I wonder about how the analysis might be enriched by perspectives from other fields within social science, and in particular, studies that are interested in values, motivation and behaviour change. The investigations seemed to show that personal relationships, especially those that either formed or were validated outside the work sphere, were critical enablers of industrial symbiosis outcomes. This resonates with our own work and the work of others around espoused values versus values in action – the idea that there is for most of us, a gap between what we say and what we do.

In the chapter by Gibbs, I wonder about the opportunity to strengthen the focus on the socio-technical paradigm shift, and deepen the analysis against this theoretical frame, especially since in the set of EIPs chosen, half were not yet operational at the time of the data collection in 2002–2004. In other work, I have found Rip and Kemp's (1998) frame quite compelling, perhaps because of its interdisciplinary foundations, and eschewing of the presumption that we can precisely plan or control the paths of either artefacts or societies. A deeper analysis of a handful of successful and unsuccessful EIPs could be quite enlightening.

CONCLUDING REMARKS

Any field that seeks to create real change must engage across the spectrum of ways of knowing, acting and being: that is, across disciplines and epistemologies, as well as across personal and professional roles. These are the characteristics of transdisciplinary research. These characteristics, alongside the idea of explicit planning for and evaluating outcomes in the three spaces of the situations, the stock of knowledge, and the practitioners involved, may offer some useful insights for industrial ecology. Doing good work across these domains is predicated on establishing effective collaborative partnerships. It is essential to avoid the trap of technically trained specialists doing well-intentioned but poor quality qualitative work. The richest and most effective insights and outcomes will be associated with work that makes space for a real breadth of conversations, and encourages the reflective development of the epistemological stances of all involved, that is, an awareness of the impact of one's history and beliefs on one's interpretations and decisions.

The opportunity in industrial ecology and many other fields seeking to create change towards sustainable futures is to fearlessly engage with questions of what quality means in qualitative work, and to treat qualitative work as an equal to quantitative work.

The concept behind this book is a wonderful initiative in this direction, so I offer my congratulations to the editors, and humble thanks for the opportunity to participate in this most unusual of chapters. May the initiative do much to make room for social science perspectives in industrial ecology.

ACKNOWLEDGEMENTS

The thinking reported here has developed through countless conversations, meetings, workshops and retreats with my colleagues and students at ISF and elsewhere. In particular, I'd like to acknowledge Dr Juliet Willetts for her insightful contributions to these processes. The responsibility for the expression of these thoughts rests with me.

NOTES

1. I am rather enamoured of Lawrence Stenhouse's definition of research: systematic inquiry made public.
2. When strawberry runners grow, they branch in what appear to be haphazard ways.
3. I note with some irony two meanings for neophyte: 1. beginner: a beginner or novice at something, and 2. recent convert: a recent convert to a religion. http://encarta.msn.com/dictionary_/neophyte.html accessed 22 March 2008.
4. I am currently completing a fellowship from the Australian Learning and Teaching Council for a project entitled: Zen and the Art of Transdisciplinary Postgraduate Research.

REFERENCES

AtKisson, A. (1999), *Believing Cassandra: An Optimist Looks at a Pessimist's World*, White River Junction, VT: Chelsea Green.
Boix Mansilla, V. (2006), 'Interdisciplinary work at the frontier: an empirical

examination of expert interdisciplinary epistemologies', *Issues in Integrative Studies*, **24**:1–31.

Ison, R.L. (2008), 'Methodological challenges of trans-disciplinary research: some systemic reflections', *Nature, Sciences, Societies*, **16**: 241–51.

Kuhn, T.S. (1970), *The Structure of Scientific Revolutions*, 2nd edn, Chicago, IL: University of Chicago Press.

Meadows, D.H., D.L. Meadows and J. Randers (1993), *Beyond the Limits*, White River Junction, VT: Chelsea Green Publishing Company.

Morgan, D. (2007), 'Paradigms lost and pragmatism regained: Methodological implications of combining qualitative and quantitative methods', *Journal of Mixed Methods Research*, **1**(1):48–76.

Nicolescu, B. (2002), *Manifesto of Transdisciplinarity*, Albany, NY: State University of New York Press.

Palmer, C., J. Gothe, C. Mitchell, C. Riedy, K. Sweetapple, S. McLaughlin, G. Hose, M. Lowe, H. Goodall, T. Green, D. Sharma, S. Fane, K. Brew and P. Jones (2007), 'Finding integration pathways: developing a transdisciplinary (TD) approach for the Upper Nepean Catchment', *5th Australian Stream Management Conference*, May 2007, Albury, NSW, Australia.

Rip, A. and R. Kemp (1998), 'Technological change', Chapter 6 in S. Rayner and E.L. Malone (eds), *Human Choice and Climate Change*, vol. 2, Colombus, OH: Batelle Press, pp. 327–99.

Taylor E.W. (1998), *The Theory and Practice of Transformative Learning: A Critical Review*, in ERIC Clearinghouse on Adult Career and Vocational Education (ed.), Information series no. 374, vol. 2006, 27 September, Center on Education and Training for Employment, Columbus, Ohio, viewed 27 September, 2006 http://www.cete.org/acve/mp_taylor_01.asp.

Willetts, J., N. Carrard, K. Abeysuriya, C. Mitchell, A. Macrellis, S. Johnstone and R. Pinkham (2008), *Guidance for Establishing Successful RMEs: Scoping Paper*, available at www.werf.org.

Third intermezzo Regional eco-industrial development: views from different stakeholders

Anthony Chiu

Eco-industrial developmental (EID) schemes have been thought of as a means to operationalize industrial ecology, and early studies using this approach focused mostly on resource flows. At times EID took the form of industrial symbiosis (IS), describing activities undertaken to alter resource flows, and at other times it was applied within some spatial constraint, such as an eco-industrial park (EIP), eco-industrial estate (EIE), or simply in a virtual network. Such exercises helped to identify resource relocation and matching, shared utility, or shared service alternatives. The end objectives included optimizing economic and ecological benefits within and around a particular operating system. Physical science issues dominated the industrial ecology research in the early stages, with much emphasis on using materials flow analysis (MFA), Input–Output Analysis (IOA), and life-cycle analysis (LCA) as the measuring tools.

My exposure to the industrial ecology field started in 1998 with the United Nations Development Program (UNDP) project in the Philippines called PRIME. PRIME stands for PRivate enterprises Involvement in the Management of Environment. I became a member of the Technical Working Group (TWG) on Industrial Ecology (IE) Module, and in 2001 I coordinated the UNEP-UNDP-EU conference workshop on EID which involved 90 EID players in the Asia Pacific region from China, Sri Lanka, Malaysia, Nepal, Thailand, Vietnam, Indonesia, Philippines, Pakistan and India. In the succeeding years, I had the good fortune to get involved with and interact in several EID projects or to provide training workshops to around 20 governments. A significant one was the four demonstration project sites in China, where the UNEP team looked at resource flows, environmental management systems (EMS), awareness and preparedness for emergencies at the local level (APELL), and cleaner production (CP). A Taiwanese case came up later with three projects that heavily involved environmental businesses and eco-product design. The Korean,

Japanese and Thai EID programmes, on the other hand, reflect EID programmes in different stages. I was involved in expert meetings and training workshops with them for a few years while reviewing their EID policies, implementation plans and programmes.

Working with these projects has been really eye-opening; I observed that differences in the country's stage of development led to adoption of different EID policy and strategies; which in turn required different support mechanisms. Through the years I also gained insight into other Asian countries' EID plans and programs when I was editing the *Journal of Cleaner Production* second special issue on industrial ecology. Together with my other co-editors, Don Huisingh, Ed Cohen-Rosenthal (who passed away during the process), and Jouni Korhonen, I received very good papers, especially those that added to our EID databank from Singapore and Australia. This past ten years of observation led to my findings that showed that Asia Pacific EID could follow a continuum developmental framework with the economies clustered into three EID developmental hubs (Chiu 2009).

In several attempts to implement eco-industrial development projects in the Asia Pacific region, country project management teams observed several concerns and barriers. In the 2001 UNEP-UNDP-EU conference workshop, 90 eco-industrial development project stakeholders and experts identified seven areas of concern for Asia Pacific EID projects (AP7) (Chiu 2001). These were: terminology for EIP indicators and reporting, communications among the stakeholders, policies of the authorities, financing the EID, research and development on indigenous resources, management of EIP, and the future of EID.

I noticed that the majority of the seven concerns centered on social dimensions, leading me to conclude that eco-industrial development (EID) implementation must address two important streams of activity (Chiu 2001; Chiu and Pascual-Sison 2001). These are, first, addressing resource flow accounting, industrial metabolism, and information flow; and, second, addressing stakeholders' involvement in issues such as policy, management, communications, capability, political will, finance, and the like. I will use the above framework to evaluate and support some findings of the three chapters included in this section.

INTERTWINED ISSUES OF DEFINITION, BOUNDARY, AND SYSTEM OPTIMIZATION

In the three chapters in this section (4, 5 and 6), and in most classical industrial ecology literature, industrial symbiosis occurring within a boundary such as an EIP or industrial region is defined as covering system-level resource exchange, utility sharing and service sharing. Common findings in these chapters include the observation that, while many of the resource exchanges happened within the boundary studied, a number of transboundary resource exchanges also existed. Chertow and Ashton's chapter also shows that, although some EIPs were theoretically suited for resource exchange, few or no exchanges had actually come into being. Paquin and Howard-Grenville's chapter showed that a facilitating organization could increase resource exchange in a regional industrial symbiosis network. These findings add to the evidence that issues of resource use and boundaries need to be revisited in trying to understand appropriate scales for eco-industrial development.

A second issue raised in the chapters, notably that by Gibbs, is that there is a need to quantify EID outputs using parameters such as environmental performance indicators (EPI). This is also reflected in the experience, in 2001, of the UNEP expert team which was launching the first EIP project in four Chinese parks. Then State EPA (SEPA) officials expressed concern that the continuous improvement notion was very ambiguous and suggested a need for common metrics and performance indicators. This interesting issue led to an investigation of what different stakeholders look for in the development of and the delivery out of industrial symbiosis.

Korhonen (2001) has suggested four important success factors in industrial ecology, two of which are cooperation and roundput. Roundput involves the recycling of material and the cascading of energy within an industrial ecology. With the seven issues identified of concern by the Asia Pacific EID conference workshop, I argued that cooperation may be helpful at firm level for inter-firm interactions, but when one elevates the system analysis to park-level, cooperation is insufficient. There is the need for cooperation and coordination in such circumstances. Under the coordination notion, the roundput factor and the EPI concern of the Chinese government become self-revealing. In the inter-firm scenario, the optimization of resource use (both primary supply chain products and secondary by-product flow) is subjective to the individual players. However, what would be optimal to each player might not be the best solution for the entire system. This was tested using game theory (Chew et al. 2007). These two-level goals are clearly differentiated from each other if we visit the three classes of industrial symbiosis development outlined in Paquin and Howard-Grenville's chapter. Their classification was almost identical to the approach the Asian Productivity Organization (APO) and UNEP used in the training for about 20 governments between the years 2004–2006. Christensen and I (Chiu 2005; Chiu and Christensen 2004) labelled the serendipitous scenario as bottom-up, the goal-driven scenario as top-down and facilitative scenario as sideways-in.

In each of these forms of industrial symbiosis development, there is almost always a so-called 'champion' in the network. This entity may be the public or private developer (for example Thailand IEAT), facilitator (for example UK NISP), policy maker (for example China Guiyang city government), anchor tenant (for example Kalundborg Statoil), community activist/NGO (for example Philippine Business for Environment), professional organization or facility network (Puerto Rico BRWTP), research institution (for example Halifax Dalhousie University), or others. However, the goals of these champions vary at different levels. Paquin and Howard-Grenville made a sound observation by identifying that NISP does have a political, economic and ecological mandate. NISP's business model approach took into consideration the cost-benefit and measurable sustainable performance output of potential projects. Their facilitating role and involvement as an active partner in some projects contributed to a significant shift in the system. The data presented in Chapter 5 suggest that the facilitating and business roles of NISP influenced the choice of certain projects and hence the overall development of regional industrial symbiosis.

In my expert meeting participation and keynote speech to the Kawasaki forums, I was confronted with the question of the optimal scale of a system boundary to successfully operationalize industrial ecology. The ideal answer I believed was the scale at which roundput would be achieved. First I observed the industrial park scale (for example Tianjin TEDA), next I extended the boundary to include multiple parks (for example Philippine 5-park BPX), then I looked at a regional example (for example Upper Styria), and, finally, I also considered approaches in a city (for example Guiyang) and at the national policy level (for example Sound Material Society). For example, I asked questions such as: How many resource loops are closed in the system boundary in Guiyang (phosphorous, aluminum)? What is the efficiency of the water recycle/reuse in Kalundborg? In most cases, voluntary resource matching will not be successful 'within the park wall' boundary. Resource flow optimization needs to operate on a much wider scale, and this was clearly depicted by the local-regional resource flow in the Gibbs chapter. To better manage such resource flows within a designated perimeter, coordinating or facilitating interventions would be very helpful, such as those demonstrated in the NISP case.

This roundput issue would not be a priority at the inter-firm network level, but surely is a priority at the park level if there is a system optimization goal set by the facilitator or higher authority under the top-down or sideways-in scenarios. In summary, a different level stakeholder may bring either a micro- or macro-view of resource utilization and/or optimization to the system, and this will affect how the primary stream definitions of resource flow and industrial metabolism are operationalized and addressed. A macro-view of resource utilization would involve both product and by-product utilization in the system boundary, thus both product supply chain and by-product supply chain would theoretically be merged into one roundput consideration. This scenario has yet to be operationalized.

IMPORTANCE OF INFORMATION FLOW AND COMMUNICATION CHANNELS

Geographic proximity is not a dominant success factor in industrial symbiosis, but 'short mental distance' is. Chertow and Ashton's chapter demonstrates that some firms in the same vicinity do not know each other, and some do not even want to know each other. In some cases communications existed among supply chain partners, but these firms looked at the product material flow and did not pay attention to the by-product and utility/service resource flow. Under these circumstances, industrial symbiosis for resource exchange, shared services and utilities often is not very promising. A catalytic facilitator such as NISP may be successful in such situations, for it can provide firms with a broader inter-firm and strategic perspective (see Chapter 5). In another example in Asia Pacific, the Industrial Estate Authority of Thailand (IEAT) holds periodic meetings with companies in the Map Ta Phut Industrial Park. Importantly, IEAT also organizes plant tours to visit the companies' environmental facilities, but not their production lines which are sometimes treated as confidential aspects of their businesses. Similar activities of simply meeting were cited in the Chertow and Ashton chapter about Cataño Mayor. Communication is such an important factor in eco-industrial development but its effectiveness depends very much on who is involved in the communications process. In a conventional networking gathering among firms, for example, supply chain network, the company representatives are the procurement and production officers. These people are not responsible for overseeing the overall resource flow within the company wall; moreover, they do not have any 'beyond the wall' thinking (Chiu 2005). In these conventional networking meetings, the participants share information on product flow, and not by-product flow. Hence, developing the right role and right platform for firm representatives to speak a common language on resource flow becomes an important step to realize industrial symbiosis objectives. Too many networking channels that do not fit into a resource flow purpose are ineffective in developing an eco-industrial development scheme.

It is noteworthy here to again link supply chain relationships with resource flow. As in the evolution from quality management systems (QMS and ISO9000) to environment management systems (EMS and ISO14000), supply chain has been used as the conduit. Supply chain in the 1980s was used to target higher quality and productivity of production systems through the centre-satellite system. I call such systems the first generation or CSS-1 (Chiu and Christensen 2004). Embracing all resource flows this time (product, service and by-product) along the supply chain stream, a second generation of resource flow system cited in literature as corporate synergy system (CSS-2) (Chiu et al. 1999) surfaced in the late 1990s. This out-of-the-box thinking aims to integrate all resource flows within a system, with individual firms considering optimization right from the start of their product research and design stages. Eco-industrial development should not just aim for post-production by-product exchange; it should also explore firm-level optimization, inter-firm level optimization, and system-level optimization.

TRIPLE BOTTOM LINE AND MARKET MECHANISMS

Since the Brundtland report, there has been an increasing trend in the business community towards corporate social responsibility. The report introduced the notion of sustainable development and in recent years this has been associated with the idea of triple bottom lines (TBL), namely economic, ecological and social bottom lines. Inasmuch as business firms would want to devote to the TBL, the three bottom lines in reality are not additive in characteristics. Often ecological and social components come in only after the economic bottom line is met. For example, Gibbs (Chapter 4) cites Sterr and Orr, saying that 'expecting firms to relocate to a site specifically to procure secondary materials is perhaps unrealistic'; business decisions such as location still rest with conventional corporate business strategy. Gibbs' own empirical work also bears this out. Given that this is the realistic market mechanism, enhanced eco-industrial development will not take off simply through bottom-up and top-down approaches. Reflecting the strength of the market mechanism, Gibbs cites a respondent saying that 'what we are trying to do is mandate co-operation and you really can't do that'. In recent years, most models for eco-industrial development have advocated either a retrofitting model (bottom-up) or master planning (top-down) approach that installs a strong champion to facilitate and generate the much needed catalytic effect. My observation of Asia Pacific EID events, suggests, however, that there is no such thing as a purely bottom-up or top-down model. All EID initiatives involve significant multi-stakeholder participation through a champion facilitator. The facilitating model may prove to be the most realistic for future EID efforts, and Gibbs' scale-intervention model would serve as a significant contribution in this endeavour.

REFERENCES

Chew, I.M.L., R. Tan, D.C.Y. Foo and A.S.F. Chiu (2007), 'Game theory approach to the analysis of eco-industrial water conservation, reuse, and recycle networks, in G.Q. Tabios and L.Q. Liongson (eds), *Proceedings of UNESCO-IHP International Conference on Hydrology and Water Resources Management for Hazard Reduction and Sustainable Development* (HRSD-2007) (pp. 215–19). Intercontinental Hotel, Makati, Metro Manila, Philippines, 19–23 November 2007.

Chiu, A.S.F. (2001a), 'Ecology, system, and networking: walking the talk in Asia', *Journal of Industrial Ecology*, **5**(2): 6–8.

Chiu, A.S.F. (2001b), 'Overview of eco-industrial networking in Asia', *Proceedings of the New Strategies for Industrial Development: An International Conference and Workshop*, 3–6 April, Manila, Philippines.

Chiu, A.S.F. (2005), Training Package for NCPC on CP/Environmental Management of Industrial Estates. Ver 3.3. UNEP/InWEnt, Paris, France, http://www.uneptie.org/pc/ind-estates/events/announcement.htm.

Chiu, A.S.F. (2009), 'Emerging role of eco-industrial development in the Asia Pacific: Towards national and regional green economics', in P.S. Low (ed.), *Global Change and Sustainable Development: Asia-Pacific Perspectives*, Cambridge University Press (forthcoming).

Chiu, A.S.F. and V. Christensen (2004), *Planning Issues in EID*, Training Manual of APO Greening Productivity – Industrial Ecology Module (GP-IE), 21–25 June. Manila, Philippines.

Chiu, S.Y., J.H. Huang, C.S. Lin, Y.H. Tang, W.H. Chen and S.C. Su (1999), 'Applications of a corporate synergy system to promote cleaner production in small and medium enterprises', *Journal of Cleaner Production*, **7**(5): 351–8.

Chiu, A.S.F. and G. Pascual-Sison (2001), 'Asia Pacific ecological industrial development', *Proceedings of the 3rd Asia Pacific Roundtable for Cleaner Production*, 28 February–2 March, Manila, Philippines.

Korhonen, J. (2001), 'Four ecosystem principles for an industrial ecosystem', *Journal of Cleaner Production*, **9**(3): 253–9.

PART III

Product chain approaches

7. Transgenic crops in Brazil: scientific decision-making for social ambiguities?

Jeremy Hall and Stelvia Matos

INTRODUCTION

The social aspects of new technologies have become an increasing source of concern for managers, policymakers, researchers and other stakeholders, especially in developing countries. In the context of industrial ecology, one of the challenges consists in integrating social factors into its analytical processes. In this chapter, we discuss these challenges. We argue that sustainable development, the recognition of interactions among economic, environmental and social parameters, has replaced the narrow environmental management perspective where industrial ecology emerged. Sustainable development is more complex, a situation where there are many interacting variables, and often ambiguous, i.e. where it is difficult to identify key variables and how they interact with each other (Hall and Vredenburg 2003; Matos and Hall 2007). We use the biological analogy suggested by Frosch (1992) and Frosch and Gallopoulos (1989) and Graedel (1994) to interpret the core concept of industrial ecology. We suggest that, as in biological systems, industry, society and ecology are complex systems with many variables and many interactions (Spiegelman 2003). Such complexity indicates that imperfect information is the norm rather than something that can be assumed away. Under these circumstances, the underlying industrial ecology optimization strategies based on assumptions and heuristics advocated by orthodox economics, scientists and engineers have limitations: a search for satisfactory solutions is more appropriate (Simon 1969). We thus define industrial ecology as a managerial approach that aims to avoid and reduce wastes by considering the interactions amongst and within complex systems (for example, manufacturing processes, industries and economies).

The purpose of this chapter is to continue with this book's focus: the recognition of the need to bridge social science contributions with the engineering/natural sciences to industrial ecology, by emphasizing the challenges of complexity and ambiguity in sustainable development, an issue that traditional social and engineering/natural scientists tend to avoid. Second, we illustrate these challenges of sustainability with data collected in the developing economy of Brazil, where the 'dirty details' of imperfect information led to major problems with the acceptance of agricultural biotechnology,[1] which in turn was shaped by previous controversies over 'Green Revolution' technologies, where chemical intensive, large-scale farming vastly improved agricultural output, but subsistence farmers' skills were disrupted. Many have argued that biotechnology offers environmental benefits for agriculture (Magretta 1997), and could facilitate industrial ecology applications (Bull 1996; Morrissey et al. 2002; OECD 2004). The science-based, optimization and technological deterministic approaches underlying biotechnology and Green Revolution technologies also draw close parallels with industrial ecology. What lessons can be learned for industrial ecology from these previous initiatives, and what are the implications for developing countries?

Brazil, one of the world's largest food exporters, has an active but often controversial agricultural biotechnology sector. Like most other jurisdictions, their attempts to promote and regulate the technology were based on scientific evidence and economic benefits, yet these approaches did little to placate those opposed to the technology. A major concern in Brazil was the wider social impacts of such technologies on, for example, small-scale subsistence farming. We suggest that the analysis of scientific information without consideration for such social uncertainties erodes the utility of industrial ecology principles. We discuss the implications of these limitations, suggest indicators for dealing with social uncertainties in industrial ecology, and conclude with implications for policy and research.

INDUSTRIAL ECOLOGY: THE OPTIMIZATION PROBLEM OF GLITTERING COMPLEXITY

The seminal paper by Frosch and Gallopoulos (1989) recognized that industrial processes could be transformed into a more integrated model where, for example, waste streams from one manufacturing process may be used as raw materials for others. Since that time, industrial ecology has been recognized as a 'new unifying principle for operationalizing sustainable development' (Ashford and Cote 1997), and that it is the 'science of sustainability' (Allenby 1999). An important contribution of concern to this chapter, and one that has since been discussed within the industrial ecology discourse, is the recognition that manufacturing systems should optimize the total industrial material cycle (see Graedel 1994; Ayres and Ayres 1996), analogous to biological systems. For example, Graedel and Allenby (1995: 5) argue that industrial ecology is 'a systems view in which one seeks to optimize the total materials cycle from virgin material, to finished material, to component, to product, to obsolete product and ultimate disposal. Factors to be optimized include resources, energy and capital'. According to Okoku (2004), these authors typically take a technological deterministic view, which is based on the conviction that 'the social world basically is rational, and therefore can be explained by scientific methods' (p. 323), and deny ideological and moral criteria.

A number of authors have taken issue with this perspective. For example, Halluite et al. (2005) argue that in 'an idyllic closed loop industrial ecosystem' (p. 33), there is an exact balance of inputs and wastes, but in reality, well intentioned industrial ecology practices often create unintended and negative consequences. According to Betts (2007), leading industrial ecology scholars such as Ehrenfeld and Chertow have acknowledged that there are no successful highly planned approaches to industrial ecology symbiosis in the US and Europe, whereas the few functioning examples come about organically. We suggest that such shortcomings are due to the lack of appreciation for the complex nature of sustainable development, particularly for social issues. Salmi and Toppinen (2007) argue that industrial ecological systems are only meaningful when contextualized and linked to localized needs and political implications. Such contextualization presents greater dimensions of complexity, an issue identified by a number of industrial ecology scholars (see Allenby 1998; Bey and Isenmann 2005; Lifset 2005). For example, Frosch (1992) recognizes the 'optimization problem' of balancing production costs with waste disposal (p. 801) due to its 'glittering complexity' (p. 802). Spiegelman (2003) argues that complex systems analysis could provide more rigorous methodological tools for the industrial ecologist, and Ehrenfeld (2007) argues that the classical ecology models used in industrial ecology lack sufficient power to address the goals of sustainability. Below, we discuss some of the underlying constructs of complexity and how the complex and often subjective social dimension of sustainability may be considered in the context of industrial ecology.

INDUSTRIAL ECOLOGY AND AGRICULTURAL BIOTECHNOLOGY

Many argue that biotechnology has a significant role in promoting advances in industrial ecology. Bull (1996), for example, argues that cleaner processes, products and ecological remediation can be achieved through biotechnology. Specific examples include the development of genetically modified organisms (GMOs) for *in situ* waste bio-treatment and the reduction of chemical herbicides and pesticides by using herbicide-resistant traits in plants. Morrissey et al. (2002) identify the opportunity of using genetically modified microbial inoculants that can reduce the usage of agricultural chemicals and remediate polluted sites. Many other scientific studies show the application of techniques such as gene manipulation, gene transfer, DNA typing and cloning of plants for environmental improvement in agricultural production and the food industry (see McFall-Ngai and de Lorenzo 2007; Adrio and Demain 2002; Kern 2002; Kuipers 1999). Inter-governmental organizations such as the Organization of Economic Cooperation and Development (OECD) and the United Nations' Food and Agriculture Organization (FAO) have emphasized the importance of biotechnology for sustainability in the agri-forestry, industry and waste treatment sectors, especially in developing countries (OECD 2004; FAO 2000). Although the above studies suggest the importance of social aspects, their analyses focus only on environmental aspects of the technology.

Other studies are less enthusiastic about the consequences of biotechnology. From an environmental perspective, a review of scientific studies by Wolfenbarger and Phifer (2000) found that it is currently impossible to determine the benefits and hazards of genetically modified organisms, due to a lack of understanding of ecological and metabolic systems. Further research is needed to reveal the risk of changing functional properties of the organism, changing bioactive compounds, epigenic silencing of genes, altering levels of antinutrients and potential allergens and toxins (Doerfler et al. 1997; Inose and Murata 1995; Lapeé et al. 1999; Novak and Haslberger 2000). From a social perspective, Stone (2004) identified negative impacts such as skills disruption of local Indian farmers due to a decrease in information flows, inconsistency with local agricultural practices, and overly rapid technological change. As we will show below, similar problems occurred in Brazil during the 1960s and 1970s with the introduction of 'Green Revolution' technologies and later biotechnology, where modern technologies encouraged large-scale farming and vastly improved agricultural output, but subsistence farmers' skills were disrupted. First, we will discuss the theoretical underpinnings of sustainability.

INDUSTRIAL ECOLOGY FOR ENVIRONMENTAL MANAGEMENT OR SUSTAINABLE DEVELOPMENT?

The initial focus of Industrial Ecology articulated by, for example, Frosch and Gallopoulos (1989) and Ayres (1989) concerned environmental improvements in manufacturing systems from a theoretical and technical perspective. Since that time, we argue that there has been a shift from improving environmental performance towards concerns over sustainable development (Matos and Hall 2007), and more specifically within the context for industrial ecology (Ashford and Cote 1997; Allenby 1999). The Brundtland Commission's (WCED 1987) recognition of the relationship between present social needs without compromising future generations' needs emphasized the importance of analysing environmental problems in the wider context of economic and social interactions; the popular 'triple bottom line' suggested by Elkington (1998). Although this transition from looking at environmental problems in isolation towards a holistic approach more accurately reflects reality, it presents greater dimensions of complexity and imperfect information. Understanding these imperfections are crucial, but typically disregarded under theoretically elegant approaches such as industrial ecology. The next sections explore the theoretical underpinnings of some of these 'dirty' imperfections.

THE COMPLEX AND AMBIGUOUS NATURE OF SOCIAL UNCERTAINTIES

An underlying construct of industrial ecology is the management of risk. According to Knight (1921), *true risk* is probabilistic, where both the variables and probabilities are known, while *uncertainty* is where the variables may be known, but not the outcome probabilities. True risk is rare in the real world. Managing uncertainty is perhaps the dominant managerial task, and the foundation for industrial ecology, where there is an implicit assumption that scientific methods can be used to convert uncertainties into probabilistic risks through such techniques as actuarial sciences, market surveys, laboratory testing, simulations, and so on (Matos and Hall 2007). Unfortunately, such techniques may not be conducive for social uncertainties, which in many cases are ambiguous,[2] in that neither the variables nor probabilities can be identified or estimated. Ambiguity, particularly the inability to identify key stakeholders, is becoming an increasingly important business challenge, yet one not sufficiently addressed by traditional decision-making approaches (Hall and Vredenburg 2005; Stone and Brush 1996). For example, few policy-makers or business managers were able to anticipate beforehand the influence of NGOs in the Brazilian biotechnology regulatory process. Such risks are further exacerbated under high degrees of complexity, a situation where there are many interacting variables (Simon 1969). Under high degrees of complexity, it is difficult to understand fully the implications of how the variables interact, which may lead to compromises or less than ideal options (Frenken 2001; Gatignon et al. 2002), or increased political influences (Rosenkopf and Tushman 1988). Simon (1962, 1969) argues that because of complexity, actors are limited in what they know (bounded rationality) and thus what they can do. He suggests that under complex environments, decision-makers should seek satisfactory solutions rather than follow optimization strategies.

Environmental issues often involve considerable complexities, because of the very nature of ecosystem interactions (Wolfenbarger and Phifer 2000). Technologies with sustainable development implications such as biotechnology are that much more complex, because there must be consideration for environmental, economic and social variables from an intergenerational perspective. Furthermore, many sustainable development pressures are ambiguous, because it is not always easy to identify key variables, particularly those that are subjective (Matos and Hall 2007). Secondary stakeholders, those that are not directly involved in the business relationship but may have an effect on the firm (Freeman 1984) may not always be easily identified. Secondary stakeholders also do not always have the same rights, claims or interests (Clarkson 1995), and thus may present conflicting pressures. For example, the demands or concerns of market-related stakeholders such as customers (for example farmers), suppliers (for example seed suppliers), complementary innovators (for example food processors) and shareholders are relatively similar and unambiguous (that is, they are primarily concerned with financial gain). See Chapter 9 for a discussion of stakeholder categorizations and their relationship to external pressures and incentives. We have argued elsewhere that non-market stakeholders such as anti-globalization activists, safety and environmental advocates are sometimes much more ambiguous, as they are often not always identified as key stakeholders in early phases, nor do they have the same interests or market-driven values as market-related stakeholders (Hall and Vredenburg 2003).

Technologies with wide ranging implications – and thus wide ranging stakeholders – such as biotechnology involve not only technical uncertainties, but also non-technical ambiguities (Hall and Martin 2005). The key distinction is that technical uncertainties involve situations where the primary interacting variables can be identified, and therefore scientific methodologies underlying industrial ecology are appropriate. As social pressures are often ambiguous, scientific approaches, and indeed the majority of economic and managerial decision-making tools, have major limitations. Even Popper (1945) recognized the limits to his influential scientific methodology. He proposed an extension of his conjecture-refutation approach, what he called *piecemeal social engineering,* recommending that politicians should attempt to correct generally accepted social ills in an ad hoc or piecemeal manner, rather than seek to impose a utopian 'good' or 'optimum' solution. If industrial ecology is to deal with the complex and sometimes ambiguous issues of sustainable development for policy advice, there must be a recognition of compromises and searches for satisfactory solutions. Under ambiguous situations, Gavetti et al. (2005) and Matos and Hall (2007) suggest the use of analogical reasoning; the ability to transfer useful wisdom from a broad range of previous similar settings.

METHODOLOGY

The data presented in this chapter is part of a broader programme of research investigating the interactions between social pressures, public policy, firm dynamics and innovation. The specific project concerns the impact of Green Revolution and transgenic technology on various stakeholders from the perspective of a developing economy, Brazil. Transgenic technology is the application of genes from one species to another, and is considered one of the more controversial applications of biotechnology. Although these technologies were not developed explicitly under industrial ecology principals, their application was based on similar scientific principles following optimization strategies, and thus provides a close analogy for industrial ecology and how it may be improved to reflect social attributes. As discussed above, biotechnology has been identified as having a significant role for developing countries (OECD 2004; FAO 2000) and in promoting advances in industrial ecology (Bull 1996; Morrissey et al. 2002; McFall-Ngai amd de Lorenzo 2007; Adrio amd Demain 2002; Kern 2002; Kuipers 1999). However, few studies have explored these issues and the social characteristics of developing countries in the context of industrial ecology.

Given the exploratory nature, we followed a grounded theory approach (Glaser and Strauss 1967) and case study methodology (Yin 1984; Eisenhardt 1989) employing qualitative instruments (Robson 1993). We started with desk research and information gathering that included data from government documents and reports, the academic literature and the Brazilian and international press. Site visits were conducted in Brasilia, Campina Grande, Manaus, Petrolina, Porto Alegre, Recife, Rio de Janeiro and Sao Paulo in 2003–2005. Interviews were conducted with approximately 70 key informants (senior and middle managers, government officials, industry experts, NGO officials, trade association members and other stakeholder representatives), identified as key stakeholders from our desk research and through the snowball technique (Berg 1988). We also conducted interviews with 23 individual farmers and four focus groups totalling 45 subjects. A semi-structured interview guide that investigated the key issues and perspectives of innovation management, public policy, stakeholder relations and strategy was used. Interviews required between one and three hours, and were recorded, translated (if necessary) and transcribed in summary form. To verify the data, we applied a triangulation approach where we interviewed and compared a broad range of stakeholders' varying opinions and interests, and made comparisons between primary data (interviews) and secondary data (official documents and reports).

AN OVERVIEW OF BRAZILIAN AGRICULTURE AND 'GREEN REVOLUTION' DISRUPTIONS

Brazil is the world's fifth largest country by land area (8 456 510 sq km) and population (178 million people). Agriculture is a key sector in the country's growing economy, accounting for 13 per cent of its GDP, and it is a major producer of a variety of crops and livestock (Borges da Fonseca 2003). The importance of agriculture is reflected in two influential federal agencies, the Ministry of Agriculture (responsible for large-scale industrial farming) and the Ministry of Agriculture Development (responsible for small scale, family and subsistence farming). The latter was initiated by the left-of centre President Luiz Inácio 'Lula' da Silva to deal with the social problems of subsistence farmers. The Green Revolution industrialization of Brazilian agriculture during the 1960s and 1970s vastly improved agricultural output and exports, but the benefits of agricultural productivity was not equitably distributed (Lee 2005), nor was it designed to meet specific local environmental and socioeconomic conditions of farmers (Aerni 2002). Millions of subsistence farmers were dislocated; many of whom migrated to urban centres seeking other opportunities, but often ended up destitute and living in *favelas*, or shantytowns (Ferraz 1999). These squatter communities are infamous for high crime rates and other social problems such as drug abuse and prostitution. Our prior studies (Hall et al. 2008) found that the economic success of Green Revolution technologies tended to overshadow the social downside, and there was a concern among many Brazilians that biotechnology would follow a similar path.

Although Green Revolution technologies were not designed under industrial ecology principles, the underlying logic of applying scientific principles and heuristics remains similar. Although recently criticized for overuse of chemical inputs and disruption of subsistence farmers, the initial stimulus of Green Revolution pioneer and Nobel Laureate Norman Borlaug was to provide affordable food for the world's poor (de Castro

2004). The elegant industrial ecology approach now deals explicitly with environmental impacts, but one must question whether some yet undefined social problem will emerge that overshadows these environmental improvements, as was the case for biotechnology, discussed next.

Brazilian Agricultural Biotechnology Policy Controversies

Brazilian biotechnology policy emerged in 1995 with the Federal Government's Biosafety Law (Law 8-974), which established safety rules and inspection mechanisms for all activities related to genetic engineering technology, including research, production, storage, transportation and commercialization of biotech products. In 1996, the government created the National Technical Commission for Biosafety (CTNBio) responsible for technical evaluations of safety, inspections and approval of biotechnology products for commercialization. CTNBio is part of the Ministry of Science and Technology and was composed of scientists and representatives from the government and civil society (consumers, labour representatives and entrepreneurs). However, our interview data indicated that their participation in the approval process was somewhat irrelevant since decisions were based purely on scientific evidence.

In 1998, CTNBio approved the commercialization of Monsanto's Round-up Ready soybean, a transgenic product that contained a gene from the bacterium *agrobacterium*. The decision was based exclusively on scientific evidence, as was the mandate of CTNBio. Of note, Monsanto had not conducted any environmental assessments, even though the Brazilian constitution requires impact assessment studies and licensing of activities that 'potentially' affect the environment. However, the government at that time interpreted the law as not applicable for transgenic seeds. A problem with the legislation is that it does not clearly define which activities are potentially hazardous to the environment. In response, the non-governmental organization (NGO), Institute for Consumer Defense (IDEC), legally contested CTNBio's approval with the Public Ministry (the ministry responsible for legal issues). They argued that the government should have identified transgenics as a case where impact assessment and licensing are required (Lazarinne 2004). In addition to scientific uncertainty, NGOs were also concerned about wide-ranging detrimental social impacts. Soon afterwards the Federal Justice Department ruled that no commercial GE activities should be authorized until environmental impact assessments were undertaken and regulations more clearly defined.

Despite the judicial resolution, farmers from the state of Rio Grande do Sul (RGS), a major large-scale agricultural producer, started growing transgenic seeds illegally imported from Argentina. RGS farmers and politicians then requested changes in the federal law, arguing that the state would suffer major economic damage if they would not be allowed to sell their crops. In response, the federal government launched a provisional measure in 2001, lifting the ban applicable only to those that planted transgenic soybeans (Medida Provisória 2.137).

In 2002, the Federal Ministry of Environment's National Environment Council established a policy that transgenics would require an environmental license. However, political pressure from RGS farmers continued, and they managed to get government approval to plant transgenic seeds for the 2003–2004 growing season through yet another provisional measure (Law No. 10.814, 2003). This led to the government's reevaluation of the national biotechnology policy, resulting in the National Policy on Biosafety (Law No. 11.105, 2005). This law is based on the precautionary principle and changes the decision-making system, where CTNBio is responsible for a pre-evaluation of technical and safety issues, and is no longer responsible for commercialization approval. CTNBio participants have been increased to include more representatives from consumer rights groups, small-scale agriculture and industry, as well as experts on health, environment and ethics. Such an approach encompassing a wide range of stakeholders is perhaps unusual for a regulatory agency, but indicated that the regulatory system was attempting to account for social aspects and more generally sustainable development issues, which were a major concern in the country. Once a transgenic product is considered technically viable and safe by CTNBio, the final decision regarding commercialization is given by the National Biosafety Council. This Council is comprised of 12 ministry representatives, including the Ministries of Environment, Agriculture, Agriculture Development, Health, Trade and Hunger Defense (a Ministry dedicated to reducing poverty).

To complicate matters, during this time a GM-labelling law came into force, stipulating that all human and animal food containing more than 1 per cent transgenic soy must be labelled. Products that use transgenic soybeans harvested in 2003 must state the following: 'this may contain ingredients produced by transgenic soya'. Products made from the 2004 soya harvest must be identified with a 'T' – for 'transgenic' – on the label, and enforced by the Ministry of Agriculture with the National Health Surveillance Agency and the state consumer-protection organization responsible for controlling and imposing fines. However, local scientists and some government officials questioned the viability of implementing this law due to the complexities of label inspection for all phases of the production chain (Strauss 2004).

The legislation process became very contentious due to widespread opposition from a variety of stakeholders for a variety of reasons.

Such conflicts were reflected in the inconsistent positions taken by the government ministries. For example, before approval, the Ministries of Science and Technology, and Agriculture recognized biotechnology as a key pillar in its innovation strategy and supported biotechnology research (Blackburn 2004). In contrast, the Ministries of Environment and Agriculture Development were opposed to the technology. The Ministry of Trade appeared to be caught in the middle of European and American disagreement (representatives from this ministry refused to speak to us). Both jurisdictions recognized that the scientific evidence suggests transgenic soybeans were safe, although the rejection of these products by many European consumers led to very different regulatory stances and outcomes. Perhaps unique to developing nations is the Ministry of Hunger Defense, concerned with poverty issues. Counter to the claims of proponents, biotechnology was not seen as a solution for hunger by this Ministry, as there are many more pressing issues such as access and distribution problems.

The government rift reflected wider disagreement in Brazil. During the time of our research, there was a large and influential industry presence composed of major multinationals (Monsanto, Aventis, Syngenta, BASF, Bayer CropScience, Dow AgroScience and Dupont Pioneer), plus approximately 300 smaller local biotech enterprises. Farmers' opinions varied – most in the technologically advanced soybean producing southern states were in favour, although the governor of one of the most advanced states, Parana, was opposed to the technology. North and north-east farmers (60 per cent of which were small and medium sized), were not growing soybeans, but were mostly opposed, especially the subsistence farmers, who feared another 'Green Revolution' disruption. A consumer acceptance study conducted in 2002 found that 41 per cent have never heard about transgenics (IBOPE 2002). Of those that have, 71 per cent would not consume transgenics if they could choose, while 92 per cent think that GM food should be labelled. In 2003, there were about 15 active anti-transgenic NGOs, although Greenpeace and the nationally based IDEC were the most dominant. They focused their efforts on environmental, health, economic, social (particularly small farmer implications) and national sovereignty issues.

Table 7.1 summarizes the claims and interests of a sample of stakeholder groups in a pairwise comparison modified from our previous analysis (Hall et al. 2008). A pairwise comparison is a useful approach to illustrate key stakeholders and their relationships with each other (Handy 1992; Phillips et al. 2003). Stakeholders with similar claims and interests represent unambiguous relationships (+). Those with different claims and interests (–) represent in some cases uncertainty, where for example

Table 7.1   Pairwise comparison of sample stakeholder groups (before Law no. 11.105, 2005)

Stakeholders	1	2	3	4	5	6	7	8	9	10
1. **Large Scale Farmers**										
2. Subsistence Farmers	−									
3. **Biotech Industry**	+	−								
4. IDEC	−	X	−							
5. Greenpeace	−	X	−	X						
6. **EMBRAPA**	+	−	+	−	−					
7. **Ministry of S&T**	+	−	+	−	−	+				
8. Ministry of Environment	−	X	−	+	+	−	−			
9. **Ministry of Agriculture**	+	−	+	−	−	+	+	−		
10. Ministry of Ag. Development	−	+	−	X	X	−	−	X	−	

Notes:
Based on key informant interviews conducted in Brazil, 2003/4
Bold text = Proponent of transgenic technology
Roman text = Opposed to transgenic technology in Brazil
Pairwise comparison:
(+) = Similar claims and interests
(−) = Different claims and different interests
(X) = Similar claims but different interests

scientific knowledge was not fully understood and some decided to follow a precautionary principle (for example Ministry of Environment) whereas others believed this was insufficient to halt the technology (for example, Ministry of Science and Technology, Ministry of Agriculture and EMBRAPA). In these examples, all groups used the same scientific variables, but interpreted the results differently, as would be the case for other scientific approaches like industrial ecology. The solution for such an impasse would be more scientific information – highly complicated, but relatively unambiguous, or the enactment of law, as was the case here (Law no. 11.105, 2005). Indeed, after this law, all government agencies had to follow the same policies (thus eliminating the negative pairwise relationships in Table 7.1).

Examples that are more ambiguous include the relationship between Greenpeace versus EMBRAPA and large-scale farmers, where Greenpeace would not find the technology acceptable regardless of the scientific data or legal status, but rather shift their opposition to other issues such as the impact on subsistence farming. Situations where stakeholders have the same position towards transgenic technology but different interests and objectives (X) are also ambiguous and sometimes contentious. For example, consistent with the precautionary principle, IDEC claimed to be willing to change their opposition to the technology with sufficient scientific evidence, whereas Greenpeace would not.

A general source of opposition to transgenics was due to the technology's perceived dominance by foreign multinationals, a particularly contentious issue for developing economies. For example, EMBRAPA established a joint venture with Monsanto, believing that each could offer valuable complementary assets – 'a match made in heaven' according to one senior EMBRAPA official. However, the widespread distrust of foreign multinationals, particularly Monsanto, became a main deterrent to public acceptance of the technology, and eroded EMBRAPA's reputation as a national technology contributor. All but one key informant agreed that the technology would not have been so controversial had it been developed independently by a national enterprise. Note that this issue has nothing to do with scientific evidence, yet the proponents continued to use scientific criteria for what was essentially social ambiguity, that is, a key variable, opposition to foreign multinationals, was not recognized.

Another key issue for developing countries was the distinction between subsistence and large-scale farming, adding a degree of complexity (that is, more variables) with different claims and demands (that is, more ambiguity). Indeed, some of the most powerful opposition arguments were based on previous negative experiences with supposedly beneficial Green Revolution technologies. The underlying scientific, optimization approaches of Green Revolution technologies and biotechnology closely resemble the technological deterministic view (Okoku 2004) of industrial ecology, and will likely encounter similar problems unless these social factors are addressed.

CONSIDERING SOCIAL FACTORS IN INDUSTRIAL ECOLOGY

In practice, one way to introduce social factors into industrial ecology is to add social parameters in the implementation of common analytical tools for industrial ecology such as life-cycle assessment (LCA), materials flow analysis (MFA), risk assessment, and so on. The practitioner may chose to add social parameters into the scope of the analytical tool or investigate these parameters *ex ante* as in a screening process to evaluate the degree of social uncertainty related to the case in study. The point here is to adopt a preventive attitude by 'searching' for social issues (and satisfactory, rather than optimal solutions) and avoiding major setbacks in trying to fix problems after they occur. In our previous work (Matos and Hall 2007), we suggest that when managing for sustainable development, social factors may determine the appropriateness of LCA, and likewise industrial ecology. We argue that if there are any potential environmental or social impacts that are unknown or require specific investigation, practitioners should consider uncovering such ambiguities before applying such tools. As we observed in Brazil, opponents used scientific uncertainties of biotechnology as fuel for their anti-transgenic campaigns, and often complicating the issue by linking these scientific uncertainties to more ambiguous issues such as rights of subsistence farmers and anti-Monsanto/globalization concerns.

Hobbes et al. (2007) present another example of incorporating social factors into analytical tools. They propose the application of material flow analysis in a social context by examining the connections between material flow and key stakeholders' actions. For example, they selected a Vietnamese village and developed maps of stakeholders' options (for example support, negate, ignore, bribe, etc.) and motivations (for example income, social return, no risk, etc.) for logging and bamboo production. These maps provide useful information for policy design and show the importance of multidisciplinary approaches for industrial ecology that includes environmental, natural (including ethics) and social sciences.

Social parameters can be investigated using social indicators but should be developed in accordance with specific characteristics and needs of the system. Better yet are sustainability indicators because they involve not only economic, social and environmental factors, but also interactions among these three dimensions (Wilson et al. 2007). Table 7.2 lists examples of sustainability indicators that can be incorporated into tools for industrial ecology. Note that the use of these indicators is intended to open the discussion and not to limit practitioners' scope for identifying relevant issues that are specific to the case in study. In fact, some special cases may instead require a 'drop out' from conventional tools and the adoption of alternative approaches (see Chapter 9). These alternative options may be developed for the specific case in place, or be inspired by other disciplines. For example, management scholars such as Rivkin and Siggelkow (2003), and Levinthal and Warglien (1999) have applied biological concepts in their research.

Although collecting and examining social parameters are not easy, and ambiguous issues may still come out from unexpected sources, practitioners, researchers and policy makers need to realize the importance of going beyond the environmental focus of industrial ecology and recognize the importance of considering the interconnections among environmental and social factors.

We suggest that when introducing social factors into industrial ecology, appropriate social indicators need to be developed. These indicators will

Table 7.2   Examples of sustainability indicators

Indicators for the economic dimension
- Employment growth
- Unemployment rate
- Income distribution/capital
- Rate change of purchase of local products/value and variety
- Capital formation in the community/investment
- Availability of local credit to local business
- Entrepreneurial opportunities for local residents
- Per cent of profit/revenue reinvestment in reserved natural and cultural area management and protection
- Nature of demand per cent of repeat visitors
- New GDP (index of sustainable economic welfare)
- Local community economic stability labour/company and job conditions
- Social cost/benefit at community level for examining net benefit to local economy
- Equal opportunity employment and promotion to women and local residents

Indicators for the social dimension
- Continuance of traditional activities by local residents
- Resident/non-resident ownership of homes (2nd homes/part time residents)
- Level of congruency among stakeholders
- Change in community structure evident of a community breakdown and alienation
- Change in family cohesion
- Per cent employed in sex tourism
- Community attitude toward sex tourism
- Community resource degradation/erosion of natural and cultural resource
- Per cent of managerial employment from local residents
- Community health and safety litter/pollution (air, water, etc.)
- Crime rate
- Loss of traditional lifestyle and knowledge via modernization
- Levels of satisfaction with community life in general

Indicators for the ecological dimension
- Amount of erosion on the natural sites
- Number of good air quality days
- Rate of ecosystem destruction/degradation
- Per capita water/energy consumption data
- Per cent under protection designation or environmentally managed
- Natural environment accounting and life-cycle analysis
- Number of endangered species
- Reuse/recycling rates
- Renewable resources used
- Recycling rate

Table 7.2   (continued)

- Fisheries utilization
- Health of human population
- Formal control required over development of sites and use densities
- Type and amount of environmental education training given to employee
- Per capita discharge of waste water
- Per capita discharge of solid waste
- Loss of non-renewable resources

Source: Based on Choi and Sirakaya (2006)

need to be specific to the technology or application under analysis. A starting point would be to listen to local concerns so the technology can be used meaningfully for that community, in an attempt to avoid or pre-empt problems. Users should be encouraged to participate in analytical processes, building cooperation and credibility. Many of the problems we observed have to do with a poor or non-existence approach from practitioners in considering the interactions among economic, environmental and social aspects of the technology, and the lack of credibility and influence of environmental arguments because of their failure to understand the needs of the community. Unfortunately the subjective nature of these social indicators may not translate into 'hard' numbers, and may therefore be deemed less valid than economic or environmental indicators that are assumed to be more robust. Indeed, this is a common phenomenon we have observed in this and other industrial settings, where the use of scientific data correlates to due diligence, but does not necessarily lead to satisfactory outcomes.

IMPLICATIONS AND CONCLUSIONS

We began this chapter by arguing that more complex sustainability pressures have overtaken environmental management as the key issue for policy, and questioned whether conceptually elegant approaches such as industrial ecology are sufficiently equipped to cope with these added complexities and ambiguities. From our perspective, the 'dirty realities' of imperfect information is the key challenge for policy and management, yet typically ignored within the orthodox academic discourse. We illustrated these challenges with the application of Green Revolution technologies and later biotechnology in Brazilian agriculture. Both technologies apply similar heuristics as industrial ecology, and the latter has been identified as a facilitating technology for promoting advances in industrial ecology. Like in other developing economies, agriculture fulfils significant economic and social roles, and over the years, Brazil has accumulated globally competitive competencies, although increases in competitiveness came at a cost. The introduction of technologies that focuses only on scientific parameters and fails to consider the social dynamics of sustainable development are likely to encounter considerable opposition.

The implications for industrial ecology are threefold. First, as an analogy (Gavetti et al. 2005), the experiences of previous generations of new agricultural approaches such as Green Revolution technologies and biotechnology illustrate the potential detrimental social side-effects that were poorly addressed during the initial phases of introduction. Arguably both of these approaches to agriculture, although driven by economic opportunities, presented social benefits in the form of increased food production for the poor in the case of the former, and reduced chemical inputs for transgenics. Green Revolution technologies, although now widely diffused, have come under scrutiny in Brazil and other developing countries, and many interview subjects argued that this experience led to concerns over transgenics. We suggest that industrial ecology applications will likely encounter the same problems if they follow a similarly scientifically myopic approach. Given the precedence, developers of industrial ecology applications do not have the luxury of claiming that they only see their efforts as a scientific issue rather than one that could involve ethical, religious, cultural, social and economic issues, as was the case for former Monsanto CEO Robert Shapiro (2000).

Second, we caution the proponents of conceptually elegant concepts, such as industrial ecology, that are developed in the context of modern industrial societies and then expected to apply equally in developing economies. Brazilian agriculture highlights the heterogeneous nature of many developing economies, with globally competitive and subsistence farming operating in the same jurisdiction, but with vastly different practices and societal goals. A generic application, based on scientific heuristics across all settings, will erode the utility of industrial ecology applications. Furthermore, developing economies like Brazil have major concerns over globalization pressures, particularly in strategically and socially important sectors like agriculture. To the best of our knowledge, there have been limited applications of industrial ecology in this sector, and although promising, current industrial ecology approaches may not have the heuristics to deal with these concerns. More research is needed in this area.

Lastly, there is a need to include social indicators that should be developed in conjunction with the more technical industrial ecology parameters. We however recognize that there remains an issue of prioritization, where hard scientific and/or economic data will usually trump 'soft' but equally important social concerns. We also realize that under such complex circumstances that involve important social ambiguities, the implementation will remain messy and unpredictable. The key issue is to avoid being caught in 'optimization traps' and focus efforts on identifying satisfactory solutions.

As a final remark, the use of biological analogies to industrial systems of production is undoubtedly a useful and insightful approach to understanding sustainable development. However, we suggest that the biological analogy used in industrial ecology has not been fully exploited. For example, the evolutionary perspective advocated by biologists such as Kauffman (1993) has been applied as analogies to new product development (Frenken 2001), firm strategies (Gavetti et al. 2005), supply chains (Choi et al. 2001) and environmental life-cycle assessment (Matos and Hall 2007). In these studies, the biological analogy is used to describe the evolutionary, path dependent characteristics of complex systems, with a focus on identifying satisfactory solutions rather than following optimization strategies. These approaches would apply equally well to industrial ecology, and perhaps provide a partial explanation of Betts' (2007) observation as to why planned (as opposed to organic) approaches to industrial ecology have yet to succeed.

NOTES

1. Biotechnology is defined as 'the manipulation (as through genetic engineering) of living organisms or their components to produce useful, usually commercial, products (as pest resistant crops, new bacterial strains, or novel pharmaceuticals); *also*: any of various applications of biological science used in such manipulation' (www.webster. com). Agriculture biotechnology is the application of such technology in the agriculture sector.
2. Ambiguity is sometimes referred to as Knightian Uncertainty. To avoid confusion, we use ambiguity (see Knight 1921; Camerer and Weber 1992; and Alvesson 1993).

REFERENCES

Adrio, J.L. and A.L. Demain (2003), 'Fungal biotechnology', *International Microbiology*, **6**(3): 191–9.
Aerni, P. (2002), 'Stakeholder attitudes towards the risks and benefits of agricultural biotechnology in developing countries: a comparison between Mexico and the Philippines', *Risk Analysis*, **26**(6), 1123–37.
Allenby, B. (1998), 'Context is everything', *Journal of Industrial Ecology*, **3**(1): 6–8.
Allenby, B. (1999), *Industrial Ecology: Policy Framework and Implementation*, NJ: Prentice-Hall.

Ashford, N. and R. Cote (1997), 'An overview of the special issue on industrial ecology', *Journal of Cleaner Production*, 5(1/2): i–iv.

Ayres, R. and L. Ayres (1996), *Industrial Ecology. Towards Closing the Material Cycle*, Cheltenham, UK and Northampton, MA, USA: Edward Elgar.

Ayres, R.U. (1989), 'Industrial metabolism and global change', *International Social Science Journal*, 121: 363–73.

Berg, S. (1988), 'Snowball sampling', in S. Kotz and N.L. Johnson (eds), *Encyclopaedia of Statistical Sciences*, Vol. 8, New York: John Wiley.

Betts, K. (2007), 'Quantifying industrial ecology', *Environmental Science & Technology*, 39(17): 354–5.

Bey, C. and R. Isenmann (2005), 'Human systems in terms of natural systems? Employing non-equilibrium thermodynamics for evaluating industrial ecology's "ecosystem metaphor"', *International Journal of Sustainable Development*, 8(3), 189–206.

Blackburn, P. (2004), 'Brazil maps Arabica coffee genome to improve quality', *Reuters*, 20 April.

Borges da Fonseca, F. (2003), 'Brazil exporter guide annual 2003. USDA foreign agricultural service GAIN report', www.fas.usda.gov, accessed 11 August 2003.

Bull, A.T. (1996), 'Biotechnology for environmental quality: closing the circles', *Biodiversity and Conservation*, 5(1), 1–25.

Choi, T., K. Dooley and M. Rungtusanatham (2001), 'Supply networks and complex adaptive systems: control versus emergence', *Journal of Operations Management*, 19: 351–66.

Clarkson, M. (1995), 'A stakeholder framework for analyzing and evaluating corporate social performance', *Academy of Management Review*, 20, 92–117.

de Castro, L.A.B. (2004), 'A strategy for obtaining social benefits from the gene revolution', *Brazilian Journal of Medical and Biological Research*, 37: 1429–40.

Doerfler, W., R. Shubbert, H. Heller, C. Kamner, K. Hilger-Eversheim, M. Knoblauch and R. Remus (1997), 'Integration of foreign DNA and its consequences in mammalian systems', *Trends in Biotechnology*, 15: 297–301.

Ehrenfeld, J. (2007), 'Would industrial ecology exist without sustainability in the background?', *Journal of Industrial Ecology*, 11(1): 73–84.

Eisenhardt, K. (1989), 'Building theories from case study research', *Academy of Management Review*, 14(4): 532–50.

Elkington, J. (1998), *Cannibals with Forks: The Triple Bottom Line of 21st Century Business*, Gabriola Island, BC: New Society Publishers.

FAO (2000), 'Statement on Biotechnology', http://www.fao.org/biotech/stat.asp, accessed 27 September 2007.

Ferraz, J.M.G. (1999), 'A insustentabilidade da revolução verde, informativo meio ambiente e agricultura (EMBRAPA)', 8(26), 25–28, http://www.cnpma.embrapa. br/ informativo/mostra_informativo.php3?id=108, accessed 22 October 2005.

Freeman, R.E. (1984), *Strategic Management: A Stakeholder Approach*, Boston: Pitman.

Frenken, K. (2001), 'Understanding product innovation using complex systems theory', PhD thesis, University of Amsterdam.

Frosch, R.A. (1992), 'Industrial ecology: a philosophical introduction', *National Academy of Sciences*, 89: 800–803.

Frosch, R.A. and N.E. Gallopoulos (1989), 'Strategies for manufacturing', *Scientific American*, 260: 144–51.

Gatignon, H., M. Tushman, W. Smith and P. Anderson (2002), 'A structural approach to assessing innovation: Construct development of innovation locus, type, and characteristics', *Management Science*, **48**(9): 1103–22.

Gavetti, G., D. Levinthal and J. Rivkin (2005), 'Strategy making in novel and complex worlds: the power of analogy', *Strategic Management Journal*, **26**(8), 691–712.

Glaser, B.G. and A.L. Strauss (1967), *The Discovery of Grounded Theory: Strategies for Qualitative Research*, Aldine Atherton.

Graedel, T. (1994), 'Industrial ecology – definition and implementation', in R. Socolow, C. Andrews, F. Berkhout and V. Thomas (eds), *Industrial Ecology and Global Change*, Cambridge: Cambridge University Press, pp. 23–41.

Graedel, T. and B. Allenby (1995), *Industrial Ecology*, Englewood Cliffs, New Jersey: Prentice Hall.

Hall, J. and H. Vredenburg (2003), 'The challenges of innovating for sustainable development', *MIT Sloan Management Review*, **45**(1), 61–68.

Hall, J. and H. Vredenburg (2005), 'Managing stakeholder ambiguity', *MIT Sloan Management Review*, **47**(1): 11–13.

Hall, J. and M. Martin (2005), 'Disruptive technologies, stakeholders and the innovation value chain: a framework for evaluating radical technology development', *R&D Management Journal*, **35**(3): 273–84.

Hall, J., S. Matos and C. Langford (2008), 'Social exclusion and transgenic technology: the case of Brazilian agriculture', *Journal of Business Ethics*, **77**(1): 45–63

Handy, C. (1992), 'Balancing cooperate power: a new federalist paper', *Harvard Business Review*, November–December, 59–67.

Halluite, J., J. Linton, J. Yeomans and R. Yoogalingam (2005), 'The challenge of hazardous waste management in a sustainable environment: insights from electronic recovery laws', *Corporate Social Responsibility and Environmental Management*, **12**(1): 31–7.

Hobbes, M., S. Stalpers, J. Kooijman, T. Le, K. Trinh and T. Phan (2007), 'Material flows in a social context: a Vietnamese case study combining the material flow analysis and action-in-context frameworks', *Journal of Industrial Ecology*, **11**(1): 141–59.

IBOPE (2002), 'IBOPE – Instituto Brasileiro de Opinião Pública e Estatística. Pesquisa de Opinião Pública sobre Transgênicos', http://www.idec.org.br/files/pesquisa_transgenicos.pdf, accessed 12 August 2003.

Inose, T. and K. Murata (1995), 'Enhanced accumulation of toxic compound in yeast cells having high glycolytic activity: a case study on the safety of genetically engineered yeast', *International Journal of Food Science and Technology*, **30**: 141–6.

Kauffman, S. (1993), *Origins of Order: Self-Organization and Selection in Evolution*, Oxford: Oxford University Press.

Kern, M. (2002), 'Food, feed, fibre, fuel and industrial products of the future: challenges and opportunities. Understanding the strategic potential of plant genetic engineering', *Journal of Agronomy and Crop Science*, **188**(5): 291–305.

Knight, F. (1921), *Risk, Uncertainty and Profit*, Beard Group.

Kuipers, O.P. (1999), 'Genomics for food biotechnology: prospects of the use of high-throughput technologies for the improvement of food microorganisms', *Current Opinion in Biotechnology*, **10**(5): 511–16.

Lapeé, M., E. Bailey, C. Childress and K. Setchell (1999), 'Alterations in clinically important phytoestrogens in genetically modified, herbicide tolerant soybeans', *Journal of Medicinal Food*, 1: 241–5.

Law no. 10.814 (2003), 'Estabelece normas para o plantio e comercialização da produção de soja geneticamente modificada da safra de 2004, e dá outras providências', www81.dataprev.gov.br/SISLEX/paginas/42/2003/10814.htm, 15 December.

Law no. 11.105 (2005), 'Lei de Biosseguranca', www.ctnbio.gov.br/index.php/content/view/ 3671.html, 24 March.

Lazarinne, M. (2004), Executive coordinator of IDEC. Personal communication.

Lee, D. (2005), 'Agricultural sustainability and technology adoption: issues and policies for developing countries', *American Journal of Agricultural Economics*, 87(5): 1325–34.

Levinthal, D.A. and M. Warglien (1999), 'Landscape design: designing for local action in complex worlds', *Organization Science*, 10(3): 342–58.

Lifset, R. (2005), 'Industrial ecology and public policy', *Journal of Industrial Ecology*, 9(3): 1–3.

Magretta, J. (1997), 'Growth through global sustainability: an interview with Monsanto's CEO, Robert B. Shapiro', *Harvard Business Review*, 75(1): 78–88.

Matos, S. and J. Hall (2007), 'Integrating sustainable development in the supply chain: the case of life cycle assessment in oil & gas and agricultural biotechnology', *Journal of Operations Management*, 25(6): 1083–102.

McFall-Ngai, M. and V. de Lorenzo (2007), 'The ultimate rendezvous: microbial ecology meets industrial biotechnology', *Current Opinion in Microbiology*, 10(3): 205–6.

Medida Provisoria 2.137. Governo do Brasil. Available at: http://www.planalto.gov.br/ccivil/mpv/Antigas_2001/2137-4.htm, accessed 12 October 2007.

Morrissey, J.P., U.F. Walsh, A. O'Donnell, Y. Moenne-Loccoz and F. O'Gara (2002), 'Exploitation of genetically modified Inoculants for industrial ecology applications', *Antonie Van Leeuwenhoek International Journal of General and Molecular Microbiology*, 81(1–4): 599–606.

Novak, W. and A. Haslberger (2000), 'Substantial equivalent of anti-nutrients and inherent plant toxins in genetically modified novel foods', *Food and Chemical Toxicology*, 38: 473–83.

OECD (2004), Meeting of the OECD Committee for Scientific and Technological Policy at Ministerial Level. Report: Biotechnology of Sustainable Growth and Development, January 2004.

Okoku, H. (2004), 'Policy implications of industrial ecology conceptions', *Business Strategy and the Environment*, 13: 320–33.

Phillips, R., R. Freeman and A. Wicks (2003), 'What stakeholder theory is NOT', *Business Ethics Quarterly*, 13(4): 479–502.

Popper, K. (1945), *The Open Society and its Enemies*, London: Routledge.

Rivkin, J. and N. Siggelkow (2003), 'Balancing search and stability: Interdependencies among elements of organizational design', *Management Science*, 49: 290–311.

Robson, C. (1993), *Real World Research*, Cambridge, Blackwell.

Rosenkopf, L. and M. Tushman (1988), 'The coevolution of community networks and technology: lessons from the flight simulation industry', *Industrial and Corporate Change*, 7: 311–46.

Salmi, O. and A. Toppinen (2007), 'Embedding science in politics: "Complex utilization" and industrial ecology as models of natural resource use', *Journal of Industrial Ecology*, **11**(3): 93–111.

Shapiro, R. (2000), 'The welcome tension of technology: the need for dialogue about agricultural biotechnology', *Business Leaders: Thought and Action CEO Series*, Issue 37, Center for the Study of American Business, Washington University.

Simon, H. (1962), 'The architecture of complexity: hierarchic systems', Proceedings of the American Philosophical Society, December, 467–82.

Simon, H. (1969), *The Sciences of the Artificial*, Cambridge, MA: MIT Press.

Spiegelman, J. (2003), 'Beyond the food web: connections to a deeper industrial ecology', *Journal of Industrial Ecology*, Winter 2003, **7**(1): 17–23.

Stone, G.D. (2004), 'Biotechnology and the political ecology of information in India', *Human Organization*, **63**(2): 127–40.

Stone, M. and C. Brush (1996), 'Planning in ambiguous contexts: the dilemma of meeting needs for commitment and demands for legitimacy', *Strategic Management Journal*, **17**: 633–52.

Strauss, L.R. (2004), 'Fiscalização da rotulagem será parcial', Folha de São Paulo, São Paulo, 6 April 2004.

WCED, World Commission on Environment and Development, (1987), 'Our Common Future', Oxford and New York: Oxford University Press.

Wilson, J., P. Tyedmers and R. Pelot (2007), 'Contrasting and comparing sustainable development indicator metrics', *Ecological Indicators*, **2**(7): 299–314.

Wolfenbarger, L. and P. Phifer (2000), 'The ecological risks and benefits of genetically engineered plants', *Science*, **290**: 2088–93.

Yin, R. (1984), *Case Study Research: Design and Methods*, Beverly Hills, CA: Sage Publishing.

8. Commodities, their life-cycle and industrial ecology

Timothy M. Koponen

INTRODUCTION

There are similarities between industrial ecology and commodity chain analysis. I attempt to outline the practices that commodity chain research has developed over the past years, and to introduce or refine them for the industrial ecologist looking to perform ecological mapping and policy making in industrial fields.

Foremost, commodity chains offer a link from the technical to the social that developed from the global scope embedded in World Systems theory and the developments in the social studies of science as to the social nature of scientific discovery. What they share with industrial ecology is the combination of technical and social analyses, in that both fields focus on the process of production as a sequential, spatial system.

Four commodity chain techniques allow an understanding of production: Network Exchanges, Technological Lock-in, Action at a Distance and Locally Constructed Values. I apply these, in truncated form, to the case of an undifferentiated good in two production constructs: Zimbabwean agriculture in the 1990s, and present day American agriculture. The ways in which an undifferentiated good, maize, is differentiated by technical and social access and values is developed by the parallel comparison of the two distinct chains of production.

WHAT INDUSTRIAL ECOLOGISTS AND COMMODITY CHAIN ANALYSTS HAVE IN COMMON

Within the broad field of industrial ecology (IE) is a mandate to accurately map and assess the relationships – spatial, contractual and social – among firms in an industrial field. Industrial Ecology is particularly interested in:

how the industrial system works, how it is regulated, and its interaction with the biosphere; then, on the basis of what we know about ecosystems, to determine how it could be restructured to make it compatible with the way natural ecosystems function. (Dayal et al. 1997: 1)

There is a direct connection in the mapping of the linkages between producers and their products, the sources and sinks of their manufacture, and the social circumstances that define legal regulation, social regulation and the values imposed by that regulation on the ecology of any industrial system. This mapping of social connections directly relates to the ways in which modern commodities are made through 'chains' of firms, governments and other actors in a social system that can have varying spans of space and regulatory regimes.[1]

Commodity chains are linked to the more technical/scientific aspects of industrial ecology. In their *Scientific American* article that inspired the field, Frosch and Gallopoulos state that it is the use and reuse of industrial ecologies that will allow for more efficient and sustainable manufacturing throughout the entire manufacturing system. This system is closed and therefore must be treated as an integrated whole: an ecology (1989). More recently, Ehrenfeld redefines the scope and goals of Industrial ecology. Academically, it combines 'the study of the flows of materials and energy in industrial and consumer activities, of the effects of these flows on the environment, and of the influences of economic, political, regulatory and social factors on the flow, use and transformation of resources' (Ehrenfeld 2007: 73). Ehrenfeld points out he is focused on using this ecological metaphor developed by Frosch and Gallopoulos to understand better the waste and potential environmental impact of industrial society – locally, and writ large.

My interest in industrial ecology comes through a research agenda that highlights 'commodity chains' (Gereffi et al. 1994). This holistic methodology and the theories that are associated with it were developed as tools to analyse global flows of goods and the distribution of profits and power in the world system (Hopkins and Wallerstein 1986). In this chapter, I hope to show how commodity chain analysis can effectively improve the scope and understanding of this ecology of industry by bringing *social ties* that determine production flows, energy usage, and reuse of commodities to the fore.

Recently, developments in commodity chain research have linked the global, sequential production of goods to a variety of moral issues. These have ranged in scope from the labour and environmental regimes through which commodities pass in a global system (Anner 2007; Bartley 2007) to the moral consequences of consumption of goods made in systems that violate consumers' notions of 'fair trade' (Dolan 2007; Hughes 2006). Large and long-term studies have attempted to view the globe as one economic system, and to use a holistic approach to look at the distribution of economic benefits (Mahutga 2006).

In general, industrial ecology and commodity chain analysis share a perspective in that they address problems in trying to evaluate the ecological footprint and comparative advantages of various industrial production systems. Traditional economics has not dealt with these issues of resources and externalities openly. From Adam Smith, Ricardo and Say, to Samuelson and even the 'ecological economists' of the present (Bergh and Janssen 2004; Mayumi and ebrary Inc. 2002), an integrated look at the system of production has not viewed resource use as an ecological problem: a problem of multiple inter-relationships. There are several reasons for this.

What Economists Can Learn From Ecologists

I argue that most of this problem arises from economic systems analyses that assume one univalent goal in economic life. While most of the time this is the maximization of profit, some others assume that there may be some other goal. Nevertheless, the analysis of economic action is done in such a way as to achieve one singular value that must be maximized.

Gary Becker, and the application of economics to social action in general, is the leading edge of this 'not economic, but at least maximizing' style of thinking that has misled us to look into the production process in ways that do not allow other and especially multiply-linked goals to be set by several parties in a productive system. The recent popular book, *Freakonomics*, is the most popular example of this type of thinking (Levitt and Dubner, 2005). Concurrent with this view is one that takes neither the good nor the market as the basis for analysis, but looks into the social institutions of production and their linkages as primary. Among historians, this is well represented by the work of Alfred Chandler et al. (1998). In sociology, seminal works are those of Powell (1991), Granovetter (1992), and Zucker (1987). A fairly complete introduction to this field would be Menard and Shirley's *Handbook of Institutional Economics* (2005). Within economics as a discipline, there are dissenting voices making the case for institutional economics and close attention to historical specificity (Hodgson 2001; 2004). However, the dominant mode of economic thinking focuses upon univalent motives and ahistorical calculations.

Interestingly, one of the roots that ties economists to this univalent economics is the use of 'advanced' mathematics in economic analyses. The general model of production systems has not changed in its assumptions since Leontief's multivariate linear algebras of the 1960s (Leontief 1966). This univalent economics includes the input-output models developed separately in western economics and in the Soviet Union to describe how various goods and products can be turned into a matrix of inputs and transformed into outputs. Through matrix algebra, and using sophisticated techniques involving ever more complex equations, models can then maximize the N-by-M matrices to find optimal solutions for *any particular value* one wishes to maximize across the entire system.

These systems are impressive, and the tracking of mathematicians with their computers from the mathematics departments of universities and into the economics departments has given a grand scientific look to economics. These sophisticated models link their predictive powers to the belief that mathematics is the queen of the sciences. The crucial problem is that these models give simplistic models of human economic activity a veneer of credibility, while the axioms and assumptions about *complex human behaviour* remain hidden under the overarching singular value that drives social science thinking when it comes to economic issues.

The problems that arise from this particular model-family are twofold. First, the models only maximize one value, and most or all measurement is done with one metric. The second is the social science presumption that generally corresponds to the first: that the diversity of humankind can be modelled within one set of values, and thus by these sophisticated systems of linear equations.

Two things go awry in this approach when attempting to adapt them for analysing production systems as ecologies of relationships. Economic models are no longer about human exchange, but about maximizing something, infinitely if possible, beyond any perceived need or cultural norm. The other effect is that everyone, from the peasant who sells his/her children for debt in an Asian or African village, and the CEO of the apparel or toy manufacturer living comfortably in Hamburg or New York, have the same motivation: to maximize whatever one single value we impose on the system.[2]

In such a system, it is no wonder that the economic combine has made, in its very image, a cold calculating machine, devoid of humanity and culture. Such a system is rational in its stated goals, like a Weberian Iron Cage (Weber [1903] 1987), but it is not rational in its implications, especially when looking at the single-minded drives that seek to unify the global economy, while the things that make the globe a set of different visions of humanity are swept away through misunderstanding.

How about more than one economic value system?

The use of univalence in economics works well, so long as there is no contest about the values actors use within various production and exchange systems. These models 'work' when all the preparation to get all significant actors to agree about values is done before the model is run. What is lacking is a sort of unearthed knowledge about relationships of production, and the built-in ability for economic actions to be valued in several ways by different agents in production chains. Then the issue becomes how do we track and account for these multiple values that lead folks into production chains. Do we need to commensurate them? How do we measure them?

We need an ecology of values that identifies what drives actors to participate along the production chain. Beside marginal economics is the critical twentieth-century tradition that has forsaken the monolithic approach to economic value, production and exchange. This approach has in its roots the economic anthropology of Marcel Mauss (1954), and follows a path through the understanding of commodities as having a life of their own, as changing social objects (Appadurai 1986b).

COMMODITY CHAINS: TYING TOGETHER THE PHYSICAL AND SOCIAL WORLDS OF THINGS

The purpose here is to look at economic exchange from an anthropological or sociological perspective. I attempt to use two variations on one case, that of agricultural production of maize. The variation is between the production system of industrial corn in the United States, and the production system of Zimbabwe's maize production system, circa 1990.[3] I wish to use the similarities and variation of the two systems to explain how we can aspire to a more contextual, accurate and multivalent form of economic analysis: a system of socio-technical-economic analysis best understood as 'commodity chain analysis'.[4]

Commodity chain analysis provides a mélange of alternative perspectives on economic production and exchange. It presents valuable tools in understanding the various ways human actors work creating stable and efficient (and unstable or repressive) production cycles and technical capabilities. The focus of the commodity chain is to make a 'biography of a thing' (Kopytoff 1988) that follows the commodity and tracks it through its stages of being a raw material or set of raw materials up to the point that it lands under the control of an end user.

More salient to the issues involved in industrial ecology, the commodity is also tracked into its demise as a valuable social object, through a set of sequential technical operations that transforms it from a set of raw materials and labour relations into a commodity, and eventually into a post consumption phase as 'waste/potential raw material'. This makes the industrial commodity chain, especially for manufactured goods a 'commodity cycle' instead of a commodity chain, as is shown in my work on the recycling industry in the United States (Koponen 2002).

The essential procedure of a socio-techno-economic view of goods in production/consumption is that it takes the 'thing' or 'good' itself to be self-evident. The job is to look at the presentation of the good on hand in various loci of production. The task is to explain the *changing* social values represented by the good. As this is done, we can assess the rationales of exchange along the production/consumption process as variables. These variables become the social and physical meaning of production. In social constructivist fashion, they determine the meaning of the thing in its local context (Berger and Luckmann 1966).

These different values, modes of production, technologies and exchanges expose the system of production as a value-imbued social system, with multiple values being used in various nodes. In short, by focusing on the goods produced rather than their commensurate value ('market' values, carbon footprint, or 'domestic content' as examples), one can see how the styles and meaning of production evolve or compare, without having to impose value assumptions on the process before one gets started. Instead of assuming the values and looking for the mix of goods, we look at the goods and search for the mix of values.

This allows a leap to an ecological understanding of local systems of values and production/consumption. The ecological view then must track the good as it translates among value systems. The task is to look, not at the market value, but at the meaning of the thing in its social situation. Malinowski did this with the Kula, for instance, in the trade of the Trobriand Islanders (1984).

One begins by understanding the various values that motivate trade and production in that particular niche. Then the task is to translate that set of values through space and time, between the maker, the trader, the shipper and the interested PhD candidate in New York who buys the object for money. Now, we thread the value that the Kula, as fetish for the educated, exhibits on the mantle of the student's home, into the web.

The Technical Aspects are Value-Laden Too . . .

The means by which many of these transformations happen are the technology of each particular system. When discussing values, we can look at ethnographic data to determine the motivation of actors to work or sell. Similarly, we can look at the design and patrons of particular technologies to understand whose advantage is embedded in them. To do so, I adopt the coupling of techno-science, culture and control inspired by Bruno Latour (1993, 1999), John Law (1999) and Michel Callon (1991, 1998a, 1998b). When wedded to economic anthropology, we combine both the sociology of value in exchanges to the command and control of long commodity chains (Hopkins and Wallerstein 1986, 1987; Polanyi 1971, [1957] 1985, Pearson 1957).

Overall, commodity chains (some refer to Actor Network Theories) allow a robust analysis, disassembling the component parts of a commodity's lifespan. Social analysis of these chains offers a rich text through which alternative models of economic action become necessary and apparent. These alternative models are often in direct opposition to market/greed driven models and to necessity-based Marxian models. In order to join the sociology of value and the anthropology of technology, I posit four components that help the serious industrial ecologist map out impacts and pathways that form social and technological relationships among humans, and that form industrial culture.

FOUR PRINCIPLES

My take on commodity chain practice looks at each social actor in a production process and maps him or her along the path of the product itself. One starts at the raw material or idea/conception phase, and ends with the good being consumed. Each actor applies technological expertise and skill to the material that is becoming the final good. Actors are not assumed to have overarching reasons (like profit motive, minimization of the carbon footprint or transcendent altruism for the human race) which motivate them to participate; instead, all available motivations are suspect for any individual actor.

Concretely, the reasons that a peasant farmer may be growing maize in communal lands in Rhodesia are not assumed to be the same as the motivation for traders in maize to buy and sell that product further down the line. The social system, distribution of surplus and the values that motivate are empirical questions and results of investigation – not axioms. Four features arising from applications of this approach distinguish commodity chain analysis from economic analysis. This set of principles also views technology as more than techniques for making things. Technology becomes part of a social system that confines certain interests and controls social actors. The technology adopted for a particular commodity chain dictates requirements of raw materials, energy inputs, skills and 'appropriate division of labour' that technologies carry with them. This effectively makes technology a pervasive basis for social control as well as the means by which values are imposed on materials, not an add-on aspect of economic analysis.

Each of the following principles relaxes various standard economic presuppositions in order to understand the social reality of production. They do so by making the reality comprehended more complex, and well . . . human. The four aspects of commodity chain analysis that distinguishes it from economic/market analysis are: Network Relations for Exchanges, Technological Lock-in, Action at a Distance and an emphasis on Locally Constructed Values.

1. Networks, Not Markets

We look at the progression of goods from one supplier of raw or semi-finished products to another. In this way we can look at the manufacturer of glass involved in the production of automobile windshields, then to the producer of the windshields from such glass, and then to the assembler of the automobiles themselves, as a *directed network* of value-creating producers. These are not markets or even intermediate markets, but are linked chains of technologically bound entities that need to use prolonged cooperation and mediation to sustain the industrial production chain.

Using the simpler exchange-based models, allows us to peer into contract relationships in modern economies without categorically trying to explain them as failures or variations of market exchanges. By focusing on the networks of exchange, before denoting motivation for exchange, we can treat contracts, or barters, and so on *prima facie* as (social, legal and economic) relations in-and-for themselves.

2. Technologies that Control Behaviour and Determine Relationships

Technologies play a key role in this scheme, and not only as they allow certain raw materials to be used, or as technology allows for greater productivity. The crucial role in forming economic activity along a particular commodity chain is to tie technologies and technical knowledge together in the production stream. This 'locks-in' technical aspects of production, and is the most salient way to force production in general to travel along a specific technological pathway. Petroleum-based vehicles, with all their ancillary gas stations, roadways, tire manufacturers, parts suppliers, and so on, form a salient example of how technologies beget families of related and dependent technologies in order to support them. Infrastructure, habit or education then locks in favoured technology. Monopolies form along the path, or alternative technological paths for production are discounted because of huge costs in 'unlocking' the production of goods from a settled pathway of skills and technologies. As wealth accumulates to those in possession of a monopoly/oligopoly, the political and social 'inevitability' of these technological arrangements become more 'real'. They are made real by the investment of time and labour. They are constructed to be real.

In general, this principle can be seen in high relief in 'technological battles' such as seen in the collective decision to adopt 'competing' technologies. Whether it is BetaMax versus VHS tape, or BlueRay versus HD-DVD, or formats for HDTV, all allow technical control of resources and social interactions that exist in the culture in which the exchanges are embedded.

3. Acting through Technological Controls: Objectifying Another's Place in the System

These networks of quasi-firms or commodity chains couple with the technical lock-in of actions along the chain. This leads to two phenomena. One is that technologies themselves, through machines, standards and established divisions of labour, allow the intent of the technician or designer to act through non-human actors. One can design a production process and control what happens in a faraway place through technical means. Standards for steel, tomatoes, maize, coal or other commodities extend the influence of an actor from the place the standards are established. By expressing the 'good' goods and the 'bad' goods, standards often act to imply technologies, practices and capital use in such a way to control the technologies of production. A positive example of this, from the standpoint of sustainability, is the technological dictates of 'organic' standards in food production, or the 'green building standards', like LEED, that reduce choices of inputs and techniques for building high performance buildings. This makes it possible for actors along the commodity chain to determine actions both upstream and downstream from their actions by using standards as tools to act at a distance (Bingen and Busch 2006). Forces outside a particular market exchange along a commodity chain can determine value and technical requirements without being part of demand or supply. The automobile manufacturer determines the quality and kind of brake pads that the brake manufacturer buys from the brake pad manufacturer. Yet, the automobile manufacturer is not 'party to the exchange' (Johnson 2001).

4. 'Scientific' (Universal) versus 'Moral' (Local) Values

This networked global system also has within it values of each local production manager and values of cultural, environmental and profit motives that exist within local actors themselves. These local values that drive production are not the same along any particular commodity chain. This forms not only an industrial ecology of manufacturing and production, but also reveals a chain of value negotiations that allow an interface among actors along a particular production chain. In modern child indenture, the parents receive money in an exchange for a child; their desperation has turned into a child-for-money market. The coal (or movies) that the child's labour is changed into is purchased for use to generate electricity, or the movie fulfils a bourgeois prurient interest: there has been a change of what that child has meant in that transformation and the parents would hardly recognize the final result as their daughter.

Combined, these principles let us see how the economy works in practice. They move significantly beyond market analyses to reveal a more varied political economy in action.

WHEN SOCIAL SCIENCE HITS TECHNICAL CONTROL: THE CASE OF MAIZE

In order to briefly give the reader some sense of how this works, I show two cases of the 'same' commodity: *Zea Mays* (corn or maize, depending from which part of the English speaking world one hails). I will show how to follow the maize/corn in production, and highlight one of these aspects of commodity chain analysis in each node of the two commodity chains. My intent is to show how such a rethinking of economics as a political and moral economy leads us to better understand the reasons for and construction of commodities, but also enables one to explain the ecology of production and the ecological impact of the entire system.

Methodologically, I want to show that commodity chain analysis is a robust set of constructs that are methodologically agnostic. My Zimbabwean case is constructed from a year of participant observation and interviews, historical analysis of documents (primary and secondary sources) and statistical trends in capital formation and market access/production statistics. This research was conducted in Zimbabwe during 1992, and entails the evolution of the commodity chain of Zimbabwean/Rhodesian maize from 1890 to the then present-day (1992) (Koponen 1998).

Michael Pollan's *Omnivore's Dilemma* provides much of the details for the modern case of the United States (2007). Pollan uses much the same techniques, historical research and industry statistics, along with participant observation and interview to describe the modern American food system. I borrow heavily from the first section (pp. 15–122) which is his version of a chain or network description of the system. It is important to note that this multi-methodological approach is the most effective.

While the statistics and third-party accounts (histories) are effective to lay out the basic shape and construction of a commodity chain, the values and embedded relationships within and along the chain are revealed best through investigations that contain subjective understandings of the process by various actors. This allows analyses to marry the motivations of various actors and their values within a specific place, to the overarching structure and distribution of technical and capital advantage throughout the system *in toto*. I am also using the comparison of modern United States' maize production and historical Zimbabwean maize to highlight the ability of commodity chains to comparative and evolutionary studies of production.

Commodity chain analyses, in varying forms, can focus on the global scale of modern production (Gereffi et al. 1994) as well as form the basis for historical comparison (the seminal work for this focus is Hopkins and Wallerstein 1986, 1987).

The most important point in the comparison below is that in both cases the kind of maize is the same, an undifferentiated good that morphologically, and most would say nutritionally, are 'the same'. In order to reveal the method of analysis here, the contrast between things that are the 'same' should bring into high relief how these comparative analyses can be of value to the industrial ecologist.

The purpose of Zimbabwe's maize commodity chain looks the 'same' as the American corn commodity chain under market conditions. Internationally, each commodity has the same value (monetarily) in the market for #2 maize, and it is thought to be interchangeable on the plates of those who eat raw maize (especially Zimbabwean workers). However, each separate social system for the production of this sameness is radically different, even to the origin for *zea mays* on each continent.

Maize was introduced in Zimbabwe probably at the end of the sixteenth-century by Portuguese traders emanating from the Indian Ocean shores of Mozambique. It was adopted more rapidly than colonialism, spreading to African kingdoms in the central African plateau before guns, paper money or democratic elections. This land was occupied at the time by the 'Mashona' people, who had established a gold and ivory trade and a central state.

American corn, on the other hand, originated from the selective breeding practices of literally hundreds of generations of Native American peoples. Its ability to convert sunlight into animal-ready calories and to adapt to most agriculture friendly eco-systems in North America is a testament to the plant and the aggressive management practices of Amerindian agri-*culture*. Both Iberian based invaders of South America and Northern European invaders of the North found well adapted species that became the lifeblood of the North American conquest (continued by the newly made Afro-European tribe: the Americans).

Jumping through literally centuries of development on each respective continent, Zimbabwean maize and American maize collided in the making of the international market for goods in the late nineteenth and throughout the twentieth centuries. By 1990, these two things-that-are-same shared an interest in hybridization, international markets and technical advice from government-funded extension services. They were sold as one, in accordance with the market price of maize. At first locally, and then tied together in a sameness that only the market can create: by type (White Dent), grade (#2, #3), and water and waste content. Undifferentiable in the market, we find that each system of production, and the meaning of maize in each place, does differentiate by the commodity chain, and its *qualities* of production.

The outline of my exposition is to take one principle of commodity chain analysis, and show an example of its method at one particular production node. I have simplified the commodity chain into four basic production areas: Seeds, Reproduction (growing out), Processing and Consumption. I do this for brevity, and to show how through the comparisons made available with this method, we can see ecological differentiation in what is economically the same.

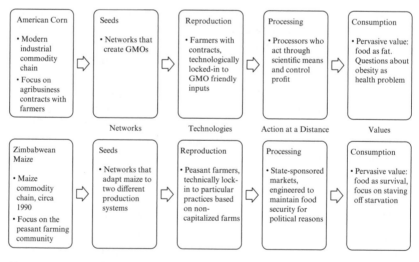

Note:	Each step should be subject to all commodity chain components in a thorough analysis.

*Figure 8.1	Simplified commodity chain comparison of American corn and Zimbabwean maize, circa 1990*

NETWORKS

As a network, the most notable difference is the length of the American commodity chain. There are two dominant commodity chains in Zimbabwe, those run by African farmers on 'communal' lands, and those run by Europeanized farmers on 'commercial' lands. In America,[5] most corn grown for the food industry is high in its petroleum footprint, all along the chains, and is subject to different monopoly or oligopoly actors who dominate terms of trade and prices. What differentiates the production chains of the commercial Zimbabwean farmer from the United States' farmer is emphatically NOT the market value of the crop. The networks of production for each 'undifferentiated good' are radically distinct, including the racial characteristics of the participants, although they share some interesting features.

Maize, in order to be a market crop, must go through several necessary steps that in the modern manufacture of maize make it a commercial crop. With the advent of the twentieth century, commercial maize was being differentiated from 'local' or 'peasant' maize by the process of hybridization. The first common path for all maize was through the 'seed' stage. Here, commercial farmers used the discovery of Dr Beal (the first to hybrid corn) that corn could use the genetic diversity of North and South American breeds and adapt itself to virtually every possible farm plot in the world (an amazing feat . . . no pun intended). In Rhodesia (the colonial nation that preceded Zimbabwe on the world stage), this meant that the breeding of desert-ready maize – that peasant Africans could grow with reliable yields, and light loads of fertilizer and pesticides – was now possible. For Rhodesian commercial farmers, there were the irrigable, high-yielding varieties of maize, dependent eventually, on petroleum based fertilizer and Euro-American methods of post Second World War agriculture.

The paradigm of the Rhodesian maize system has evolved into the dominant American food system (organics aside). The United States, from Earl Butz's stay at the United States Department of Agriculture to the present, has focused on the industrialization of the 'food system'. The USDA's Extension Service became the sellers of a modernistic dream: high inputs and high yields, with price supports accessed by the highest yielding farms to the tune of millions of dollars . . . if only the farm were large enough to sustain this industrial farm enterprise. While Zimbabwe's blacks were producing in the petroleum-free, no-till agriculture of the past, the same crop was being grown in the petroleum-soaked food system across the Atlantic.

Each land-grant university provided free technology and technical help to construct the American industrial maize mold. While in Zimbabwe, the 'English' farmers of the commercial highlands[6] were linked to international markets and the emerging petroleum economy, the Americans were embedded within that market and the growing ocean of oil that would keep big agri-business afloat.

From finely tuned hybrid seeds, the growers of maize itself formed another common node in the industrial maize chain. Again, the common point of reference, 'maize producer', masks network connections and political support.

Growers in Zimbabwe and the United States are encouraged by their representatives (i.e. their elected governments) to produce maize. Maize growers in Zimbabwe however, are primarily food growers. They grow maize to feed people in African industry and working African farms. American growers do not in general produce food for people.[7] They produce food for two other guts: one set fattening the meat industry (most often beef, then chicken, then pork), and the other set made of chemical digestion of the 'food industry' (as raw material that will become the chemicals from which processed food alchemy is practiced).

It is at this point where African maize and American maize fall so far apart. The same type of maize used by Americans to feed cattle is the preferred type of maize for direct consumption by Africans. White Dent maize is the leading component of the ubiquitous #2 maize of international trade. In America, it means feedlots, coupled with antibiotics and cows. In Zimbabwe, it means millers and direct consumption of maize as *sadza* course maize, similar to grits) by human beings, working in factories or making tobacco and more maize. This leads us to another essential difference in the making of this undifferentiated good: who makes the money from this chain? And who controls the production system?

TECHNOLOGICAL 'LOCK-IN'

Technologies that regulate behaviour and make investment decisions for us are crucial to keep commodity chains stable. Just as action-at-a-distance through political controls determines the distribution of profits and overall shape of commodity chains, so too do the structural aspects of ordering the commodity chain through technology (Arthur 1986; Callon 1991, 1992).

Not only does title give advantage in capitalization to the White Zimbabwean farmers of the 1990s, it also allows the farmers to become what I like to call 'chained to the chain'. That extra capital land title affords the farmer access to world markets, and title allows the government to give the Rhodesian/Zimbabwean farmers cheap credit. It also locks him or her into a complex arrangement of fertilizers and pesticides, and labour practices that are dictated by the crops that 'grow well' under very specific conditions, and grow poorly under the natural conditions of the plateau. The dependency of farmers on irrigation and labour arranged in plantation fashion begins to form the mold into which all other farming practices must fit. This is true in the irrigated highlands of Zimbabwe and in the African owned desert lands below where the needs of the farmer for drought-resistance are beginning to yield to profits from small-scale fertilizer crops for the sellers of fertilizers. However, nowhere is this more true than in the United States.

The United States corn commodity chain is dominated by food processors and by seed companies. Together, they lock in the inputs and the rotations (or lack of these) to keep the US producing more corn than any other country. About 85 per cent of the United States crop is currently grown from genetically modified seed. The main thrust is that the seeds of these new types of maize resist either common area pests or diseases. In addition, some newer generation seeds create high proportions of certain proteins, enhancing the crop for use in animal feed.

The kind of seed grown is tied very closely to the specific kind of herbicides and pesticides that may be used. Some GMO seeds demand more fertilizer than do non-GMO types. What happens with the United States' GMO corn is that the entire chain becomes one technology. The linkages between the seed and the market become firm, and the losses of more extensive and expensive petroleum inputs are offset by fewer losses to specific pests, or higher prices due to specialized characteristics in the corn itself (as in the case of protein enhanced corn).

This technical lock-in is an extreme case of the general idea that technology is also an agent that can force producers into serving the interests of firms or 'nodes' in a commodity chain far away from their place. This action at a distance is not mandated simply by government pricing and policy. The technological lock-in occurs in-depth, locking in the need for farmers to use petroleum to make corn, and locking the prices of the farmers' production to the proprietary markets of the GMO creator. Where we see this tendency in the United States, those farmers tie themselves to the new GMO commodity chains; we see the opposite in many other countries. In Zimbabwe, GMO maize is not used due to the robust seed research conducted through the government and the adaptation of certain hybrids to the microenvironments of the Plateau.

American farmers become 'stuck' in terms of their inputs and markets to committing more land to GMOs, which then pay for themselves through increases of yield, but often do not make the farmer better off than before. The profits instead fall to the seed producers and food processors. Whereas in Zimbabwe, the social group that benefited from the commodity chain in the early 1990s is the commercial farmers; mostly white ex-Rhodesians with large farms, access to capital and international markets, and some cash crop as well as maize in their mix of farming. These farmers have the technical knowledge and capital that allows them to set prices for maize in such a way as to recoup their costs and to keep African Farmers out of the same markets. By bundling actions through credit and titles, seed development and input credits keep African farmers locked into a labour-intensive, yet input and capital poor production process on their farms. Because of this, African farmers are more exposed to environmental risks, and have less net income than do the commercial farmers. This keeps Africans in a subsistence mode of production, with their small surpluses adding to a surplus of maize produced by commercial farmers. The parity board in Zimbabwe, the Grain Marketing Board (GMB), then sets a price that allows the commercial farmer to recoup their costs, and places the burden of high levels of unpaid labour at the feet of the peasant. This effec-tively means that profits from corn are located in the commercial sector; while a credit starved communal (African) sector is left to supply subsist-ence needs of the workforce, cutting wage levels in farm work as well.

ACTION AT A DISTANCE

From the seed stage, maize is grown and then processed on both continents. More important is the way dominant consumers and producers hold sway over the pricing and subsidies for each crop in its respective agriculture. This use of seed science to create classes of farmers is done, at a distance, in Zimbabwe and the United States. The goals of this differentiation are themselves different in each place.

In both countries, the processing of maize into food maintains and feeds the agricultural and industrial workforce. As the locally hybridized seed is planted in each distinct agricultural system, it is shaped into the purpose for which it is grown.

In the Zimbabwean example, maize from African farms in communal lands and from Highland commercial farms ends up primarily as ground cornmeal. This cornmeal is subsidized by the Government (in 1992), and used to keep the workforce fed, while granting oligopic power to millers over the processing.

The biggest proponents of this government control over the millers and the placement of grain are farm organizations in the commercial sector. These predominantly white-owned farms have an interest, stemming from Rhodesian colonial days, to keep workers well fed and as placated as possible, while living in the pallor of third world wages. The crop 'maize' is not seen as a commodity as it is in the United States. In Zimbabwe, maize is fuel for growing tobacco. Maize-fed farm workers grow and harvest the tobacco that then fuels the entire agricultural export economy in this Southern African nation.

In the United States, the way that corn is grown is not dictated by the needs of employers for a cheap fuel for labour. On the contrary, the hegemonic forces behind US corn production are stockholders and managers of increasingly complex and private food processing companies. Cargill and Archer Daniels Midland (ADM) are the two dominant players in this corn driven food chain. The food processors do not care for cheap food in the same way that Zimbabwean producers of tobacco (along with industrial employers) do. Their concern is for corn that can be used as an industrial input in the making of raw organic material to transform into *expensive* foods (relative to inputs) sold in processed food supermarkets across the United States (with their water misters for fresh corn, and rows of aisles for the cornucopia of maize based 'food'). This leads to different kinds of control that extend government policies governing maize research and maize pricing.

Action-at-a-distance is one of the key concepts in understanding how commodity chains are organized, and it is in the growing-out and post-harvest phase of maize on each continent that the methods of long-distance control become so very evident.

In Zimbabwe, white farmers and government bureaucrats use regulation, research and market control over millers to stabilize the workforce and create foreign exchange essential to the payment of Zimbabwe's 'development debt'. Two distinct seeds, one for irrigated farms, and one for desert conditions, are grown by White farmers and Black farmers respectively. The seeds for white farmers are more productive and more difficult to farm without expensive farm equipment. Zimbabwean farmers in the predominantly white commercial sector have title to their land, and that land title is used to capitalize the farm. In the communal area, black farmers are not given title to their land. They therefore have no capitalization through mortgages, and thus are stuck growing drought resistant seed maize that has lower yields, and keeps these farms poorer.

In the United States, farmers are given a choice between genetically modified maize seeds (GMO corn), which increase yields through recombinant DNA manipulations. These seeds possess certain qualities (such as a corn that is 'super-sweet' or one with high vitamin C content). Food processors want that extra sugar to sell in their fresh food bins, and they want the vitamin C to extract and add to other synthetic foods like Tang – an *ersatz* orange juice made of a variety of processed organic material and petroleum products. The way each of these actors, the tobacco farmers of the 1990s and the ADMs of today, control the chain is through positioning themselves in certain places on the long commodity chain where they have an unregulated or favoured monopoly control over what is in the profitable sectors of the economy and what is not.

While a self-governed settler colony, Rhodesia used the government explicitly for maintaining farmer profits and African acquiescence. In the modern Zimbabwean economy, the needs of the farmers were tied to the government's need for foreign exchange (up to the taking of commercial lands in the late 1990s and 2000s). African ministers needed to worry about the credit worthiness of their nation, and in order to avoid hyperinflation and economic collapse, farmers were able to control the terms of regulation and research to their advantage . . . acting on millers and others that were separate from them economically, but controlled through policymaking and rules.

Americans are coerced into GMO manufacture by the same technique: hegemony over regulation and research agendas, but for a different clientele, and to a different end. The USDA and land-grant university research agendas are set by lobbyists and foundations funded by agri-business, to the detriment of American farmers. By disallowing the labelling of substances as 'GMO-free', no markets decisions of consumers can allow for niche markets of non-GMO foods. By demanding foodstuffs with the qualities and especially the quantity delivered by GMOs, farmers in alternative farming practices can be excluded from markets, and thus the flow of food-as-organic-stock-commodity-chain maintains itself over the cheaper food-as-food-chain. Agents, regulation and control over research priorities are crucial to the very different chains.

VALUES

The maize or corn eventually ends up in the bellies of folks for whom it was grown. The paths to these separate African and American bellies are tied to the commodity chain that makes the food. It is here that we can tease out values used in the consumption of food in each place. It is easy to see the undifferentiated qualities of each type of maize. Both the maize grown for the American market and the African market is White Dent maize. However, as the production and processing of the glut of GMO and hybrid corn is processed in America, there is a goal to cheapen the cost of the corn as an input of the processing industry.

Cheap maize in Zimbabwe is not the goal of the commercial farmers. They, distinct from their counterparts in the United States, are gaming to get markets and price arrangements, technologies and policymaking actors, to offer a higher price for their food in order to encourage a steady supply of the staple food for their workforce. The dominance of one actor over another changes the playing field as well as the meaning of 'fair price' in each context.

Changed too is the meaning of the food itself. American maize will become the corn syrup of Coca-Cola and other soft drinks. It will become the basic components for the *Twinkie* and American concoctions of various chemicals and organic components that are eaten with such relish by American youth. In America, one *meaning* of corn is that it threatens the health of the nation through the consumption of excess corn-based calories, and in Africa, the meaning focuses on the fact that the paucity of maize instead creates starvation, malnutrition and government instability.

In general, the values imposed upon various goods by their production chain actors have to do with the values exchanged along the chain as a whole. The comparison here is that the changes of values represented by each commodity chain of the same good end in such radically different meaning for the local consumer of *sadza*, the traditional side dish of the Zimbabwean Plateau, and the *Twinkie*, the representative fat and sugar soaked food of the nutrient-short American diet.

Within the issue of values, it is important to understand why there are 'fat-free' foods made from corn in the United States, and why there is imported food-aid (of the same type of *zea mays*) in Zimbabwe to stop starvation. Nevertheless, the importance of the multiple values in production does not begin at the end of the chain . . . in the market. Rather, value comes from the way peasant farmers in Zimbabwe have been placed on their land. The history of colonialism that backs European farmers on both non-European continents, and the various ways that American farming has grown to be sharecropping for the food processing industry are all part and parcel of the pockets of values that are difficult to commensurate in the maize market.

The problem that is ignored is that in every exchange, the understanding and meanings of the good is exchanged along with the good (Appadurai 1986a; Kopytoff 1988). Thus, we resolve in monetary terms the relative value of something that is incommensurable. The Maize means no starvation to a poor Zimbabwean, and cheaper Coca-Cola to a fat American. But it also means staving off bankruptcy for an American farmer, and healthy shareholder profits for the food processor, as well as the industrial workday of the 'agricultural' worker who is packaging the corn flakes.

It is in looking at the differentials of value in these commodity chains that we see the biggest value of using commodity chain analysis in industrial ecology. In part, to understand how the productive systems fit together, we need to see how these values are exchanged, and who controls the value of the chain overall.

DISCUSSION

Commodity chain analysis, with its focus on *combining* technical abilities and constraints and social/ethical values should bring some value to industrial ecology by introducing the ways that the relationships between the things of production and the social systems of production can lead to a sustainable productive economy and ecology. Commodity chains are, however, not prescriptive. Their value is in part that the baseline description of a particular commodity chain links various actors together in an industrial ecology, and allows for the recognition that technical controls determine production requirements in far-flung nodes of the chain. This is something that I think will resonate with industrial ecologists in general.

The ability to analyse the technical (perhaps more 'supply chain' driven) aspects of the commodities open research avenues into various ways of doing the 'same thing'. Contrasts between different maize chains, as above, indicate that one can use this technique to look at the oil or carbon footprint of an industrial commodity, and compare it to some modification of production that would suggest superior ways to manufacture and distribute goods. The completeness of the chain (from raw material to consumed product, or perhaps through product recycling) allows an understanding of how various parts form the whole, and permits a focus on 'dysfunctional' nodes or controls, as well as an account of the process overall.

One caveat, embedded in the method above, is that each commodity chain comes with its institutional local values and knowledge, and that those form as difficult barriers to overcome, as do technical barriers and constraints. So, while one could find a low carbon farming or manufacturing example in one place, its translation to another place is not merely a task of reproducing the physical and technical practices, but also of fitting the proposed changes into an existing cultural milieu.

In this comparative case, I have focused on two very different production systems in order to maximize the social and technical differentiation of an undifferentiated good. That was polemical. It could be just as useful for analyses to focus on the variety of systems in one particular economy, as Michael Pollan does in his ongoing critique of the American food system. These cases, comparative, yet bounded by national or regional boundaries (perhaps NAFTA or EU bordered), can illuminate the possibilities of an industrial ecology without the large value translations that distinguish the maize case above.

Deeper than the technical aspects of one method or another, commodity chains, with a focus on the distribution of power and profits, have a moral similarity to industrial ecology. The shared moral claim is simply threefold: that technical solutions to problems are not necessarily the best solutions, that local values have *value* in the sustainability of production processes, and that social and ecological sustainability are important to evaluate, in addition to, and balanced with univalent values imposed through economic analysis in the narrow sense.

What is needed, and what I am attempting to explain here, is a more humanistic and less imposed economic analysis. In order to understand the ecology of industry, we must look for and find the internal logic of each member of the niche. In order to look for things that the economists have explained away to make their analyses simple enough to model as linear ecology, we need to point out the non-linearity of the system, in order to understand its grace and the distribution of power along the way. The need to integrate human relations, technical requirements and the ability of actors to act at distances will help establish models that reflect the realities of modern production.

NOTES

1. Regulation here is to be taken broadly, as the State regulation of enterprises, the large scale regulation of exchanges, or the social regulation of work patterns and common values.
2. Of course, the way around this is to impose various multiple constraints. I will explain that that just compounds the problem of universal values by multiplying the number of them, not their different weights in various social milieu.
3. The choice of cases is constrained by my work in Zimbabwe, and as an informed observer of the American food system.
4. Methodological note: My point in taking these two cases is to apply this 'quick and dirty' analysis of two goods that are 'economically the same'. The corn in Iowa from last year's crop, and the corn from Zimbabwe in 1990, are morphologically the same (even if the American crop is 80 per cent GMO's, they look and supposedly taste the same). I then use this sameness of the resulting crop to contrast the respective production systems. Varying time, place and culture . . . to produce the same.
5. On certain aspects of extensive, petroleum rich farming, I can make a common cause between the farmers of the United States, and those living in Canada. When I refer to 'American' agriculture, I exclude the practices of peasant farmers in Mexico, but include all Anglo-colonial farmers connected to the world markets.
6. Wetter, more fertile areas taken by fiat by colonial governments . . . another characteristic shared by the two sets of euro-descended farmers.
7. At least most of American farmers do not grow food for people. About 80 per cent plus of corn in America is fed to the machine described below.

REFERENCES

Anner, M. (2007), 'Forging new labor activism in global commodity chains in Latin America', *International Labor and Working-Class History*, **72**(Fall): 18–41.

Appadurai, Arjun (1986a), 'Introduction: commodities and the politics of value', pp. 3–63 in *The Social life of Things: Commodities in Cultural Perspective*, edited by A. Appadurai. Cambridge: Cambridge University Press.

Appadurai, Arjun (1986b), *The Social Life of Things: Commodities in Cultural Perspective*, Cambridge: Cambridge University Press.

Arthur, W.B. (1986), 'Competing technologies, increasing returns and technological lock-in by historical events', *Economic Journal*, **99**: 116–31.

Bartley, T. (2007), 'Institutional emergence in an era of globalization: the rise of transnational private regulation of labor and environmental conditions', *American Journal of Sociology*, **113**(2): 297–351.

Berger, Peter L. and Thomas Luckmann (1966), *The Social Construction of Reality: A Treatise in the Sociology of Knowledge*, Garden City, NY: Anchor Books.

Bergh, Jeroen C.J.M. van den and Marco Janssen (2004), *Economics of Industrial Ecology: Materials, Structural Change, and Spatial Scales*, Cambridge, MA: MIT Press.

Bingen, J. and L. Busch (eds) (2006), *Agricultural Standards: The Shape of the Global Food and Fiber System*, The international library of environmental, agricultural and food ethics, Dordrecht: Springer.

Callon, Michel (1991), 'Techno-economic networks and irreversability', in John Law (ed.), *A Sociology of Monsters: Essays on Power, Technology and Domination*, New York and London: Routledge and Kegan Paul, pp. 132–61.

Callon, Michel (1992), 'Variety and irreversability in technique conception and adoption', in Dominique Foray and Christopher Freeman (eds), *Technology and the Wealth of Nations: The Dynamics of Constructed Advantage*, New York: St. Martin's Press, pp. 232–68.

Callon, Michel (1998a), 'Introduction: the embeddedness of economic markets in economics', in M. Callon (ed.), *The Laws of the Markets*, Oxford, UK: Blackwell Publishers, pp. 58–68.

Callon, Michel (1998b), *The Laws of the Markets*, Oxford and Malden, MA: Blackwell Publishers/The Sociological Review.

Chandler, A., J.P. Hagström, et al. (eds) (1998), *The Dynamic Firm: The Role of Technology, Strategy, Organization and Regions*, Oxford and New York: Oxford University Press.

Dayal B.S., J.F. MacGregor and S. Erkman (1997), 'Industrial ecology: an historical view', *Journal of Cleaner Production*, **5**(1–2): 1–10.

Dolan, C.S. (2007), 'Market affections: moral encounters with Kenyan fairtrade flowers', **72**(2) (June): 239–61.

Ehrenfeld, J.R. (2007), 'Would industrial ecology exist without sustainability in the background?', *Journal of Industrial Ecology*, **11**(1): 73–84.

Frosch, R.A. and N.E. Gallopoulos (1989), 'Strategies for Manufacturing', *Scientific American*, **189**(3): 152

Gereffi, G. and M. Korzeniewicz (eds) (1994), *Commodity Chains and Global Capitalism*, Westport, CT: Greenwood Press.

Gereffi, Gary, Miguel Korzeniewicz and Roberto P. Korzeniewicz (1994), 'Introduction: global commodity chains', in Gary Gereffi and Miguel

Korzeniewicz (eds), *Commodity Chains and Global Capitalism*, Westport, CT: Greenwood Press, pp. 1–14.

Granovetter, M. (1992), 'Economic institutions as social constructions: a framework for analysis', *Acta Sociologica*, **35**(1): 3–11.

Hodgson, G.M. (2001), *How Economics Forgot History: The Problem of Historical Specificity in Social Science*, London and New York: Routledge.

Hodgson, G.M. (2004), *The Evolution of Institutional Economics: Agency, Structure, and Darwinism in American Institutionalism*, London and New York: Routledge.

Hopkins, T.K. and I.M. Wallerstein (1986), 'Commodity chains in the world-economy prior to 1800', in *Review (Fernand Braudel Center)*, vol. 10, pp. 157–70.

Hopkins, T.K. and I.M. Wallerstein (1987), 'Capitalism and the incorporation of new zones into the world-economy', *Review*, **10**: 763–80.

Hughes, A. (2006), 'Learning to trade ethically, knowledgeable capitalism, retailers and contested commodity chains', *Geoforum*, **37**(6): 1008–20.

Koponen, T.M. (2002), 'Commodities in action: Measuring embeddedness and imposing values', *The Sociological Review*, **50**(4): 543–69.

Kopytoff, Igor (1988), 'The social biography of things', in A. Appardurai (ed.), *The Social Life of Things*, Cambridge: Cambridge University Press, pp. 64–94.

Latour, Bruno (1993), *We Have Never Been Modern*, Trans by C. Porter, Cambridge, MA: Harvard University Press.

Latour, Bruno (1999), 'On recalling ANT', in J. Law and J. Hassard (eds), *Actor Network Theory and After*, Sociological Review Monograph Series, Boston, MA: Blackwell Publishers, pp. 15–25.

Law, John (1999), 'After ANT: Complexity, naming and topology', in J. Law and J. Hassard (eds), *Actor Network Theory and After*, Sociological Review Monograph Series, Boston, MA: Blackwell Publishers.

Leontief, Wassily W. (1966), *Input–Output Economics*, New York: Oxford University Press.

Levitt, S.D. and S.J. Dubner (2005), *Freakonomics: A Rogue Economist Explores the Hidden Side of Everything*, New York: William Morrow.

Mahutga, M.C. (2006), 'The persistence of structural inequality? A network analysis of international trade, 1965–2000', *Social Forces*, **84**(4): 1863–89.

Malinowski, B. (1984), *Argonauts of the Western Pacific: An Account of Native Enterprise and Adventure in the Archipelagoes of Melanesian New Guinea*, Prospect Heights, Ill: Waveland Press.

Mauss, Marcel (1954), *The Gift: Forms and Functions of Exchange in Primitive Societies*. Trans by I. Cunnison, Glencoe: The Free Press.

Mayumi, K and ebrary Inc. (2002), 'The origins of ecological economics: the bioeconomics of Georgescu-Roegen', in *Routledge Research in Environmental Economics; 1*, London and New York: Routledge, pp. xii, 161.

Menard, C. and M.M. Shirley (eds) (2005), *Handbook of New Institutional Economics*, Dordrecht: Springer.

Pearson, H.W. (1957), 'The economy has no surplus', in C.M.A. Karl Polanyi and Harry W. Pearson (eds), *Trade and Markets in the Ancient Empires*, Glencoe, IL: The Free Press, pp. 320–41.

Polanyi, K. (1971), *Trade and Market in the Early Empires; Economies in History and Theory*, Chicago: Henry Regnery Co.

Polanyi, K. [1957] 1985, 'The economy as instituted process', in M. Granovetter and R. Swedberg (eds), *The Sociology of Economic Life*, Boulder, CO: Westview Press.
Pollan, M. (2007), *The Omnivore's Dilemma: A Natural History of Four Meals*, New York: Penguin.
Powell, W.W. (1991), 'Expanding the scope of institutional analysis', in W.W. Powell and P.J. DiMaggio (eds), *The New Institutionalism in Organizational Analysis*, Chicago: University of Chicago Press, pp. 183–203.
Weber, M. [1903] (1987), *Economy and Society*, edited by G. Roth and C. Wittich, Berkeley: University of California Press.
Zucker, L. (1987), 'Institutional theories of organization', *Annual Review of Sociology*, **13**: 443–64.

9. Sustainable supply chain management

Stefan Seuring, Romy Morana and Yan Liu

INTRODUCTION

The management of product and supply chains has become a dominant paradigm in business practice. Materials, information and financial resources flow in supply chains around the globe connecting distant parts of the world economy. Products often move through several continents before reaching their point of consumption. While these products bring economic value and benefit to the customer, there is an economic and social burden created during the different stages of production

Several approaches have emerged in the scientific literature that address the economic and social considerations of the product lifecycle. These include industrial ecology, integrated chain management, lifecycle management and sustainable supply chain management. While these concepts are closely interrelated, each of these approaches has its major strength. This chapter aims to provide insights into the historical development and current status of sustainable supply chain management. First, sustainable supply chain management is put into the context of related concepts. Integrated chain management as a particular line of development in the German speaking area will be discussed here as it serves as a suitable example of political embeddedness. Second, a framework summarizing the current status of sustainable supply chain management is presented, based on a literature review of the field. Third, an examination of the organic cotton supply chain of Otto, a German mail-order company, is used to illustrate sustainable supply chain management. Finally, the topics of this chapter will be discussed in the context of social embeddedness.

INTERORGANIZATIONAL APPROACHES TO SUSTAINABILITY

A range of concepts for interorganizational sustainability management have been developed. The most prominent of these can be seen in integrated chain management. In our review of the field, which is based on German doctoral and habilitation theses (Seuring and Müller 2007), we provide an analysis of the research literature. This indicates how political initiatives drove the concept of integrated chain management in Germany. The works of the Enquete-Commission of the German Bundestag (national parliament), and the Dutch National Environmental Policy Plan (NEPP) of the Netherlands (1989) were both key policy milestones (Wolters et al. 1997).

One line taken up in integrated chain management is life-cycle assessment (ISO 14040, 2006). Life-cycle assessment was developed in the 1970s and 1980s due to the increased need for a means of total system analysis. The environmental impacts of systems were of particular interest (Hunt and Franklin 1996; Oberbacher et al. 1996). Later on, this developed towards the study of life-cycle management (Hunkeler et al. 2003; Remmen et al. 2007). The tool was developed by researchers mainly as a way of describing systems and analysing all of the related environmental impacts. In many cases, the starting points for tool development were practical cases, such as the question of which liquid packaging system would be preferable from an environmental point of view (Oberbacher et al. 1996). Later, existing approaches were brought together in an effort to unify them; in these efforts the Society of Environmental Toxicology and Chemistry (SETAC), and the reports commissioned under its purview, have been highly influential.

The historical background of supply chain management is a mixture of practical and academic developments. The term, as it is commonly known, was first used by Oliver and Webber (1982). It is sometimes seen as an extension of previous logistical thought, where cooperation and partnerships among companies become much more important (Cooper et al. 1997; Mentzer et al. 2001). Interestingly, the integration of environmental and sustainability issues emerged around the same time that the conceptual developments of supply chain management were becoming mainstream.

The core concepts of supply chain management are often stated in terms of the focal companies. Two criteria determine focal companies (Handfield and Nichols 1999: 2):

- The focal company organizes the supply chain, as it designs and develops products and services, selects suppliers and decides which distribution channels to use; and

Table 9.1   Comparing industrial ecology to related concepts

Concept	Historical Back-ground	Distinctive Feature	Actor Network	Material Flows/ System Boundaries	Time Frame
Integrated Chain Manage-ment	Emerged driven by political initiatives	Stakeholder integration	Companies involved in and stake-holders affected by material flows	Material flows within their societal and legal boundaries	Societal and Legal Systems (decades)
Life-cycle Manage-ment	Managerial application of LCA	Product design as most important decision phase	All production stages involved in designing and producing products and services	Material flows that are related to a product life-cycle	Product Life-cycle (months to years)
Supply Chain Manage-ment	Mix of consulting, practical and academic develop-ments	Managerial activities needed within the actor network	All production stages directly involved in fulfilling customer demands	Operational material and information flows to satisfy customer needs	Supply Chain Develop-ment (months to years); Delivery Cycle (hours to weeks)

Source: Based on Seuring (2004: 314)

- The focal company provides access to the end customer or is visible to the end customer through its brands.

Seuring (2004) compared the different approaches – integrated chain management, life-cycle management and supply chain management – and pointed towards their differences and interrelations which are summarized in Table 9.1. The approaches have considerable overlap. As one example, life-cycle analysis (LCA)-type methods and results are often referenced in the sustainable supply chain management literature. They usually provide the environmental data needed to identify strategies for product-based green supply (Bowen et al. 2001) or the subsequently discussed 'supply chain management for sustainable products' (Seuring and Müller 2008b). In this respect, LCA is used to create strategic and operational improvements to the supply chain. This also holds for the intersection of life-cycle management and integrated chain management.

POLITICAL EMBEDDEDNESS: THE EMERGENCE OF INTEGRATED CHAIN MANAGEMENT

As highlighted in Table 9.1 integrated chain management carries the notion of stakeholder integration as a core element of related managerial activities. This is emphasized in the definition given by the Enquete-Commission (1994: 549) of the German Bundestag: 'Integrated Chain Management' (Stoffstrommanagement) is the management of material flows by stakeholders [to be] the goal-orientated, responsible, integrated and efficient manipulation of material flows. Set targets derive from the ecological and economic realm, under consideration of social aspects. Goals are set on the level of the individual firm, within the supply chain of actors, or on the public policy level. A second major distinctive feature is the inclusion of the policy level as a means of political embeddedness.

We pointed this out based on a comprehensive literature review of related books (mainly PhD and habilitation theses) and special issues of journals published in German from 1990 to 2005 (Seuring and Müller 2007). While the work of the Enquete-Commission was published between 1993 and 1995, related research emerged beginning in 1994. In subsequent years, research gained momentum; now there is an almost constant output of related publications.

The sequence of political action followed by academic research has been called 'political inception' (Seuring and Müller 2007) since the concept of integrated chain management developed against this background. Three major schools of thought can be distinguished this way. First, the 'regional industrial network school' has a clear connection to industrial ecology. Indeed, the development of integrated chain management – with its wide definition and relation to life-cycle management and industrial ecology – has absorbed much of the related developments in Germany (Isenmann 2003). The application of integrated chain management was also clearly promoted by the state (Baas and Boons 2006). In particular, the funding of related research projects has encouraged many related PhD and habilitation theses.

In this respect, there might be an element of spatial and temporal embeddedness, which in this case is centered on the German speaking area where integrated chain management (Stoffstrommanagement) has been adopted as generic term. It is rather hard to explain this phenomenon. Many of the early researchers had a background in life-cycle assessment. Initiated by the environmental political work of the German Bundestag, they moved on to integrated chain management. Other researchers 'added' the environmental or sustainability dimension to their existing research in the areas of, for example, production or logistics management. As supply chain management developed at the same time, there was no initial influence. This leads to the second point addressed in this chapter.

THE CURRENT STATUS OF RESEARCH

Almost obviously, both sustainability management and supply chain management form the background against which the field developed. This has been influenced by all of the different approaches already mentioned. In particular, the link to life-cycle assessment and management is clearly established, and the close link to integrated chain management has already been mentioned (Seuring 2004). Research reviews which aim at identifying and summarizing major lines of research in these areas have been limited. Based on a Delphi-Study we conducted in 2006 with international experts (Seuring and Müller 2008a), we identified four major topics:

1. Pressures and incentives for sustainable supply chain management.
2. Identifying and measuring impacts on sustainable supply chain management.
3. Supplier management (particularly addressing issues at the supplier–buyer interface).
4. Supply chain management (issues across all companies involved in the supply chain).

Taking this one step further, we present a conceptual framework here in three parts. The first part offers the background, while parts two and three outline distinct strategies:

1. Triggers for sustainable supply chain management;
2. Supplier management for risks and performance (a more reactive strategy); and
3. Supply chain management for sustainable products (a more proactive strategy).

The framework is developed against (1) a literature review (Seuring and Müller 2008b) as well as our own empirical research (see some of the references given in this text). To illustrate the strategies, the case of the organic cotton textile chain at Otto, based in Hamburg, Germany is used.

TRIGGERS FOR SUSTAINABLE SUPPLY CHAIN MANAGEMENT

As an initial step, the triggers for the field and related action are identified (see Figure 9.1). This can be broken down into pressures and incentives as well as barriers and enablers which will be outlined in full before detailed aspects are subsequently discussed.

The starting points are external pressure and incentives set by different groups, which are based on stakeholder theory (Freeman 1984). This can be comprehended as structural embeddedness as it is a consequence of the interrelation of actors. While stakeholders form the widest possible description, three groups are of particular relevance. On one hand, customers are of great importance; operating the supply chain is only justified if the products and services are finally 'accepted' by customers. On the other hand, all modes of governance which can be enacted by local municipalities, national governments, or multinational organizations are of great relevance. This forms part of the political process and embeddedness that has already been discussed in the context of integrated chain management. Third, non-governmental organizations (NGOs) are of great importance; their campaigns can reveal companies' misconduct and drive related change (Roberts 2003; Argenti 2004). All three groups can elicit pressure, but can also be a source of incentive for companies. These incentives are straightforward if customers prefer to buy products that are superior from a sustainability point of view. For example, organic food products have seen strong market growth in recent years, such that today demand outstrips supply (Hamm and Gronefeld 2004).

An early paper pointing towards this normative level is by New (1997). He 'advocates an expanded scope for supply chain management research which accounts for the social function and the political and economic implications of supply chain developments'. Others call for focal firms to monitor new developments and trends in the environmental and social realm, and observe changes in pressure exerted by external stakeholders (Koplin et al. 2007). Roberts (2003) emphasizes that action from NGOs which holds focal companies responsible for environmental and social problems at earlier stages of their supply chain can lead to a reputation loss for the focal company.

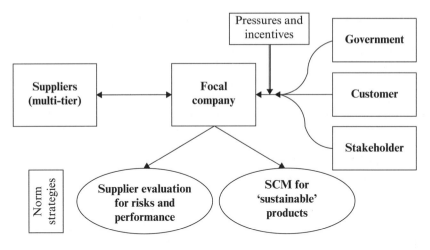

Source: Seuring and Müller (2008b)

Figure 9.1 Triggers for sustainable supply chain management

When the focal company is pressured, it usually passes this pressure on to suppliers. Here, one distinctive feature of sustainable supply chain management emerges. Looking at the overall supply chain (or life cycle) of the product, the focal company quite often has to take a longer part of the supply chain into account than needed for 'pure' economic reasons (see for example, Handfield et al. 1997; Kogg 2003; Seuring 2004a; Preuss 2005). Monitoring n-tier suppliers and demanding certain product attributes, which form part of typical criteria for organic products, would require that the focal company maintain close contact with suppliers. This is one of the clear links to the other concepts of inter-organizational sustainability mentioned already. Once again, barriers and supporting factors can support or hinder the cooperation with suppliers (see for example, Lamming and Hampson 1996; Carter and Dresner 2001). This holds true for both gaining information on the environmental and social performance at the individual production stages, and for improving the performance of n-tier suppliers.

Based on these factors, a range of strategies can be identified for how companies deal with such issues. For our purposes, two different strategies summarize the key distinctions. The two strategies are labelled as 'supplier management for risk and performance' and 'supply chain management for sustainable products'. While these strategies may seem to oppose each other at first, they are not mutually exclusive. This relationship between them is outlined below.

Environmental and, increasingly, social management systems play an important role for monitoring suppliers (Koplin et al. 2007). They serve as a tool for companies that aim to reduce related risks (see for example, Min and Galle 2001; Cousins et al. 2004; Rao and Holt 2005). First, companies may face increasing fears of boycotts if environmental or social problems in their supply chain are reported. This might also lead to a loss in reputation and therefore business opportunities. There is a second aspect of customer demands. Focal companies increasingly ask their suppliers to perform according to guidelines set by environmental and social standards contained in management systems for environmental (for example, ISO 14001) and social (for example, SA 8000) issues.

Management systems play an important role in this regard and impose at least minimum standards on suppliers. They mainly centre on environmental management, through systems such as ISO 14001 (Corbett and Kirsch 2001; Chen 2005). Socially related approaches, such as SA 8000 (Social Accountability 8000, see Graafland 2002; Courville 2003) or codes of conduct (Davies and Crane 2003) are now increasingly being implemented. Even so, social aspects in the discussion are much less developed than environmental ones.

While the previous discussion looks more at the factors that are external to the supply chain, there is also the internal perspective. To achieve set goals, it is important to know which factors act as barriers and which acts as supports. Understanding this demands active management and accordingly leads firms to incur higher costs (Seuring 2001). The resulting coordination effort and complexity of the supply chain are also critical issues in understanding internal feasibility (Seuring et al. 2004).

Higher costs are driven by the additional need for monitoring suppliers (Koplin et al. 2007) although joint efforts of all supply chain partners can help to control costs (see, for example, Seuring 2001; Goldbach et al. 2004). Two strategies for implementing related action are outlined next.

SUPPLIER MANAGEMENT FOR RISKS AND PERFORMANCE

Increased global development and competition have pushed many industries to operate on a much more global level. With increased outsourcing, the number of companies involved in a typical supply chain has greatly increased. As a response to the above-mentioned pressures and incentives, a number of companies have introduced supplier evaluation schemes which integrate environmental and social criteria (Trowbridge 2001; Beske et al. 2008). This explains the need for supplier management as identified in our Delphi-study (Seuring and Müller 2008a). This closely interlinks with current research on supply chain risk management (for example, Tang 2006). Economic risks mainly relate to the disruption of the supply chain which might be caused by disasters (Kleindorfer and Saad 2005).

Related measures are supplier self-evaluation schemes (Trowbridge 2001) where suppliers have to declare how they deal with environmental and social issues, often through the use of environmental and social standards. The goal is to improve overall supply chain performance whereas frequently, the focus has been on the relationship between environmental factors and economic performance (Green et al. 1998; King and Lenox 2001; Rao and Holt 2005; Zhu et al. 2005; Hervani et al. 2005; Vachon and Klassen 2006). In many cases, a positive correlation between these two dimensions is observed, although this might be a bit too simplistic. Currently, long term studies are not yet available, and the social dimension has been rarely addressed, leaving the relationship between the environmental and social dimension rather unclear. In a first evaluation of expert opinions, Seuring and Müller (2008a) point towards a win–win situation among these two dimensions. Thereby, a second distinctive feature of sustainable supply chains can be identified. Performance tradeoffs exist among the 'usual' operations objectives such as quality, speed, dependability, flexibility and cost (White 1998). Increasingly, these performance measures have to include environmental and social objectives (also Kleindorfer et al. 2005), taking the trade-off debate among different performance objectives to a broader level. The resulting trade-offs are not so much within the economic dimension any more, but rather, among the three dimensions of sustainability.

Further insights are offered on how these dimensions relate to each other. Newton and Harte (1997) have criticized much of the related environmental management publications for pointing out only the 'easy wins', and feel that these should not be mistaken as long term results. A more critical assessment is needed, such as the work of Wagner and Schaltegger (2004) who point out that at first, easy wins might be gained, but following these wins, additional effort and investment will be needed to improve environmental performance.

In line with operations management thought, where the concept of order qualifiers is used, environmental and social performance can be seen as the prerequisite for determining suitable suppliers. Order qualifiers allow staying in the market (Hill 2000). From the focal company's perspective, this implies that environmental and social criteria for supplier evaluation guarantee that the supplier acts according to set standards (Laming and Hampson 1996; Min and Galle 2001; Cousins et al. 2004). The complementing order winners are typically based on economic performance, i.e. the third dimension of sustainability.

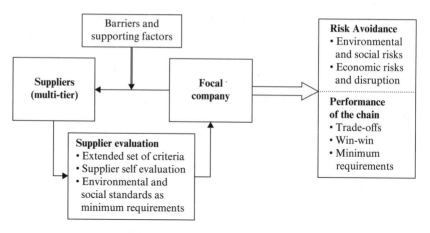

Source: Seuring and Müller (2008b)

Figure 9.2   Supplier management for risk and performance

Standards both for management systems (i.e. ISO 14000, SA 8000, codes of conducts) which suppliers have to implement upon focal company/ customer request, or specific products (for example, coffee: Blowfield 2003; Courville 2003) play a central role in supplier selection. In one recently published example, Mamic (2005), collected data from 22 multi-national companies and 74 of their suppliers to gain insight in to how such standards (i.e. codes of conduct) are implemented in the footwear, apparel and retail industry. One step of greening the supply process (Bowen et al. 2001), is requiring such comprehensive supplier audits (Min and Galle 2001; Graafland 2002; Rao 2005; Mamic 2005; Zhu et al. 2005; Koplin et al. 2007). These might even trigger further partnering where joint process improvements are conducted (Handfield et al. 1997). Such process and product improvements form a central part of the more pro-active strategy.

SUPPLY CHAIN MANAGEMENT FOR SUSTAINABLE PRODUCTS

The second strategy is called 'supply chain management for sustainable products'. 'Sustainable product' is the term used to describe all kinds of products that have or aim at an improved environmental and social quality while of course fulfilling economic requirements. The ultimate aim is to satisfy customers and gain a competitive advantage in the market (Meyer and Hohmann 2000; Goldbach et al. 2004; Kovács 2004; Rao and Holt 2005).

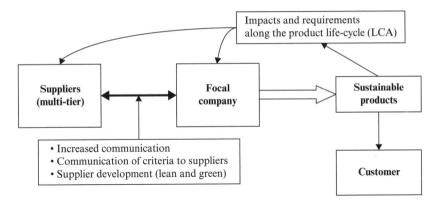

Figure 9.3   Supply chain management for 'sustainable' products

For specifying product-related requirements, life-cycle assessment is the method to be relied on most often (Lamming and Hampson 1996; Pesonen 2001), clearly confirming the affinity to life-cycle management (Seuring 2004b). Again, the focal company is in charge of addressing this and requesting it from suppliers, but joint initiatives would help to implement this product-based green supply (Bowen et al. 2001; also Handfield et al. 1997).

In line with this, cooperation with suppliers increases in importance. This does not just extend to first-tier suppliers who are often the focus of conventional supply chain management. In supply chain management for 'sustainable' products, ensuring the quality of the product and the performance of the operational processes might be as much of an issue as building partnerships for new product introductions, so the complete supply chain from raw materials to final customers has to be integrated (Meyer and Hohmann 2000; Seuring 2001; Kogg 2003; Goldbach et al. 2003; Seuring 2004a; Preuss 2005). Criteria for improvement do not only relate to the final products. Environmental criteria of a product, for example, being free of contaminants, can be tested. However, this is not possible for the environmentally harmful processing technologies applied, nor for social impacts such as child labour. This links the issue not only back to the use of environmental and social standards, but also extends beyond this.

As several cases report, supplier changes were required before focal companies were even able to offer 'sustainable' products to their customers. Several authors report that textile and apparel producers/retailers had to make sure they had an organic cotton supplier before they were able to offer such products (Meyer and Hohmann 2001; Kogg 2003; Goldbach et al. 2003). This triggered considerable investments at partner locations to develop this supply structure and to help improve their production facilities and processes, and was required before they could meet the set environmental standards for the production processes as well as the final product. What is implied is that suppliers are trained and their overall performance is improved even though the focal company usually buys less than 10 per cent of the total output (Walton et al. 1998; Holt 2004; Preuss 2005). King and Lenox (2001) characterize these as 'lean and green' suppliers (also Simpson and Power 2005). This demands much 'deeper' information flows along the supply chain where suppliers have to gain detailed insights into the subsequent stages of the life-cycle and supply chain as a way to comprehend why such improvements are required (Pesonen 2001). DeBakker and Nijhof (2002) offer a framework on how internal (that is, inside the focal company) as well as external (that is, along the supply chain) capabilities have to be developed to reach such goals. Overall, there seems to be a need for cooperation among a wider range of companies along the supply chain than is usually discussed in conventional supply chain management literature.

COMPLEMENTING ISSUES AMONG THE TWO STRATEGIES

As already mentioned in the previous sections, the two strategies are not mutually exclusive. While they emerge as two different, distinguishable approaches, their relation to each other might be called ambivalent, thereby opposing, but also supporting each other at the same time. In the following example of organic cotton production, some of the companies aimed for environmentally improved and socially sound products. When they started to offer them in their product line, they experienced the need to monitor the environmental and social performance of the suppliers (Handfield et al. 2005). Conversely, companies starting with supplier development initiatives for risk minimization (Min and Galle 2001; Cousins et al. 2004; Mamic 2005) might then see opportunities for further win-win-win situations, and look at product performance as well.

The Example of Organic Cotton

Otto GmbH & Co. KG is the largest mail-order business in the world. Otto was founded in 1949 in Hamburg, Germany. While the headquarters remain there to date, the Otto group presently consists of 123 companies in 19 countries, employing more than 51 000 people worldwide with a turnover of €15.2 billion in 2006. Exceeded only by Amazon.com, Otto runs the second-largest online shop in the world. The products sold by Otto cover a wide range, including clothes, electronics, and household appliances (for more information see www.ottogroup.com). The case is part of our longer term research. The initial case study research process is summarized in Seuring et al. (2005). An update was conducted in 2006 in a wider research project on supply chain integration of organic cotton chains. Findings are partly incorporated here.

Conventional cotton carries tremendous environmental problems, such as the use of a vast amount of water. This has led, for example, to the drying up of the Aral Sea. Further, large amounts of pesticides are used in cotton farming (see for example, Meyer and Hohmann 2000; Seuring 2003).

The main trigger for Otto to introduce organic cotton apparel was the internal decision to strengthen the company's sustainability activities. There was a feeling that customers might demand such products in the long run, but also the awareness that this is not the case at the moment (see the related analysis in Meyer and Hohmann 2000). In this particular case, pressures and incentives have been limited, but barriers and supporting factors played a central role. The relation to suppliers had to be redeveloped, so that higher cost for the related production processes could be overcome (Goldbach 2002; Goldbach 2003; Seuring et al. 2004). One major effort for Otto was that they had to set up a new supply chain and engage in this supply chain. Conventional cotton is readily available and apparel products can be purchased from manufacturers. Even though they are frequently produced according to design defined by focal companies, the focal companies are not involved in organizing the supply chain. This increased need for cooperation is now seen as one major factor distinguishing traditional supply chains from sustainable supply chain management (Seuring and Müller 2008b).

When starting to organize the organic cotton chain, Otto had to realize that they also need measures for risk mitigation. These included measures towards environmentally and socially sound production at the suppliers' level and measures to reduce additional costs (Seuring 2003; Goldbach et al. 2004). Supplier selection was based on such criteria so that environmental and social standards could be met as well as meeting economic goals. Therefore, Otto introduced a supplier evaluation scheme where suppliers were qualified as 'approved eco-suppliers'. Such a scheme, which covers a wider range of products, reduces the need to evaluate the supplier for each order while allowing issues of sustainability to be generally addressed at the supplier level (see for example, Koplin et al. 2007).

Such measures should enable focal companies to jointly reach set sustainability goals by identifying win-win situations among the partners in the supply chain (Seuring 2001). This triggers the need to change the relationship from one that is dominated by power to one that uses trust as an alternative coordination mechanism (Goldbach 2003). As Goldbach (2003) shows, such measures can be analysed building on positive principal–agent theory.

The end goal of Otto was the introduction of organic cotton apparel products. The criteria were initially environmental, based on life-cycle assessment concepts (Bunke et al. 2002), but were extended to include social issues (Goldbach et al. 2004). While Otto was driving the development of such criteria, they had to be communicated along all stages of the supply chain, even reaching cotton farmers in Turkey and India. The wider scheme of 'approved eco-suppliers' also extends to other product lines, but for the initial stage of the organic cotton project, Otto even engaged consultants and sent them to their suppliers to help them improve their production processes. Such measures are beneficial to the suppliers as they, of course, use the improved processes for all of their production, while they supply less than 10 per cent of their total output to Otto.

As already mentioned, trust has to be built among supply chain partners before they engage in such measures. Such measures can be explained using theories of structuration (as done in Goldbach 2003).

SOME REFLECTIONS ON EMBEDDEDNESS

In the first chapter of this book, five dimensions of embeddedness are identified:

- Cognitive embeddedness (bounded rationality, systems thinking, characteristics of change agents);
- Structural embeddedness;
- Spatial and temporal embeddedness;
- Cultural embeddedness (collective cognitive maps, development of consumer preferences, legitimacy, sustainability);
- Political embeddedness (state promotion of industrial ecology, market power, stakeholders).

We briefly discuss these different forms of embeddedness and how they relate to the previous parts of the chapter.

Cognitive Embeddedness

As pointed out in the first part of this chapter, supply chain management and industrial ecology are closely linked. The particular perspective of supply chain management can add to the wide spectrum of industrial ecology thought. The focus on the theoretical as well as the empirical side of supply chain management has drawn on concepts from operations management. The number of research papers that have taken a wider theoretical perspective, taking, for example, new institutional economics as their basis, is limited even for conventional supply chain management. This suggests cognitive embeddedness which holds not only for practitioners inside companies, but also for researchers. Both might wear 'glasses' which prohibit them from seeing things differently. As Kuhn (1970) pointed out, such shifts only occur when there is a need for them.

This extends into the brief case presented. In particular, when starting the organic cotton initiative, Otto had to realize that a much wider system needed to be taken into account. One fact mentioned already was that organic cotton cannot be purchased on spot markets as is the case for conventional cotton. Our more recent research on a total of five organic cotton supply chains (Seuring, under review) provided much evidence on how focal companies act not only as change agents, but might even be required to keep the supply chain running. One example is Remei, a Swiss based company (see Meyer and Hohmann 2000, for an initial description), which by now describes itself as the 'spider in the web'.

Structural Embeddedness

This then extends into structural embeddedness which can be found both inside the individual company as well as among the different companies involved in a supply chain. The Otto example pointed out how both Otto and their suppliers had to change their behaviour. In many industries, buyer-supplier relationships are rather of a short term nature, especially when relatively simple and easy-to-imitate technologies are used. This is the case in the textile and apparel industry. Hence, this was a major shift to build supply chain partnerships across all members of the supply chain. Changing the (inter)-organizational structures and coordination mechanisms (from mainly power-based to more trust-based) (see Goldbach 2003) requires time and a significant input of resources in line with the social aspects of partnership building (Hagedoorn 2006). Such arguments return to the institutional logic on how such concepts are taken up and are implemented inside companies (Heiskanen 2002).

Spatial and Temporal Embeddedness

Further, the Otto example also relates to spatial (and temporal) embeddedness. For a start, all processes of the supply chain were operated in

Turkey. This provided a sound basis as all steps from cotton farming to final apparel production can be found in Turkey. This was observed in a similar manner for other cases of organic cotton supply chains (Seuring, under review). A high spatial focus where the different companies in the supply chain would know each other is seen as beneficial towards a more sound cooperation.

Cultural Embeddedness

Such opportunistic behaviour can be linked further to cultural embeddedness. In many countries, one would rather cheat on a foreigner than on a neighbour one has to live with for a long time. Such problems of opportunistic behaviour were observed in several cases. One strong example was that farmers would sell the organic cotton as conventional if the price for conventional exceeded that agreed with the focal company. This has happened despite the fact that such contracts usually run for several years and guarantee farmers that they would sell the organic cotton at a price well above the long term average for conventional cotton.

Political Embeddedness

The political embeddedness has been discussed here by the example of how integrated chain management came about. Regarding sustainable supply chain management, the political impacts might be limited as even supra-national organizations cannot really regulate global supply chains. Still, organizational buying by public institutions, that is, green public procurement, can trigger and thereby contribute to related developments. In this respect, governments and public administrations would exert market power without the need for an active promotion or even funding of related initiatives (Preuss 2007).

CONCLUSION

This chapter offers a brief introduction into sustainable supply chain management. Two key issues are established. On the one hand, industrial ecology has been put into the context of other concepts of inter-organizational sustainability management. The distinguishing feature is the geographical and regional approach which emphasizes the need to jointly manage related material flows. Such material flows are usually triggered by information flows, as highlighted in the definition of supply chain management given above. The field is triggered by demands from customers, governments and NGOs for the integration of sustainability issues into supply chain management. Research findings are framed in terms of two strategies which are labelled as 'supplier management for risk and performance' and 'supply chain management for sustainable products'. These strategies are also illustrated through a case study of an organic cotton supply chain. Finally, this allows to illustrate some of the different modes of embeddedness discussed in this book.

REFERENCES

Argenti, P.A. (2004), 'Collaborating with activists: how Starbucks works with NGOs', *California Management Review*, **47**(1): 91–116.
Baas, L. and F. Boons (2006), 'Industrial symbiosis in a social science perspective', in D.R. Lombardi and P. Laybourn (eds), *Industrial Symbiosis in Action*, Report on the Third International Symbiosis Research Symposium, Birmingham, England, August 5–6, pp. 77–80.
Beske, P., J. Koplin and S. Seuring (2008), 'The use of environmental and social standards by German first-tier suppliers of the Volkswagen AG', *Corporate Social Responsibility & Environmental Management*, **15**(2): 63–75.
Blowfield, M. (2003), 'Ethical supply chains in the cocoa, coffee and tea industries', *Greener Management International*, (43): 15–24.
Bowen, F.E., P.D. Cousins, R.C. Lamming and A.R. Faruk (2001), 'The role of supply management capabilities in green supply', *Production and Operations Management*, **10**(2): 174–89.
Bunke, D., M. Naschke, I. Jäger, M. Goldbach and U. Schneidewind (2002), 'Product-related environmental information systems for the optimisation of products and product-ranges', *Melliand Textilberichte, International Textile Reports*, (3), E38–E40.
Carter, C.R. and M. Dresner (2001), 'Purchasing's role in environmental management: Cross-functional development of grounded theory', *The Journal of Supply Chain Management*, **37**(3): 12–27.
Chen, C.-C. (2005), 'Incorporating green purchasing into the frame of ISO 14000', *Journal of Cleaner Production*, **13**(9): 927–33.
Cooper, M.C., D.M. Lambert and J.D. Pagh (1997), 'Supply chain management: More than a new name for Logistics', *The International Journal of Logistics Management*, **8**(1): 1–14.
Corbett, C.J. and D.A. Kirsch (2001), 'International diffusion of ISO 14000 certification', *Production and Operations Management*, **10**(3): 327–42.
Courville, S. (2003), 'Use of indicators to compare supply chains in the coffee industry', *Greener Management International*, (43): 93–105.
Cousins, P.D., R.C. Lamming and F. Bowen (2004), 'The role of risk in environment-related supplier initiatives', *International Journal of Operations & Production Management*, **24**(6): 554–65.
Davies, I.A. and A. Crane (2003), 'Ethical decision making in fair trade companies', *Journal of Business Ethics*, **45**(1–2): 79–92.
de Bakker, F. and A. Nijhof (2002), 'Responsible chain management: a capability assessment framework', *Business Strategy and the Environment*, **11**(1): 63–75.

Enquete-Kommission of the German Bundestag 'Schutz des Menschen und der Umwelt' (ed.) (1994), *Die Industriegesellschaft gestalten: Perspektiven für einen nachhaltigen Umgang mit Stoff- und Materialströmen* (Forming the Industrial Society: Perspectives for Sustainable Management of Substance Chains), Bonn: Economica.

Freeman, R.E. (1984), *Strategic Management: A Stakeholder Approach*, Boston: Pitman.

Goldbach, M. (2002), 'Organisation settings in supply chain costing', in S. Seuring and M. Goldbach (eds), *Cost Management in Supply Chains*, Heidelberg: Physica, pp. 89–108.

Goldbach, M. (2003), 'Coordinating interaction in supply chains – The example of greening textile chains', in S. Seuring, M. Müller, M. Goldbach and U. Schneidewind (eds), *Strategy and Organization in Supply Chains*, Heidelberg: Physica, pp. 47–64.

Goldbach, M., S. Seuring and S. Back (2003), 'Coordinating sustainable cotton chains for the mass market – the case of the German mail order business OTTO', *Greener Management International*, (43): 65–78.

Graafland, J.J. (2002), 'Sourcing ethics in the textile sector: the case of C&A', *Business Ethics: A European Review*, 11(3): 282–94.

Green, K., B. Morten and S. New (1998), 'Green purchasing and supply policies: do they improve companies' environmental performance?', *Supply Chain Management: An International Journal*, 3(2): 89–95.

Hagedoorn, J. (2006), 'Understanding the cross-level embeddedness of interfirm partnership formation', *Academy of Management Review*, 31(3): 670–80.

Hamm, U. and F. Gronefeld (2004), 'The European market for organic food: revised and updated analysis, organic marketing initiatives and rural development', vol. 5, School of Management and Business, University of Wales Aberystwyth, UK.

Handfield, R.B. and E.L. Nichols (1999), *Introduction to Supply Chain Management*, Upper Saddle River: Prentice-Hall.

Handfield, R., R. Sroufe and S. Walton (2005), 'Integrating environmental management and supply chain strategies', *Business Strategy and the Environment*, 14(1): 1–19.

Handfield, R.B., S.V. Walton, L.K. Seegers and S.A. Melnyk (1997), '"Green" value chain practices in the furniture industry', *Journal of Operations Management*, 15(4): 293–315.

Heiskanen, E. (2002), 'The institutional logic of life cycle thinking', *Journal of Cleaner Production*, 10(5): 427–37.

Hervani, A.A., M.M. Helms and J. Sarkis (2005), 'Performance measurement for green supply chain management', *Benchmarking: An International Journal*, 12(4): 330–53.

Hill, T. (2000), *Manufacturing Strategy, Text and Cases*, 3rd edn, Boston: McGraw-Hill.

Hunt, R.G. and W.E. Franklin (1996), 'LCA – how it came about – personal reflections on the origin and the development of LCA in the USA', *International Journal of Life Cycle Assessment*, 1(1): 4–7.

Hunkeler, D., G. Rebitzer and A. Inaba (2003), *Life Cycle Management*, Society of Environmental Toxicology and Chemistry (SETAC).

Isenmann R. (2003), 'Further efforts to clarify industrial ecology's hidden philosophy of nature', *Journal of Industrial Ecology*, 6(3/4): 27–48.

ISO 14040 (2006), *Life-Cycle Assessment*, Geneva.

King, A.A. and M.J. Lenox (2001), 'Lean and green? An empirical examination of the relationship between lean production and environmental performance', *Production and Operations Management*, **10**(3): 244–56.

Kleindorder, P.R. and G.H. Saad (2005), 'Managing disruption risks in supply chains', *Production and Operations Management*, **14**(1): 53–68.

Kleindorfer, P.R., K. Singhal and L.N. Van Wassenhove (2005), 'Sustainable operations management', *Production and Operations Management*, **14**(4): 482–92.

Kogg, B. (2003), 'Greening a cotton-textile supply chain: a case study of the transition towards organic production without a powerful focal company', *Greener Management International*, (43): 53–64.

Koplin, J., S. Seuring and M. Mesterharm (2007), 'Incorporating sustainability into supply policies and supply processes in the automotive industry – the case of Volkswagen', *Journal of Cleaner Production*, **15**(11–12): 1053–62.

Kovács, G. (2004), 'Framing a demand network for sustainability', *Progress in Industrial Ecology: An International Journal*, **1**(4): 397–410.

Kuhn, T.S. (1970), *The Structure of Scientific Revolutions*, Chicago: University of Chicago Press.

Lamming, R.C. and J.P. Hampson (1996), 'The environment as a supply chain management issue', *British Journal of Management*, **7** (Special Issue): 45–62.

Mamic, I. (2005), 'Managing global supply chain: the sports footwear, apparel and retail sectors', *Journal of Business Ethics*, **59**(1): 81–100.

Mentzer, J.T., W. DeWitt, J.S. Keebler, S. Min, N.W. Nix, C.D. Smith and Z.G. Zacharia (2001), 'Defining supply chain management', *Journal of Business Logistics*, **22**(2): 1–26.

Meyer, A. and P. Hohmann (2000), 'Other thoughts; other results? – Remei's bioRe organic cotton on its way to the mass market', *Greener Management International*, (31): 59–70.

Min, H. and W.P. Galle (2001), 'Green purchasing practices of US firms', *International Journal of Operations & Production Management*, **21**(9): 1222–38.

New, S.J. (1997), 'The scope of supply chain management research', *Supply Chain Management: An International Journal*, **2**(1): 15–22.

Newton, T. and G. Harte (1997), 'Green business: Technicist kitsch?', *Journal of Management Studies*, **34**(1): 75–98.

Oberbacher, B., H. Nikodem and W. Klöppfer (1996), 'LCA – how it came about: an early systems analysis of packaging for liquids – which would be called an LCA today', *International Journal of Life Cycle Assessment*, **1**(2): 62–5.

Oliver, R. and M. Webber (1982), 'Supply-chain management: logistics catches up with strategy', Reprint in M. Christopher (ed.), *Logistics. The Strategic Issues*, London: Chapman & Hall, pp. 63–75.

Pesonen, H.-L. (2001), 'Environmental management of value chains', *Greener Management International*, (33): 45–58.

Preuss, L. (2005), 'Rhetoric and reality of corporate greening: A view from the supply chain management function', *Business Strategy and the Environment*, **14**(2): 123–39.

Preuss, L. (2007), 'Buying into our future: sustainability initiatives in local government procurement', *Business Strategy and the Environment*, **16**(5): 354–65.

Rao, P. (2005), 'The greening of suppliers in the South East Asian context', *Journal of Cleaner Production*, **13**(9): 935–45.

Rao, P. and D. Holt (2005), 'Do green supply chains lead to competitiveness and economic performance?', *International Journal of Operations & Production Management*, **25**(9): 898–916.

Remmen, A., A.A. Jensen and J. Frydendal (2007): *Life Cycle Management – A Business Guide to Sustainability*, Paris: UNEP.

Roberts, S. (2003), 'Supply chain specific? Understanding the patchy success of ethical sourcing initiatives', *Journal of Business Ethics*, **44**(2): 159–70.

Seuring, S. (2001), 'Green supply chain costing – joint cost management in the polyester linings supply chain', *Greener Management International*, (33): 71–80.

Seuring, S. (2003), 'Cost management in the textile chain – Reducing environmental impacts and costs for green products', in M. Bennett, S. Schaltegger and P. Rikhardsson (eds), *Environmental Management Accounting – Purpose and Progress*, Dordrecht: Kluwer Academic Publishers, pp. 233–56.

Seuring, S. (2004a), 'Integrated chain management and supply chain management – Comparative analysis and illustrative cases', *Journal of Cleaner Production*, **12**(8–10): 1059–71.

Seuring, S. (2004b), 'Industrial ecology, life cycles, supply chains – differences and interrelations', *Business Strategy and the Environment*, **13**(5), 306–19.

Seuring, S. (under review), 'Supply chain integration in an extreme setting – the example of organic cotton chains', *International Journal of Production Economics*, submitted for review April 2008.

Seuring, S., M. Goldbach and J. Koplin (2004), 'Managing time and complexity in supply chains: two cases from the textile industry', *International Journal of Integrated Supply Management*, **1**(2): 180–98.

Seuring, S., M. Müller, M. Westhaus and R. Morana (2005), 'Conducting a literature review – The example of sustainability in supply chains', in H. Kotzab, S. Seuring, M. Müller and G. Reiner (eds), *Research Methodologies in Supply Chain Management*, Heidelberg: Physica Verlag, pp. 95–110.

Seuring, S. and M. Müller (2007), 'Integrated chain management in Germany – identifying schools of thought based on a literature review', *Journal of Cleaner Production*, **15**(7): 699–710.

Seuring, S. and M. Müller (2008a), 'Core issues in sustainable supply chain management – a Delphi study', *Business Strategy and the Environment*, **17**(8): 455–66.

Seuring, S. and M. Müller (2008b), 'From a literature review to a conceptual framework for sustainable supply chain management', *Journal of Cleaner Production*, **16**(15): 1699–710.

Simpson, D. and D.J. Power (2005), 'Use the supply relationship to develop lean and green suppliers', *Supply Chain Management: An International Journal*, **10**(1): 60–68.

Tang, C.S. (2006), 'Perspectives in supply chain risk management', *International Journal of Production Economics*, **103**(2): 451–88.

Trowbridge, P. (2001), 'A case study of green supply-chain management at Advanced Micro Devices', *Greener Management International*, (35): 121–35.

Vachon, S. and R.D. Klassen (2006), 'Extending green practices across the supply chain – the impact of upstream and downstream integration', *International Journal of Operations and Production Management*, **26**(7): 795–821.

Wagner, M. and S. Schaltegger (2004), 'The effect of corporate environmental strategy choice and environmental performance on competitiveness and economic performance: An empirical study of EU manufacturing', *European Management Journal*, **22**(5): 557–72.

Walton, S.V., R.B. Handfield and S.A. Melnyk (1998), 'The green supply chain: Integrating suppliers into environmental management processes', *International Journal of Purchasing and Materials Management*, **34**(2): 2–11.

Wolters, T., P. James and M. Bouman (1997), 'Stepping-stones for integrated chain management in the firm', *Business Strategy and the Environment*, **6**(3): 121–32.

Zhu, Q., J. Sarkis and Y. Geng (2005), 'Green supply chain management in China: pressures, practices and performance', *International Journal of Operations & Production Management*, **25**(5): 449–68.

Fourth intermezzo Product chain management and social sciences: path dependency, cultural validity and short- and long-term feedback loops

Claudia R. Binder

This section explores the role of social sciences in product chain manage-ment, a specific branch of industrial ecology. The three contributions highlight three areas in which social sciences might enhance and support a more sustainable product chain management, namely, system understand-ing, uncertainty and goal knowledge, and management or transformation knowledge. From these contributions three key issues emerged which have to be considered if a more sustainable product chain is envisioned: (a) path dependency: development of product chains might be path dependent due to the agent network they are embedded in and the technology applied; (b) cultural validity: the technologies or strategies for optimizing product chains valid in industrialized countries might not necessarily apply for developing countries; and (c) short and long-term feedback loops: time and time frame of thinking are extremely important and induce conse-quently short and long-term feedback loops. The contributions from social science to product chain management are very similar to the ones to regional material flow management. Therefore, one subsection specifically deals with this issue.

During the last 15 years, I have developed tools for performing inter- and transdisciplinary research. Coming from a biochemistry background, I first entered the field of material flow analysis analysing the metabolism of a Colombian city and comparing it to the one of a Swiss city. It was evident that structural, cultural and development paths drove the differ-ences in resource management between these countries. Questions similar to the ones discussed below – who influences regional resource manage-ment? what might support or hinder stakeholders to engage into more sustainable resource management? – became an important part of my research programme. In my Habilitation thesis: *Concepts and Models on Material Stocks and Flows in Human-Environment Systems: A Contribution to Transitions towards Sustainable Development* (Binder 2005), the way in which the interface between regional material flow analysis and social sciences can be conceived is presented. As Assistant Professor for Social and Industrial Ecology, at the Department of Geography, University of Zurich, I have been further developing inter- and transdisciplinary methods for analysing human-environmental systems, modelling their interdependencies, and assessing potential regulation strategies from a sustainability perspective.

This 'intermezzo' reviews the three contributions with respect to their specific contribution to industrial ecology, reflects on the three key issues mentioned above, and relates the results found for product chain management to regional material flow management. We start with a reflection on industrial ecology and social sciences.

INDUSTRIAL ECOLOGY AND SOCIAL SCIENCES

> Industrial ecology is the means by which humanity can deliberately and rationally approach and maintain a desirable carrying capacity, *given continued economic, cultural and technological evolution.* The concept requires that an industrial system be viewed not in isolation from it surrounding systems, but in concern with them. It is a systems view in which one seeks to *optimize the total materials cycle* from virgin material to finished material, to component, to product, to obsolete product, and to ultimate disposal. (Graedel and Allenby 1995: 9, emphasis added)

According to the above definition, the goal of industrial ecology is to contribute to maintaining the anthropogenic system within its physical system boundaries, given the evolution of society. The focus lies clearly on restructuring the industrial system so that it will be compatible with the biosphere and sustainable in the long term (Erkman 2003). This goal relates to one specific interpretation of sustainable development 'sustainable development is the maintenance of a system within its functional limits' (Laws et al. 2002; Binder 2005: 3). The final goal as stated by Graedel and Allenby (1995) is to optimize the physical materials cycle, however, not by itself, but as part of a larger system. This goal requires that society-related factors are included into the analysis. Furthermore, it has to be considered that society might hinder or even jeopardize the optimization of the materials cycle if doing so the overall system development might not be sustainable. This definition is valid for both product chain management and regional resource management. Specifically, for studying product chains, the following questions have to be considered:

- How do product chains emerge and develop?
- How are product chains integrated in the societal system?
- Who can 'influence' the chain and how?
- To which extent do societal differences affect the management of the product chain?
- Which factors (technical, economic, social) might hinder or support the optimization of the materials cycle?
- Can we identify specific transition patterns towards optimized materials use?

THE CONTRIBUTION OF SOCIAL SCIENCES

Social sciences can contribute in three ways to improving the sustainability of production chains:

1. *System understanding*: To better understand how the underlying social system of a product chain system works;
2. *Uncertainty and goal knowledge*: To provide additional information for assessment and informed policy-making;
3. *Management or transformation knowledge*: To support management of the supply chain by understanding the drivers and hinderers of development.

The three contributions provide insights in these three dimensions. Kopenen develops an approach for understanding the underlying social dynamics of a technological system, giving insights for an improved system understanding. Hall and Matos show how indicators (including the social dimension as well as the environmental one) allow for capturing and assessing potential negative impacts of a technology, thus, supporting informed decisions. Finally, Seuring embeds one specific company into the supply chain and the social system analysing potential factors hindering or supporting more sustainable production. As he includes stakeholders and their norms in the analysis, the results might support transitions towards a more sustainable supply chain.

SYSTEM UNDERSTANDING

In his article 'Commodities, their life cycle and industrial ecology', Koponen departs from the premise that commodity chains link the physical and the social world of things. To a large extent economics has studied commodity chains, taking mostly a linear perspective and having the optimization of one parameter, for example, profit maximization as their ultimate goal (see also Kytzia and Nathani 2004; Binder 2007a for the link between economics and material flow analysis). However, he argues that this perspective might be shortsighted as it only focuses on one specific factor and neglects additional factors such as cultural differences and different preferences. That is, the contribution from social science cannot be purely an economic one, but has to cover a multivalent form of analysis.

With his socio-technical-economic perspective or commodity chain analysis, Koponen aims at broadening current economic approaches. In doing so, technology is more than a certain technique to produce goods, that is, 'technology becomes part of a social system that confines certain interests and controls social actors'. This perspective of technology requires a type of analysis which differs from the economic one by considering four main features: (a) network relation of exchanges; (b) technological lock in; (c) action at a distance; and (d) emphasis on locally constructed values. He applies this analysis to maize production in USA and Zimbabwe and highlights the main results of these studies.

Three issues strike me as being particularly relevant and interesting for industrial ecology applications. First, there is a 'path dependency of technologies'. This path dependency is mainly influenced on the one hand through the agent network in which the production system (firm, farmers, and so on) is embedded and the goals and time frames of the agents involved (see also Seuring). This has also been shown to be true in regional material flow systems such as compost or biogas production system (Lang et al. 2007) and wood management systems (Binder et al. 2004). That is, grown organizational structures provide a certain path dependency and might hinder a different type of development, even if it were envisioned. On the other hand, a technological lock in might occur as certain technologies once adopted might induce a set of other technologies and good flows. That is, even if an improvement of a material cycle could be envisioned and specific measures could be developed from an industrial ecology perspective, this might not occur due to the technological lock in. The technological lock in is also related to investment costs (including R&D costs).

Second, the agent networks are 'functional agent networks' (Hirsch Hadorn et al. 2002; Binder 2007b). That is, these agent networks and the related material cycles are not completely interlinked, implying that the involved agents do not directly interact with each other, but might have some indirect relationships. From a materials cycle perspective this could provide a positive aspect. Potentially it is possible for agents at the end point of a material chain to impact on earlier chain members even though they are not directly connected to them. This can already be observed with labelled products such as FSC (Forest Stewardship Council) for wood, or different types of food labels.

Third, 'cultural differences' have to be considered. Koponen shows that the same product, i.e. maize, can have completely different meanings in the cultural contexts such as the USA and Zimbabwe. Furthermore, the material flows in different countries also differ significantly (Graedel *et al.* 2004). Still, one open question is: how can we 'measure' these cultural differences and how can we include them in the industrial ecology context?

UNCERTAINTY AND GOAL KNOWLEDGE

Uncertainty is an additional aspect that gains relevance when shifting from technical to integrated analysis. According to Hall and Matos purely technological uncertainties can be converted into probabilistic risks, that is, the variables determining the uncertainty can be identified, measured, the potential damage and a probability of its occurrence determined. If however, a technological system is embedded into a social one, for example social pressures might become relevant and affect the system outcome. In such a case, policy advice with respect to sustainable development has to include not only technological aspects but also social ones. Hall and Matos show for their analysis on the implementation of transgenic technology in Brazil, how stakeholders, even if they have the same claims, have differing underlying interests. Furthermore they suggest a set of indicators, which allow for embedding a technological question into a socio-economic context. These two aspects are relevant for industrial ecology and will be explored in the following.

'Stakeholders' claims and interests' are indeed extremely relevant and were also considered relevant by Koponen in his agent network analysis. The analysis of the claims and interests and moreover the difference among them provides a valuable input for analysing the options and hindrances for implementing a new technology. We suggest, similar to the Structural Agent Analysis (SAA) (Binder 2007b), to additionally analyse the type of social structure underlying the claims and interest, as well as the agents' time horizon. The social structures can be differentiated according to Giddens (1994) into signification (semantic rules, i.e., stakeholders' culture and traditions), legitimation (implicit or explicit moral rules), allocative (material resources involved in the generation of power) and authoritative resources (non-material resources involved in the generation of power). The social structures affect human action but also human action itself changes or perpetuates (intended or unintended) the present social structure. That is, there is a feedback loop between social structures and human action, similar to the theory of cybernetics found in technical and natural sciences. This implies that understanding the social structure on which the claims and interests of the involved stakeholders are based on, provides a basis for improving the understanding of the potential dynamics of the social system. The analysis would be even more powerful if the time perspective of stakeholders is included. The planning horizon of agents is necessary for understanding the time within which a behavioural change can be expected. If the claims and interests of the different stakeholders are included into the analysis, we can obtain an insight into the restrictions and facilitators of each agent. Interference between agents occurs when the planning horizon, goals and structural factors among agents differ with respect to a specific flow or material goal (Scholz 2001a).

INDICATORS

It is widely agreed upon that sustainability assessments should be based on indicators and parameters if they aim at being relevant for policy-makers and involved stakeholders. These indicators should describe the important features of the environmental, economic and social aspects of the system (UN 1993; OECD 1999; Parris and Kates 2003; Wiek and Binder 2005). The challenge of elaborating such an indicators-based assessment is that of defining, determining and measuring indicators capable of translating the complexity of a system, its current status and its potential change towards sustainability. If indicators are to be used in an industrial ecology framework the following questions should be considered:

- How and who determines the sustainability thresholds (normative dimension)?
- How and who selects the indicators, are there trade-offs between the indicators and how can these trade-offs be measured and accounted for (systemic dimension)?
- How should stakeholders be included in the assessment process (procedural dimension)?

As mentioned above, indicator relevance and functional relationship might vary across cultures and should be accounted for in the indicator selection (Empacher and Wehling 2002; Binder and Wiek 2007).

MANAGEMENT OR TRANSFORMATION KNOWLEDGE

In the context of sustainable development transformation knowledge is the know-how to progress from the current to the target situation, i.e. more sustainable product chain. Seuring embeds his concept of supply chain management into the current analysis of production chains. Supply chain management departs from a specific company (focal company) as an agent and embeds this agent into the broader perspective of the whole supply chain and the political context in which the company is located. Supply chain management thereby relates to the management of material flows by the involved stakeholders. The goal is to obtain a certain ecological and economic benefit while considering social aspects. One specific characteristic of this type of supply chain management is the specific inclusion of stakeholders ranging from consumers and suppliers to politics. This allows distinguishing specific external pressures to the firm. He illustrates his approach with the example of organic cotton in Germany.

Similar to the former two approaches supply chain management includes 'stakeholders involved directly and indirectly in the production process', that is, politics, consumers, in the analysis. These stakeholders, on the one hand, put pressure on or provide incentives to the focal company for a more ecological, economic or social production. For example, consumers, play an important role in Europe. Consumer organizations might hinder that a certain product might enter the market if it does not fulfil certain characteristics (ecological or even ethical). On the other hand, the focal company depends on its suppliers who represent either barriers or supporting factors for the overall performance of the focal company. According to Seuring, a company has two potential strategies it can pursue: to avoid the risks from global supply or to supply sustainable products. Even though these strategies seem contradictory they might indeed be complementary.

Considering policymaking directly in the analysis provides 'political embeddedness'. The role of politics as described in this approach is particularly relevant for regions in Europe in which legislation might push or inhibit change towards sustainability. Again the time dimension of companies with respect to the one of politics has to be considered. Whereas companies plan at a quarterly level, until a new law is developed and implemented it can take several years. This difference in planning horizon has to be accounted for by the company as well as the decision makers. Furthermore, the role of legislation is likely to be smaller in developing countries, which again shows the relevance of including cultural aspects in the analysis.

SUPPLY CHAIN MANAGEMENT AND REGIONAL MATERIAL FLOW MANAGEMENT

Coming from regional material flow analysis and management, another branch of industrial ecology, it is interesting to see that the contribution of social sciences to supply chain management is very similar to the one to regional material flow management. Binder (2007a) presents an overview of the social science methods that have been linked to material flow analysis. Similarly as discussed by Koponen, most of the approaches linked to material flow analysis stem from economics, as these models have similar data and modelling structure than the material flow models (Binder 2007a). They usually increase the system understanding and allow for estimating the potential effects of economic policies on material flows. However, designed economic measures might not always lead to the expected improvements of the material system. That is, as discussed by Koponen for product chains, also in regional material flow management, alternative approaches are required.

In addition, the presented approaches all suggest that stakeholders have different time horizons in decision-making, implementation and effect observation, as it has been found when studying regional material flows. Still, the presented approaches fall short in specifically including this aspect in their analyses. At a regional level, one approach, which aims at filling this gap is the method of SAA (Binder 2007b), which allows for better understanding the social structures restricting or enabling strategies for managing regional material flows. The SAA complements the presented approaches as it considers explicitly 'short- and long-term dynamics' in the analysis. It does so by: (a) considering the interaction and dynamics of social structure and human agency; (b) providing a cross-level approach allowing the study of interferences among stakeholder groups; and (c) including the time scale of changes of social structure and institutions defining the options and restrictions of human action. It is thus, recommended to evaluate to which extent an adaptation of SAA might be useful for analysing product chains.

SOCIAL SCIENCES CONTRIBUTION TO PRODUCT CHAIN MANAGEMENT: PATH DEPENDENCY, CULTURAL VALIDITY AND SHORT AND LONG-TERM DYNAMICS

In this chapter it was shown that the social system might significantly affect the material flow system and could restrict the optimization of material cycles at a product chain level. In particular three issues have to be taken into account: (a) path dependency; (b) cultural validity; and (c) short- and long-term dynamics.

'Path dependency' might occur if on the one hand the stakeholder networks are rigid, that is, long-term contracts, traditions restrict changing supply or consumption partners. On the other hand certain technologies might induce certain material flows. If there were high investment costs a change towards a new technology will take time.

Stakeholder analysis mostly holds only for the specific 'cultural context' in which it was applied. Even in the same country, cultural differences among regions might exist, which have to be considered when aiming at improving material cycles. That is, technologies and strategies cannot be easily transferred to another cultural system.

Finally, 'short- and long-term dynamics' within the material cycle but also the human system have to be considered. Here a particular need was determined for developing or adapting tools which are able to include the time dimension of different stakeholders in the analysis and moreover in strategy development.

REFERENCES

Binder C.R. (2005). *Concept and models on material stocks and flows in human-environment systems: A contribution to transitions towards sustainable development*, Habilitation thesis, Department of Environmental Sciences, Swiss Federal Institute of Technology, Zurich, Switzerland.

Binder, C.R. (2007a), 'From material flow analysis to material flow management Part I: Social science approaches coupled to material flow analysis', *Special Issue: Journal of Cleaner Production*, **15**: 1596–1604.

Binder, C.R. (2007b), 'From material flow analysis to material flow management Part II: The role of Structural Agent Analysis', *Special Issue: Journal of Cleaner Production*, **15**: 1605–17.

Binder, C.R. and A. Wiek (2007), 'The role of transdisciplinary processes in sustainability assessment of agricultural systems', in F. Häni, L. Pinter and H. Herren (eds), *Sustainable Agriculture: From Common Principles to Common Practice*, Winnipeg, CA: International Institute for Sustainable Development, pp. 33–48.

Binder, C.R., C. Hofer, A. Wiek and R.W. Scholz (2004), 'Transition towards improved regional wood flow by integrating material flux analysis with agent analysis: the case of Appenzell Ausserrhoden', Switzerland, *Ecological Economics*, **49**(1): 1–17.

Empacher C. and P. Wehling (2002), *Soziale Dimensionen der Nachhaltigkeit. Theoretische Grundlagen und Indikatoren*, Frankfurt am Main: Institut für sozial-ökologische Forschung.

Graedel, T.E., D. van Beers, M. Bertram, K. Fuse, R.B. Gordon, A. Gritsinin,

A. Kapur, R.J. Klee, R.J. Lifset, L. Memon, H. Rechberger, S. Spatari and D. Vexler (2004), 'The multilevel cycle of anthropogenic copper', *Environmental Science Technology*, **38**: 1242–52.

Giddens, A. (1984), *The Constitution of the Society*, Berkeley, CA: University of California Press.

Hirsch Hadorn, G., S. Wölfling Kast and S. Maier (2002), 'Restrictions and options: A heuristic tool to integrate knowledge for strategies towards a sustainable development', *Int. J. Sustain. Dev. World Ecol.*, **9**: 193–207.

Kytzia, S. and C. Nathani (2004), 'Bridging the gap to economic analysis: economic tools for industrial ecology', *Progress in Industrial Ecology*, **1**(1/2/3): 143–64.

Lang, D.J, C.R. Binder, R.W. Scholz, K. Schleiss and B. Stäubli (2006), 'Impact factors and regulatory mechanisms for material flow management: Integrating stakeholder and scientific perspectives: The case of bio-waste delivery', *Resources, Conservation and Recycling*, **47**: 101–32.

OECD (Organization for Economic Cooperation and Development) (1999), *Environmental Indicators for Agriculture, Issues and Design*.

Parris, T.M. and R.W. Kates (2003), 'Characterizing and measuring sustainable development', *Annual Review of Environmental Resources*, **28**: 559–86.

Scholz, R.W. (2001a), 'Chancen und Dilemmata des Industriebrachenrecyclings', Paper presented at the Workshop Brachflächenrecycling, Altlasten und Raumplanung, Château Mercier, Siders/VS.

United Nations (1993), Agenda 21: programme of action for sustainable development. The final text of agreements negotiated by governments at the United Nations Conference on Environment and Development (UNCED) (3–14 June 1992), Rio de Janeiro, Brazil. New York: United Nations, Department of Public Information.

Weik, A. and C.R. Binder (2005), 'Solution spaces for decision-making – a sustainability assessment tool for city-regions', *Environment Impact Assessment Review*, **25**(6): 589–608.

Fifth intermezzo   The exchange of ideas between social science and engineering approaches to product chain industrial ecology

Bart van Hoof

The integration of social science approaches into industrial ecology reflects the constant need for engineers to invent, design, develop, produce and optimize processes, products and services of all kinds and make them acceptable to different groups of stakeholders. Since sustainability has become essential to the total quality concept, it has also become a core concept of the engineering discipline, and brings with it the need to account for social considerations.

In this intermezzo, I will try to contribute to the exchange of ideas between social scientists and engineers regarding the ongoing value of social science approaches to understanding phenomena in the field of industrial ecology. My personal reference for this discussion is based on my education in industrial engineering and 14 years of experience with applied engineering work in cleaner production and environmental improvement in small, medium and large sized companies in the Netherlands, Colombia and Mexico. In addition to this work related to industrial ecology, I am connected to academic research and teaching in the field at the Los Andes University in Bogota, and am currently in my PhD studies at the industrial ecology program of the Erasmus University in Rotterdam.

From this background, I perceive the relationship between sustainability, industrial ecology and the engineering discipline on different levels: I view sustainability as an 'umbrella concept' that provides basic values for my acting, whereas industrial ecology provides strategies and concepts which are valuable for the orientation of my activities. The engineering discipline provides 'operational tools' which enable me to implement industrial ecology strategies and contribute to sustainability.

Through the lens of this mindset, I analysed the three chapters of this book on Product Chain approaches as specific references of this intermezzo: (a) 'Transgenic Crops in Brazil: Scientific Decision-making for

Social Ambiguities?' by Hall and Matos, (b) 'Commodities, their Life-Cycle and Industrial Ecology' by Koponen and (c) 'Sustainable Supply Chain Management' by Seuring, Morana and Liu. Engineering, as well as social science disciplines play a central role in the three product chain approaches presented in these chapters. The analysis in these chapters is relevant for the dialogue between academics and researchers with different disciplinary backgrounds. The questions which guide my reflection in this intermezzo are: What is useful about the research presented regarding my own field of expertise? What are the differences in the research approaches/outcomes in these chapters? What kinds of constructive criticism can be given to the authors?

First, the three authors provide strong arguments that are useful to understanding the importance of social science approaches within industrial ecology. Hall and Matos show in their chapter how social context influences decision making in technological innovation. Their case analysis of the Brazilian biotechnology policy highlights the limitations of a technologically deterministic approach towards the introduction of a complex technological innovation with supposed environmental benefits. Especially in a diverse social context, such as that in Brazil, this technocratic approach can lead to sub-optimization. For example, the social side-effects of innovations – such as their different impacts on low income producers – can be overlooked. Similar to Hall and Matos, Koponen portrays the limitations of the traditional rationale used in economic analysis of the singular value of economic profit maximization. Due to this 'mathematical science', he stresses that the diversity of human and social elements are not generally considered. Seuring, Morana and Liu address the importance of these same social ideas in partnership building as a key process for triggering and developing sustainable supply chains.

The need to be sensitive to the diversity of different contexts and its influence on the interpretation and feasibility of sustainability goals, resonates with my personal experiences. When I moved as a Dutch trained engineer from the Netherlands to work in Colombia, South America, I experienced first-hand the differences between these countries. These differences appear in various social dimensions such as differences in cultural values and differences in the role stakeholders, such as governmental institutions, private companies and civil organizations, play in society. These differences influence decision making at all levels of society from policy making at a national level, to strategy formulation and planning at the level of individual organizations, and also to decisions and behaviour of individuals working in these organizations. As industrial ecology attempts to orient decision-making towards sustainability, its frameworks should include social concepts in order to understand and anticipate the specific conditions of diverse contexts that may influence decision-making.

While these arguments are a useful starting point for a discussion about the integration of social science approaches into industrial ecology, I consider the most important contribution of the three authors to be the claim that a paradigm shift is needed to really integrate social science into technocratic approaches. Koponen proposes in his chapter; 'In order to understand the sustainability of the production system, we need to see how economic and social values are exchanged, and who controls the value of the chain overall; Optimums are relative'. Seuring, Morana and Liu also conclude that the institutional uptake of industrial ecology requires a fundamental adjustment in how (inter-)organizational structures and coordination mechanisms are perceived. This requires a shift from power-based relations to trust-based relations, and from a short-term perspective to a long-term perspective. This rethinking of values would orient the role of engineering in sustainability, and also in industrial ecology concept, towards *improvement* as its final goal.

This paradigm shift can conflict with the focus of traditional engineering where mathematic/numeric *optimums* have been the primary focus; the existence of such optimums are a major assumption behind the use of cost/benefit analyses. Within the proposed new paradigm, engineering solutions within the industrial ecology framework would consist of the best appropriate alternatives for the context they are developed in. This appropriateness of alternatives does not only depend on technological or economical feasibility, but also on the social feasibility shown in the empowerment of the persons involved in their development and implementation. Social science concepts are needed to define and understand what is appropriate and how empowerment, and finally, improvement can be achieved.

In my consulting and research work on cleaner production implementation in small and medium-sized enterprises (SMEs) in Colombia and Mexico, and industrial ecology related strategy, the importance of appropriate solutions are clear. The technical advice is just a small part of my job. In order to achieve success in implementing pollution prevention alternatives within these companies, understanding their specific context and involving their personnel in the improvement process is critical. Cleaner production implementation in SMEs isn't only about technological alternatives, it's also about organizational change. Nevertheless, available cleaner production frameworks seldom include any tools or elements which guide engineers in a systematic way to cope with social aspects of the organizational change process.

The three authors offer interesting ways to address this gap in existing frameworks. Koponen describes an analytical model for the 'biography of a thing' in order to understand the internal logic of each member of the 'commodity chain'. In this way he analyses the logic of the distribution of power along the chain, and the integration of human relations and technical requirements. This non-linear model of modern production allows a holistic, ecological analysis of socio-technical-economic systems and its values. Seuring, Morana and Liu identify a framework of key elements for sustainable supply chain systems and the related triggers between them. They identify governments, customers and other stakeholders as main sources of pressures, incentives, barriers or supporting factors for Sustainable Supply Chain Management. Additionally, risk avoidance and development of new sustainable products are highlighted as strategies that focal companies and suppliers adopt in order to respond to the triggers. Hall and Matos contribute with their analytical framework of the understanding of what they call the 'dirty reality' of imperfect information. Through the inclusion of social indicators in their analysis, such a framework recognizes the complexity and heterogeneity of different contexts and the implications of imperfect information.

Even though these approaches provide useful and innovative thinking on how social variables should be dealt with in industrial ecology, the frameworks require further development in order to incorporate them with a set of on-hand tools which are based on the interdisciplinary conception of industrial ecology. Current tools fit easily in the mind set of engineers whose logic is often based on 'cause–effect' thinking and finding solutions. In this way the development of new interdisciplinary tools which integrate social and engineering concepts can help engineers to understand the social embeddedness of industrial ecology.

Integration of social variables in engineering tools isn't new. Just an example of a standard tool is the Quality Function Development (QFD) matrix which considers consumer/client relations, social variables, and technical requirements of newly developed products or processes. In a broader context, the field of Operational Management combines technological concepts with decision-making and organizational models.

Nevertheless, the emphasis of these traditional tools and models isn't necessarily focused on the sustainability goals industrial ecology is supposed to address. Therefore, developments of new interdisciplinary descriptive and prescriptive tools are needed to convert the important, but in an engineer's mindset, perceived 'fuzzy' social frameworks, into hands-on models that could be widely used by engineers. Ideas for the development of these tools can be based on existing theories and models of social science, organizational behaviour, business management and engineering literature. Nevertheless, it will be important that they address the specific industrial ecology goals.

Considering the Sustainable Supply Chain approaches in discussion and their perspectives to strengthen the industrial ecology tool box I propose the following ideas. The sustainable supply chain approach presented by Seuring, Morana and Liu could be useful to model the process and characteristics of the different stages in the process of achieving sustainable supply chain relations. Such a model would be useful for supply chain managers as references to analyse and evaluate their supply chains. Also further insight on the integration of sustainability criteria within existing supplier's selection and qualification tools would contribute to further development of this industrial ecology approach.

Koponen's framework tools could be developed in order to identify different types of value-creating networks and related 'lock-ins' typically related to certain kind of technologies. Regarding Hall and Matos' work, available knowledge of cultural studies could be used to provide practical guidance about particular social elements which influence uncertainty. Further, it could be developed to describe typical characteristics of social structures of complex development countries and related social indicators that might identify and describe different levels of uncertainty.

Aside from the further development of related tools and frameworks, it could be interesting to search for underlying elements of the product chain approaches discussed. If common underlying elements can be identified, how can the frameworks of the different authors contribute to each other? For example what elements of Koponen's commodity chain approach could be integrated in to Seuring, Morana and Liu's sustainable supply chain management approach? Or, how can the triggers posed by these authors be combined with Hall and Matos' framework?

One could even ask if common elements could evolve into an underlying theory. But then it would be important to consider first if the development of such a theory would contribute to advances in understanding the social embeddedness of industrial ecology? Maybe the challenge of its development could also represent its most important pitfall, as the existing business management, organizational learning and social science literature cover already an important part of the underlying theories.

From my engineering point of view, the challenge of social-embeddedness of industrial ecology is focused on introducing sustainability values to its practitioners and providing them with interdisciplinary frameworks and tools which enable them to develop their fundamental mind shift. I see it as a kind of 'bottom-up' effect; where engineers, and other practitioners, convince themselves of the value of industrial ecology including social science concepts in order to achieve sustainability goals. At least that's part of my own personal experience where the interaction with social science helped me to understand better the dimension of sustainability and its values. It also helped me in finding ways to introduce industrial ecology related strategies and alternatives to company owners and professionals with different disciplinary backgrounds. This same interaction also helped me in designing academic industrial ecology courses for business students.

Additionally, the ongoing discussion between social scientists and engineering/non-social science researchers in the field of industrial ecology is not only important to strengthen its tool box, it's also fundamental for relating its concepts with management models so industrial ecology becomes 'relevant' to a wider group of decision-makers at the top levels of business and other organizations involved in industrial developments. The focus of the exchange of ideas should not only be about 'how their disciplines could complement or benefit from each other', but also about 'how sustainability principle can be integrated into the *heart* of the involved disciplines'. This integration will be needed in order for industrial ecology to evolve into an important concept for sustainable development, rather than becoming, in the words of Hall and Matos, a scientifically myopic approach.

PART IV

The social science contribution reconsidered

10. A critical view on the social science contribution to industrial ecology

John Ehrenfeld

Before offering a critical view, I must confess that I am not a social scientist by training. My roots lie in the world of science and technology, having been trained as a chemical engineer. I have been immersed in the conversations of industrial ecology since the field was born and feel comfortable talking about it. My bona fides in social science come from more than 20 years working with and learning from students on organizational and institutional research projects, and thinking and writing about normative concerns ranging from recycling policies to the grand theme of sustainability.

At the outset of any critique, one must ask what is being examined. The title suggested to me is too general as a guide. To find a focus, let me then pose a few questions to set the context. The very first step is to ask what is this subject, industrial ecology, and then within whatever description we determine, to ask whether we are looking at social science as generating descriptions (epistemological), or prescriptions (normative), and finally, as a means for implementation (practical). There may certainly be other categories that would be useful, but these three seem to ground virtually all activities that could fall within the field. I am not writing a critique of the social sciences in general – trying to see it only in relationship to industrial ecology, but I will spill over this sharp boundary at times.

DEFINING INDUSTRIAL ECOLOGY

So then what is industrial ecology? In any social scientific work it is always dangerous to pose the ontological issue of what something 'is' without qualifying one's basic beliefs about reality. I am strongly drawn to social constructivism and pragmatism, but hopefully I will not let my mindset get in the way. I mean by the question simply how do people that are involved intentionally in the 'field' delineated by this phrase talk about industrial ecology and locate what they are doing in the field. I put the gloss on field because it has many meanings in the social sciences. A field, according to a definition I have used in the past is constituted by the following (Ehrenfeld 2004):

1. A set of foundational beliefs that lend a common meaning to all players in the field and allow communication across the boundaries of the field or, otherwise stated, a cohesive set of concepts that guide practitioners in their everyday, normal activities.
2. Practical resources or sets of standard tools and practical guides like textbooks.
3. An authoritative structure maintaining quality and conceptual coherence.
4. A community of actors playing within the first three categories above.

Although I will discuss the adequacy of the first item further, I will not raise any other questions as to whether the use of field is justifiable.

In Chapter 2, Boons probes the concept of ecology and how it shows up within different social science contexts. The meaning of industrial ecology certainly depends on how one holds the 'ecological' half of the name, but I will overlook this for the moment. As a working definition of industrial ecology, I refer to the formal definition constructed by Robert White (1994) in the first serious book on the subject appearing in the US. Earlier references to 'industrial ecology' are found in the literature, but never became embedded in the public consciousness (Erkman 1997). White defines industrial ecology as

> the study of the flows of materials and energy in industrial and consumer activities, of the effects of these flows on the environment, and of the influences of economic, political, regulatory, and social factors on the flow, use and transformation of resources. (White 1994: v)

This definition suggests a 'scientific' framing for this then new field. The focus was to be on 'the study of . . .'. Although White was not explicit in designating the scientific fields that would have to be called upon in the study process, his list of questions suggests that a wide variety will be necessary. Applied [engineering] science methodology fits the elucidation of the technical aspects of flow. Environmental sciences relate to the study of impact of the flows on the world. Social sciences apply to the determination of the influences of the four 'factors' he names.

Does this mean that industrial ecology is an interdisciplinary field? Not necessarily. If the emphasis is, as White writes, on the descriptive, the field can be, and largely is, populated primarily by 'technologists', whose work is grounded on the objective, reductionist, epistemological models of the natural sciences.[1] It takes its principal defining presupposition – material and energy flows in the industrial world are analogous to those in a natural ecosystem – from a technological source (see Frosch 1989, for example). Other fields, responding to the last set of categories in White, have contributed to the contextual and historical understanding of industrial ecology, but have added little to the field's methodological toolbox. A few examples are social ecology (Fischer-Kowalski 1998), history (Erkman 1997), geography (Desrochers 2002) and sociology (Salmi and Toppinen 2007). These voices from other fields are increasingly a part of the institutional ambit of industrial ecology as evidenced, more recently, by articles in scholarly journals, conference papers, membership in the International Society for Industrial Ecology, and/or academic collaborations.

FRAMING THE CRITIQUE

Now with this definition of industrial ecology in hand, let me turn to a more difficult question, what is to be criticized? Coordination, the process by which different people (industrial ecologists and social scientists in the context of this volume) join together to achieve a common goal, frames the rest of this critical essay. What is involved in bringing together a disparate set of actors as determined by their diverse disciplinary frameworks (the tacit beliefs and norms that delineate their fields)? What are the obstacles? As a further guide, I turn to the theories of Jürgen Habermas as being useful in exploring these subjects and exposing specific issues. Habermas was concerned, among many issues, with defending the rationality of modernity against attacks by postmodernists and in avoiding domination in normal intercourse.

Habermas (1984) argues, as others have, that models based only on objectivist, analytic, Cartesian claims are insufficient to explain how humans act in general. He deems the practical outcomes based on such claims as 'strategic action'. Such actions are constrained by the actors' pre-existing goals and determined by the relative power within the acting group. In a complex critique extending over many years and in several major works, Habermas develops a more encompassing form of rationality, which he calls 'communicative rationality', and deems the kinds of actions that flow out of it as 'communicative action'. Communicative action is consensual and moves toward a set of shared goals without dominating forces at play. If social scientists and industrial ecologists are to enter into pragmatically effective arrangements, they must base their work on consensual relationships and agreements. Shotgun marriages are very unlikely to bear fruit nor persist.

Communicative action requires the actors to raise and mutually accept the validity of claims made not only in the objective world of strategic action, but also in two additional domains: the subjective and the social (intersubjective). These claims show up as assessments made by listeners assessing the validity of a speaker's claims in three domains that underlie communicative rationality: truth (objective), truthfulness or sincerity (subjective), and legitimacy (intersubjective).

Truth entails ontological claims about the reality of the world as it is at present, and how it would become if the speaker's claims are accepted and enacted. Truthfulness corresponds to the subjective world that Habermas mentions. Claims about sincerity, reliability or competence are related forms. Truthfulness is generally an assessment about an assertion being made in the present; sincerity and competence are assessments about the speaker's intention and ability to follow through in the future. Habermas connects this domain to the subjective or dramaturgical dimension of rationality. It manifests the inner set of intentions and cognitive states of the party or parties who are attempting to coordinate action among them. The third class of validity claims, legitimacy, forms the basis of much social, as opposed to personal conflict. Legitimacy relates to the intersubjective domain and largely includes assessments about the degree to which other parties share the immediate normative concerns of the listener.

Coordination in settings involving industrial ecology is generally initiated by technologists, seeking inputs from social scientists. This asymmetry is historically based and represents the way the field is currently populated. The technological character of the field was one of the defining foci listed in the opening chapter of the *Handbook of Industrial Ecology* (Lifset and Graedel 2002). Technologists are the ones that must assess the Habermasian validity claims made by social scientists. Social scientists writing as social scientists studying industrial ecology as an object are not involved in any practical coordination, except to observe or ask questions, with the industrial ecologists. In these cases, the well-known methodological problems of understanding what is going on in a different culture inhere. I will not discuss this issue further as there is nothing remarkable about industrial ecology as such an object of research.

A fourth class of claims, that of comprehensibility, is often added to the three discussed above. This claim is fundamental; one cannot enter into a conversation leading to coordinated action without understanding the language itself or the conventional idiomatic usage of the speaker.

Two of these four – truth and comprehensibility – are broadly problematic for the embedding of social science in industrial ecology. The other two – truthfulness and normative legitimacy – are, in theory, important, but generally do not cause problems in coordination in the context of this article. Professional respect among scholars and practitioners is the norm, allowing interaction to proceed without questions of the truthfulness of the parties involved. Similarly, questions about the legitimate roles of actors in a project may arise in specific instances, but is not a general concern.

These two more problematic areas, in the context of this critique, can be further delineated as: (a) the existence of two fundamentally and incompatible ontologies of reality that separate actors within the social science world from each other and from the technologists (truth); and (b) the incomprehensibility of much language used in the social science to the technologists and vice versa (although less so). Taking up the first item, I find it very difficult to make this ontological distinction clear using words in our everyday vocabularies. The 'science' in natural science and the 'science' in much of, but not all, 'social science' is not at all the same. To make matters worse, the newly evolving complexity 'science' is still another paradigmatically distinct concept. To avoid confusion, I will limit my references to social science and natural science because I believe the real issues lie below these usual disciplinary descriptions. Instead, I will use a dichotomy to categorize the two main sources of intellectual inputs: objectivism/objectivists and historicism/historicists. Objectivists are actors whose ontological and epistemological ground is located within the predominant Cartesian dualism paradigm and consequent positive science. It applies to the technologists: those who create knowledge from this base and those who apply this knowledge in practical situations: engineers, designers, technocrats, and so on. Mainstream economics and other areas of the social sciences based on positivist theories also fall into this class. Historicists are those that believe that human action can be understood only in the context of their experience within the cultural settings into which they have been socialized. The embeddedness theme serving as the glue holding the book together is an example, par excellence, of historicism. I will use the historicism category for just about everything that does not fit neatly into objectivism. Without investigating the pedigrees of the authors of this book in depth, I would place about half into the historicist category.

For the objectivists, the standards used in making truth claims can be shrunk to an assurance that one has been faithful to the 'scientific method'. Truth in positive science is a measure of coherence to the paradigmatic methodology of one's discipline. But no such easy road is available to those whose labours lay outside of the objectivist sciences (see Baumann, Chapter 3). There are few, if any, effectively universal paradigmatic *methodologies* in the social sciences, except perhaps within mainstream economics. This social fact accounts for much disagreement and argument about whether some claims are the 'truth' or only an opinion. This consequence is caused not by less rigor and carefulness in the social sciences, but simply by the absence of a single, paradigmatic epistemological methodology. Deconstructionists, a sub-group of historicists, like Jacques Derrida, would argue neither should be privileged over the other as they are nothing but different stories.

The graduate students I worked with often asked, after labouring for a long time on their dissertations, how they could tell when they were getting done. Expecting some sort of quantitative or analytical answer they were surprised when I said, 'You are done whenever you can tell a convincing story about your studies.' You have to convince, more or less, in this order: your advisor, your committee, the academic community, and depending on how normative you aim to be, the world at large. Of course, what it takes to convince these various audiences varies considerably.

Inherent uncertainty in scientific claims is often unmentioned or ignored by the scientists making claims and overlooked by the practitioners involved. Predictions are offered by objectivists with little or no reference to the analytical uncertainty involved, or if made explicit, are soon forgotten. Unintended consequences and accidents arise out of this sociological aspect of science and technology. In all historicist social sciences, the contingency of all knowledge (Rorty 1989) is explicit, cannot be ignored, and requires great sensitivity, self-awareness and humility on the parts of the actors when they are expressing and advocating for their answers or designs. Berger and Luckman (1966: 13) offer this warning:

> How can I be sure, say, of my sociological analysis of American middle-class mores in view of the fact that the categories I use for this analysis are conditioned by historically relative forms of thought, that I myself and everything I think is determined by my genes and by my ingrown hostility to my fellowmen, and that, to cap it all, I am myself a member of the American middle class.

PROBLEM STRUCTURING IN INDUSTRIAL ECOLOGY AND ROLES FOR SOCIAL SCIENCE

One of early debates that arose within the then embryonic field of industrial ecology concerned its ontological status (Ehrenfeld 2004; Allenby 2006). Is it an emerging 'science' attempting to understand the phenomenon of material and energy flows in socio-technical-economic systems of varying spatial and temporal scales? Is it a technological endeavour developing tools and models and applying them 'objectively' to 'problems' that involve such flows? Or does it take on a normative character where its practitioners are overt or hidden advocates with an agenda for some sort of change that can be linked to or attributable to the paradigmatic structure of the field? For example, welfare economics can be said to fit all three categories. But it is not clear to me where industrial ecology lies at this still early stage in its evolution.

Industrial Ecology as Science

It is difficult to argue that industrial ecology is a science in the conventional sense of the term. There are no paradigmatic methods and models according to Kuhn's definition (1962). Algorithmic formulations do exist for determining the flows of materials (and less frequently, energy) along product chains (life-cycle assessment), among interlinked 'firms' (industrial symbiosis) or throughout a whole economy (material flow accounting), but none have the paradigmatic character of the genetic code and derivative analytic methods in microbiology. Characterizing the flows per se simply in either qualitative or quantitative terms can proceed with only the application of technical methods. This is not to say that one does not have to be clever. Quite the contrary, teasing out acceptable information from generally poor and partial data requires great imagination and means to make inferences from one set of accounting categories to another (see Graedel et al. 2004). The observation that flows in industrial systems resemble those in natural ecosystems is incidental and unnecessary in such endeavours, although as we will soon see, it has significant bearing on the questions raised in the opening paragraph of this section. Desrochers (2002) has pointed out that symbiotic waste-exchanging relationships existed long before anyone thought to describe them as analogies to ecosystems. Simply adding a social parameter, say economic efficiency, to an analysis of a technically-bound system does not require coordination with social scientists and can be handled by application of analytic frameworks alone plus the appropriate data.

Virtually all of what is labelled research in the field of industrial ecology does not conform to the orthodox methodology of science.[2] The work is fundamentally descriptive in nature as opposed to proving and disproving hypotheses. The results inevitably rest on particular assumptions and choices of the researcher. This statement is not made in any polemical or pejorative sense, but only to emphasize that such research results are a sophisticated form of opinion, different from the truths of 'pure' science. This difference becomes important, not to those that work in the field and understand this distinction, but to those stakeholders in specific projects that do not. Virtually all fields, for example, risk assessment, based on applying, rather than discovering, scientific principles face this same issue.

If the questions stray into the arena of understanding *why* the flows are whatever they are, then the social sciences must come into play since human actors are inevitably involved. White's (1994) definition implicates human actors only indirectly. In making this claim, I do not mean in any way that the field of industrial ecology need to spread far enough to envelop these social sciences and become interdisciplinary. That is another subject of interest, but not relevant here. I will argue, however, that industrial ecology must become, if it is not already, multi-disciplinary. The chapters in this book and elsewhere are evidence that this is happening. Multi-disciplinarity means that the milieu in which scholarly or applied work takes place must afford the actors a means to listen to each other sufficiently to understand the edges of their work and seek places where the edges can be joined more or less transparently. Only in this way can a whole emerge such that all the actors can share in its creation. The choice of which particular social science is relevant always depends on the peculiarities of the project at hand, again, as the work in this volume shows.

This 'scientific' aspect of industrial ecology does not fit, as I mentioned earlier, the conventional sense of the term. Modern day science has become splintered into a myriad of minute shards as knowledge of the larger chunks matures and our methods enable us to look at smaller and smaller parts. But it does begin to look like a science if we fit it into the emergent area of complexity (Ehrenfeld 2007), where science itself is being rethought. As opposed to the microscopic focus of conventional, reductionist science, complexity science looks at the world through a fisheye lens and abandons some of the basic tenets of science. Uncertainty, the consequence of the imperfections of our methods and models is replaced by an alternate ontological distinct entity, unknowability – the admission that we cannot develop a set of laws that allow prediction at all. Such complex systems can, when perturbed, move into entirely new and disconnected regimes where the relationships that previously determined their behaviour are replaced by a new set. Indeed, the world that interests many industrial ecologists is just such a complex one.

Complexity was one of the key topics discussed at the last biennial meeting of the International Society for Industrial Ecology in Toronto, June 2007. The work of the late James Kay explicitly embedding notions from complex system theory into industrial ecology broadly is increasingly cited by scholars in the field (Kay 2002: Kay et al. 1999). Evolutionary models for industrial symbioses based on self-organizing systems are taking a place alongside others based on economic theories (Boons 2008).

Industrial Ecology as a Community of Problem-Solving Practice

The second domain in which industrial ecologists work is that of problem solving, not of epistemological puzzles, but of worldly, practical problems. How can one reduce the impact of production and consumption, for example, by eliminating or reducing the materiality of some technological system, say the life cycle of the automobile? Workers here aim to change the world in some way. In this domain, the 'science' (or better, the 'sciences' (plural) of industrial ecology) serves to provide models and tools to guide the design of problem-solving exercises whether they be directed toward artefacts or policies. The designers can be objectivists or historicists. Their roles in the design process are virtually the same, but the tools they use are very different. The more interesting problems facing industrial ecologists require the services of both kinds of professionals, since they are situated in socio-technical systems like a whole economy or within firms aiming to market new products and services, for example, a carbon-offsetting transportation system.

The opening chapter invoked embeddedness as a 'metatheory' coming from social science. Embeddedness explicitly argues that human actors are influenced by the social context in which they act and also by the context into which they have historically been socialized. By socialized, we mean the milieu from which they have created and embodied their beliefs, norms and patterns of routine behaviour. Granovetter's (1985) seminal paper, cited in the opening chapter, argued that sociological factors, such as trust, could not be ignored in understanding why firms decided to obtain goods and services from the market or, alternatively, to acquire these goods and services by creating internal sources. Granovetter argued that pure economic cost/benefit models were inadequate.

Embeddedness, as an epitome of sociologically or anthropologically based theories of action, sends a warning to objectivists who argue that behaviours can be modelled and explained by an a-contextual rational calculus residing in the cognitive organs. Since we know empirically that humans do not always act in the raw rational way the basic models, such as those underlying neoclassical economics, would predict, objectivists have developed variants that can account for the 'imperfection' of human action (Simon 2000; Kahnemann 2003). Economists and other social scientists are generally aware of these two non-congruent framings for modelling and predicting individual or collective behaviour, but engineers and scientists are generally not as knowledgeable. Many engineers and scientists, even if their education or work introduced them to social science, are only familiar with economics. Very few are exposed to the historist, culturally-bound versions of behaviour. My experience at MIT as an undergraduate, although not typical today, makes the point. I was one of the first graduating classes to be required to take any courses with the label 'humanities'. But in my imprudent drive to cram in as much technical stuff, I managed to convince my advisor I did not need economics and used that slot for an advanced physical organic chemistry course.

It was only some 30 years later, on returning to MIT in an interdepartmental (but not interdisciplinary) setting, that I discovered I could not fully explore the more interesting questions in the study of environmental management in firms with only analytic tools at hand. I could identify some of these questions, for example, why firms fail to use design for environment tools in creating new products when these tools are available to them. (Lenox and Ehrenfeld 1997). But I could not develop a framework nor select effective methodologies by relying only on rational decision-making options.

More related to the topic of this book is the experience that arose from my exploration of the industrial symbiosis at Kalundborg, which is discussed in several of the chapters. Having become interested and involved in industrial ecology, I 'discovered' Kalundborg as an outcome of casual reading of the very sparse literature bearing on industrial ecology at the time. I sent a student, Nick Gertler, to Kalundborg for a month one summer to learn everything he could and in particular, to bring me back the master plan, because I was sure that such a complex web of interconnecting firms could only arise through some overlying plan. I was quite disappointed and a bit upset when he returned without such a document, telling me that there was nothing like this involved. The complex had 'simply' evolved over several decades.

I tried to get some MIT colleagues who worked with industrial organization to help understand what had happened to no avail. The evolution at Kalundborg was seen as nothing exceptional in spite of my pleas that the normative possibilities for reducing environmental impact were novel and worth studying. So Nick and I set to work with only our technical toolboxes. We did develop some 'naive' models – naive in the sense that we drew on Williamson's (1979) transaction cost economics but did not understand it well enough to go much below a superficial level of analysis (Ehrenfeld and Gertler 1997). We knew something else was going on. We mentioned a 'short mental distance' as a causative factor, but could not expand on the idea. The chapters in this volume by Gibbs, Paquin and Howard-Grenville, and Chertow and Ashton tell a much more enlightening story, and demonstrate the increasing role of the social sciences in industrial ecology.

In efforts to solve problems in industrial ecology, actors with distinctive paradigms about how their part of the world works must work collaboratively. And here too, they need to share some common language at least at the boundaries of their fields. In the first place, the problem at hand is understood and mediated through the paradigmatic structure of one's field. Problem framing depends on it (Lakoff 2002; Schön and Rein 1995). The framework of questions to be raised and answered depends on those interests and on the power structure manifest in the group. The normative interests of the players cannot be ignored although their visions for the future often lurk in the background because it is common that our culture generally requires that professional actors claim objectivity in this critical stage of every non-trivial design exercise.

But many problems of interest to the industrial ecology community spill over in the public sphere and involve ordinary citizens in the process of design. They become involved because they are concerned about the present problematic world or because they fear that some new design would interfere with their lives. Social scientists can serve this process in two ways. The first is as a part of the design team, bringing pragmatically useful models into play. The second is to act as some sort of process facilitator, using their understanding of social interactions to guide problem-setting and subsequent activities, for example, by reducing communication barriers among the many actors, especially public stakeholders. Industrial ecology is not unique in this situation. The same issues arise in every design exercise involving, as I noted, non-trivial socio-technical problems. Action research goes beyond facilitation with the social scientist participants in a project normatively involved in inducing change (Reason and Bradbury 2007).

INDUSTRIAL ECOLOGY AS A NEW PARADIGM

The last context for the field is an institutional normative frame like that of welfare economics. This subpart of the general field of economics in general would not exist without normative interests deeply involved in creating the field in the first place. For welfare economics, happiness is the normative target. For industrial ecology, the equivalent is some form of sustainability (Ehrenfeld 2007). The relevance of such a normative foundation to industrial ecology is still very much an open question.

The normative paradigm case is not fundamentally different from the problem-solving one except in scope. Actors in both have normative intentions. Problem-solving arises in limited and specific situations. Each problem needs a different set of actors with diverse specialties. In some cases, the normal choices of disciplines with their distinctive tools and concepts fail to work leaving the players frustrated (and often angry). When this happens, actors committed to solving the problems, say of unsustainability, may seek and discover a whole new paradigm to use pragmatically as Kuhn (1962) has claimed happens when scientists hit the wall. I believe this is a possibility for industrial ecology, arguing that sustainability is an emergent property of complex systems and thus, the reductionist methods of all the sciences, either in the epistemological or practical modes, do not cohere with the problems they seek to understand and solve (Ehrenfeld 2007, 2008). Kuhnian shifts persist only as long that they are pragmatically 'true', that is, if they provide answers for the seekers and methods and models for the appliers of knowledge.

The place of the normative in industrial ecology has been the subject of debate since the field started to take shape (Boons and Roome 2001). Allenby (1999: 3) argued that 'Industrial ecology should not become a normative tool rather than an objective field. Selective use of data, imposition of ideological absolutes on complex real-world systems, and simply bad science should not be a part of industrial ecology'. I argue rather that these two stances, objective and normative, should not be confused or conflated. There is no basic conflict between the normative basis for a Kuhnian paradigm shift and the pursuit of rigor and adherence to scientific standards. Although practitioners, for example, planners and designers often claim objectivity in order to avoid suspicion from sceptical stakeholders, one can argue that their mere presence in the project signals a normative stance that they think what they are doing is right.

It is certainly possible for an advocate – an actor with overt and passionate interests – to become blinded by his or her excitement and zeal. But, as Kuhn has taught us, progress in science depends exactly on the persistence and persuasiveness of normatively driven searchers and their belief that there *should* be an answer to the situation that puzzled and stymied them. In either the case of normatively-created blindness or a deliberate attempt to hide behind knowingly false or distorted scientific claims, the institutional processes in play within the field of industrial ecology will not accept the claims being made either on objective or legitimacy grounds. Peer review is an example of such a process. Anyone falsely dressing in the garb of industrial ecology will not be able to coordinate their actions with bona fide members of the industrial ecology community. But there are no more safeguards to prevent such misrepresentation about what industrial ecology is and can do as there are in any other field. Allenby's warning is a good one, but I believe the normative face of industrial ecology is important and need not undermine the integrity and reputation of the field.

RAZING THE TOWER OF BABBLE [*SIC*]

Many of the problems industrial ecologists set out to contemplate and attack involve technological systems and human agents. I have already noted that these settings generally require teams composed of both technologists and social scientists. Whether they are to collaborate (work together across time and space), cooperate (work together in real time and space), or coordinate their work (set priorities and act accordingly), all active actors must be able to speak in a language that is commonly shared. Otherwise, the results will be incoherent and successful only by chance.

This text is an example of one of the barriers to intermeshing social science into a basically technical field. Social scientists talk in many tongues and dialects. (So do technologists, but perhaps less so.) I looked at the bibliographies of each chapter and noted the keywords used by those cited publishing in the social science milieu. The list is long. Here are a few of the terms:

- Embeddedness: social, cognitive, cultural, structural, political, spatial and temporal
- Over-, under-socialization
- Trust, reciprocity
- Grounded theory
- Economic anthropology
- Stakeholder theory, ambiguity
- Social construction of . . .
- Ecological modernization
- Historical ecology
- Functionalism, functionalist
- New Ecological Paradigm
- Network analysis, social networks
- Social cohesion
- Transition management, socio-technical regimes and transitions, strategic niches, disruptive technologies

Two of the three intermezzi spoke explicitly about the need for dialogue among the various discipline-based workers in the field of industrial ecology. Dialogue, in this sense, is a conversation distinct from the oral conversations involved in the hurly-burly of normal activities. These normal conversations are meant to coordinate whatever action is going on (Habermas 1984; Searle 1989; Winograd and Flores 1986). Dialogue is distinct – explicitly designed to explore the beliefs and norms of the actors such that they begin to appreciate (understand *and* accept) those of each other.

I agree and note that most of such talk appears in academic places, especially in books and journals. But this is hardly the right place to build dialogue. Journal-bound dialogue cannot really qualify as dialogue according to the authors Boons cited in the first intermezzo and others such as Isaacs (1999) or Scharmer (2007) who see dialogue as a form of conversational practice. Dialogue has ancient etymological roots in the oral tradition. The recognition and understanding, and in the extreme, acceptance and sharing of another's beliefs and norms, comes only in spoken conversations. I have encountered real dialogical situations only rarely, like I am sure many of you have.

The most successful example in my own experience came in a seminar centred on a multi-disciplinary project at MIT exploring the place of chlorine in industrial economies. The seminar ran for several years and included students and faculties from every school at MIT. Lunch was provided as an incentive to attend. One of the group members presented his or her work each time with the specific aim to communicate to and with all the others. Bench chemists talked to political scientists and so on. By the end of the first year, a new collegiality was clearly evident and new truly interdisciplinary projects were conceived and organized. The lesson from all this was very clear. Dialogue takes time and a commitment toward mutual understanding.

From my observations as a 'steward' of the field of industrial ecology I see the dialogue expanding. I serve as an editor of the *Journal of Industrial Ecology* and have been Executive Director of the International Society for Industrial Ecology since its inception. The call for social science is ever louder. Issues like consumption, virtually impossible to do anything about, except measure it, without social scientists involved, are finding their way into journals and meetings of industrial ecologists. But one important change is not happening. Dialogue between industrial ecologists and corporate and public planners, strategists and decision-makers is rare and sporadic. No matter how well the objectivists and historicists within the field overcome their differences and more broadly coordinate action, their combined efforts will remain academic curiosities unless their works are recognized and put into practice by those with the power to do so in the larger society.

NOTES

1. For lack of a better category title for the many different kinds of actors whose intellectual frame is defined by the modern scientific epistemology – scientists, engineers, technocratic planners and so on – I will employ the term, technologists.

2. I scanned six years worth of issues of the *Journal of Industrial Ecology* to arrive at this conclusion.

REFERENCES

Allenby, B. (1999), 'Culture and industrial ecology', *Journal of Industrial Ecology*, **3**(1): 2–4.
Allenby, B. (2006), 'The ontologies of industrial ecology?', *Progress in Industrial Ecology* **3**(1/2): 28–40
Allenby, B.R. and D.J. Richards (eds) (1994), *The Greening of Industrial Ecosystems*, Washington, DC: National Academy Press.
Berger, P.L. and T. Luckman (1966), *The Social Construction of Reality*, New York: Doubleday Anchor Books.
Boons, F. (2008), 'Self-organization and sustainability: the emergence of a regional industrial ecology', *E:CO Emergence: Complexity and Organization*, **10**(2): 41–8.
Boons, F. and N. Roome (2001), 'Industrial ecology as a cultural phenomenon', *Journal of Industrial Ecology*, **4**(2): 49–54.
Desrochers, P. (2002), 'Regional development and inter-industry recycling linkages: Some historical perspectives', *Entrepreneurship & Regional Development*, **14**: 49–65.
Ehrenfeld, J. (2004), 'Industrial ecology: a new field or only a metaphor', *Journal of Cleaner Production*, **12**(8–10): 825–31.
Ehrenfeld, J. (2008), *Sustainability by Design: A Subversive Strategy for Transforming Our Consumer Culture*, New Haven, CT: Yale University Press.
Ehrenfeld, J.R. (2007), 'Would industrial ecology exist without sustainability in the background?' *Journal of Industrial Ecology*, **11**(1): 73–84.
Ehrenfeld, J.R. and N. Gertler (1997), 'Industrial ecology in practice: the evolution of interdependence at Kalundborg', *Journal of Industrial Ecology*, **1**(1): 67–79.
Erkman, S. (1997), 'Industrial ecology: a historical view', *Journal of Cleaner Production*, **5**(1–2): 1–10.
Fischer-Kowalski, M. (1998), 'Society's metabolism: the intellectual history of materials flow analysis, Part I, 1860–1970', *Journal of Industrial* Ecology, **2**(1): 61–78.
Frosch, R. and N. Gallopoulos (1989), 'Strategies for manufacturing', *Scientific American*, **261**: 142–55.
Graedel, T.E., D. van Beers, M. Bertram, K. Fuse, R.B. Gordon, A. Kapur, R.J. Klee, R.L. Lifset, L. Memon, H. Rechberger, S. Spatari and D. Vexler (2003), 'Multilevel cycle of anthropogenic copper', *Environmental Science & Technology*, **38**(2): 1242–52.
Granovetter, M. (1985), 'Economic action and social structure: the problem of embeddedness', *American Journal of Sociology*, **91**: 481–510.
Habermas, J. (1984), 'The French path to postmodernity: bataille between eroticism and general economics', *New German Critique*, **33**(3): 79–102.
Isaacs, W. (1999), *Dialogue: The Art of Thinking Together*, New York: Doubleday Business.
Kahneman, D. (2003), 'A perspective on judgment and choice: mapping bounded rationality', *American Psychologist*, **58**(9): 697–720.
Kay, J.J. (2002), 'On complexity theory, exergy, and industrial ecology: some

The social embeddedness of industrial ecology

implications for construction ecology', in G.B. Guy (ed.), *Construction Ecology: Nature as a Basis for Green Buildings*, London: Spon Press, pp. 72–107.

Kay, J.J., H.A. Regier, M. Boyle and G. Francis (1999), 'An ecosystem approach for sustainability: addressing the challenge of complexity', *Futures*, **31**: 721–42.

Kuhn, T. (1962), *The Structure of Scientific Revolutions*, Chicago, IL: Chicago University Press.

Lakoff, G. (2002), *Moral Politics: How Liberals and Conservatives Think*, Chicago: University of Chicago Press.

Lenox, M. and J. Ehrenfeld (1997), 'Organizing for effective environmental design', *Business, Strategy and Environment*, **6**(4): 1–10.

Lifset, R. and T.E. Graedel (2002), 'Industrial ecology: Goals and definitions', in R.U. Ayres and L.W. Ayres (eds), *A Handbook of Industrial Ecology*, Cheltenham, UK and Northampton, MA, USA: Edward Elgar.

Maturana, H.R. and F.J. Varela (1988), *The Tree of Knowledge*. Boston: New Science Library.

Reason, P. and H. Bradbury (eds) (2007), *The SAGE Handbook of Action Research: Participative Inquiry and* Practice, London: Sage.

Rorty, R. (1989), *Contingency, Irony, and Solidarity*, Cambridge: Cambridge University Press.

Salmi, O. and A. Toppinen (2007), 'Embedding science in politics; "Complex Utilization" and industrial ecology as models of natural resource use', *Journal of Industrial Ecology*, **11**(3): 93–111.

Scharmer, C.O. (2007), *Theory U: Leading from the Future as it Emerges*, Cambridge: Society for Organizational Learning.

Schön, D.A. and M. Rein (1995), *Frame Reflection: Towards the Resolution of Intractable Policy Controversies*, New York: Basic Books.

Searle, J. (1989), *Speech Acts*, Cambridge: Cambridge University Press.

Simon, H.A. (2000), 'Bounded rationality in social science: today and tomorrow', *Mind & Society*, **1**(1): 25–39.

White, R.M. (1994), 'Preface', in B.R. Allenby and D.J. Richards (eds), *The Greening of Industrial Ecosystems*, Washington, DC: National Academy Press, pp. v–vi.

Williamson, O. (1979), 'Transaction cost economics: the governance of contractual relations', *Journal of Law and Economics*, **22**: 233–62.

Winograd, T. and F. Flores (1986), *Understanding Computers and Cognition: A New Foundation for Design*, Norwood, NJ: Ablex Publishing.

11. The social embeddedness of industrial ecology: exploring the dynamics of industrial ecosystems

Jennifer Howard-Grenville and Frank Boons

We cannot know what the future holds, but we can know that everything we do (or say) contributes significantly to it. (Fell and Russell 1994, quoted in Ehrenfeld 2007)

In this book, we have introduced the idea of the social embeddedness of industrial ecology and explored it in conceptual and empirical ways. In the chapters on Regional and Product Chain approaches (Chapters 4–6 and 7–9), authors have demonstrated empirically how cognitive, cultural, political and structural mechanisms condition the emergence and operation of industrial ecology. In Chapters 2, 3 and 10, and a series of intermezzos, other authors have introduced and reflected on perspectives from outside the 'mainstream' of industrial ecology to consider the larger questions of the role and place of social sciences in the field. Each contribution raises at least as many questions as it answers. Thus, they bring into the open a number of opportunities for developing the field. Furthermore, they reflect the reality of a field that has been multi-disciplinary from the start and self-conscious of its stance as a scientific and normative endeavour (Allenby 1999; Boons and Roome 2000; Ehrenfeld 2007).

In this chapter, we attempt to take stock of the book's various contributions and offer some suggestions for future research and practice that can continue to explore the questions raised. The opening quote captures biologist Maturana's understanding of the natural and human world as self-organizing and emergent, a perspective that Ehrenfeld proposes may help industrial ecologists to connect to sustainability (2007). While some industrial ecologists have claimed that industrial ecology is 'the science of sustainability', this science has largely rested on developing understanding of, and designing tools for, material and energy flows in industrial systems (Ehrenfeld 2007). These technical approaches, inspired by the idea of an industrial metabolism which, like nature, operates through closed material loops, have and can go far in reducing the inefficiencies of traditional industrial practice. In this way, industrial ecology can be understood as a key approach to reducing the unsustainability of current industrial systems, with their linear approach to material and energy flows. But these approaches on their own fail to move us towards sustainability which requires significant shifts in social and cultural life (Ehrenfeld 2004).

As Commoner (1997) observed early on, the industrial ecology field has a tendency to focus on efficiency improvements that leave the more structural features of society intact. This issue is taken up in several of the empirical chapters (by Hall and Matos, Koponen and Gibbs). Social scientists have a valuable contribution to the field, given their inclination to developing a critical stance towards society as it is. In the words of the sociologist Zygmunt Baumann they tend to 'defamiliarize' (1990: 15); by analysing the structure, norms and values of groups/societies, they tend to ask questions about behavioural patterns that are so familiar to its members that they become taken for granted. Through uncovering and questioning the reasons for such patterns, sociologists tend to reflect critically on the status quo.

Such critical reflections and uncovering of taken-for-granted assumptions are essential to moving industrial ecology – and its contribution to sustainability – forward. Sustainability understood as an emergent property of human or ecological systems, rather than as an end of those systems, captures dynamic aspects such as resilience, adaptability and learning (Gunderson and Holling 2002; Ehrenfeld 2007). It is precisely these areas that can be described by social science approaches and problematized – though not necessarily *solved* – to contribute to greater wisdom about sustainability as an emergent systemic property. In their opening chapter to the edited *Handbook of Industrial Ecology*, Lifset and Graedel observe that the boundaries of industrial ecology as a field are expanded when the 'how' questions of social scientists co-mingle with the 'what' questions of natural scientists and engineers. The latter seek to characterize how technological and natural systems interact, and pose 'what-if' questions to identity the best approach to achieving a certain (broadly agreed upon) outcome. The former 'how' questions investigate processes and have the 'potential to help identify strategies that are more likely to succeed' (Lifset and Graedel 2002: 14). Lifset and Graedel remain uncommitted, however, to the value of expanding the boundaries of industrial ecology by investigating 'how' questions, preferring to leave the value of such investigations to be judged by their contributions to knowledge and practice.

In this volume, the contributors see no such clear line between 'what' and 'how' questions. The idea of embeddedness suggests that any description of 'what' is necessarily informed by understandings (implicit or explicit) of 'how'. Indeed, as we defined it in Chapter 1, social embeddedness captures the ways in which material and energy flows are shaped by the social context in which they occur. The authors in this volume have closely documented a number of empirical cases in which the social, and more specifically, the cognitive, cultural, political and structural context has influenced the development of certain patterns of production, consumption, interaction and economic exchange that necessarily shape material and energy flows. Efforts to change such flows by approaching them from the standpoint of what is strictly technically possible and desirable have fallen short of expectations. On the other hand, possibilities for change in such patterns are seen and in some cases demonstrated in the empirical chapters, with the 'how' of the change very much influencing whether and in what fashion it actually occurs. In our view, a major objective of the social science perspective is to answer these 'how' questions, and to provide insight into the dynamics of industrial ecosystems. In other words, social science approaches can and should seek to understand the way in which changes in socially embedded activities of individuals and organizations interact with changes in material and energy flows.

In the next section, we summarize the contributions of the empirical chapters to understanding the social embeddedness of industrial ecology in the two theme areas of Regional and Product Chain approaches. From this, we suggest several directions for further research. Finally, we return to a discussion of the prospects of interdisciplinary work for industrial ecology, reflecting on the arguments made in Chapters 2, 3, 10 and the intermezzos.

EMBEDDEDNESS AND INDUSTRIAL ECOLOGY

In editing this book, we chose not to impose a uniform theoretical framework to be adopted by authors. We wanted to make sure that the diversity that is present in current work of these and other authors would be captured in this volume. Embeddedness was used mainly as an organizing concept, highlighting the many dimensions of the social context from which material and energy flows emanate. As already hinted at in the first chapter, while it is analytically useful to separate the cognitive, structural, cultural, political and spatial/temporal mechanisms, uncovering the interplay between these mechanisms brings to life the way in which social contexts shape material and energy flows. This can be seen in each of the empirical chapters. The regional chapters provide this insight in geographically bounded cases in which actors seek to close material and energy loops. The technical idea of industrial symbiosis is straightforward, which may have contributed to its popularity among policymakers and practitioners. The distinct contribution of a social science perspective is in assessing the process through which regional networks evolve, and the requirements that are needed to make this happen, and the barriers that exist. Chapters 4 and 6 in particular show the relevance of such work, as the technically straightforward idea is difficult to bring into practice. Chapter 6 demonstrates how, despite geographical proximity, cognitive and cultural embeddedness can prevent individuals from seeking relationships for their businesses that might alter resource flows and improve efficiency. Chapter 4 supports this position, and adds a perspective on the need to go beyond the efficiency-gains approach and develop regional industrial ecologies as niches for more fundamental transitions. Combined with the analysis in Chapter 5, this argument has wider implications in terms of the relevant system boundary for industrial symbiosis. The network established by NISP has a much wider spatial scope than most eco-industrial parks, and thus the evolving network structure might follow a different logic than that in small-scale situations. Thus, in these chapters, the connections between aspects of structural, cognitive, cultural and spatial embeddedness are explored.

The product chain chapters (Chapters 7, 8 and 9) focus on the interconnected industrial activities along the life cycle of a product, and as a result, serve as an analysis of (parts of) industrial systems that span much larger geographical areas. Nevertheless, it remains possible to take a finer-grained look at individual actors and their goals, and the way they are influenced by their cognitive and cultural dispositions. The chapter by Koponen shows how commodities that are treated as uniform by economists and traders have different definitions of value attached to them depending on the social context from which they originate. These socially constructed values play a role in the power relationships that characterize the globally linked production chain. Likewise, the chapter by Matos and Hall takes a close look at the way in which the introduction of a new technology is shaped by its social context. In each of these cases, what is most interesting and informative is how the different dimensions of embeddedness relate to each other, and the implications they have for the particular situation. Each case offers a rich analysis, reinforcing the need to understand embeddedness as an empirical phenomenon. Based on such cases, we can develop more general insights.

First, technological 'lock-in' refers to the way that certain inputs and production techniques become standard within industries (and agriculture), making it very hard for individual actors to change their ways of doing things. Because these influences are felt through supply chain relationships, pricing and other mechanisms, they can operate at a distance (see Koponen's argument in Chapter 8) and are thus not readily changed nor even understood by the actors who perpetuate them. This is one example of cognitive embeddedness, manifesting also as political embeddedness, as existing power relations are perpetuated in the product chain. Lock-in also shapes and constrains action on a regional level because every business operating within an eco-industrial park or considering industrial symbiosis is also a participant in an industry and product chain that typically extends well past regional boundaries. Second, path dependency refers to the development of certain patterns of interaction and behaviour over time, as choices and actions from prior periods enable and constrain those available in later periods. Neither path dependency nor technological lock-in are new; both have had a long history in the social studies of science and technology (see for instance Arthur 1988; Dosi 1983). They are highly relevant to both the study and practice of industrial ecology, however, but are rarely explicitly addressed. Recognizing the importance of path dependency means paying attention to historical accumulations that have resulted from the operation of cognitive, cultural, political and structural mechanisms. This does not mean that nothing can change, but simply that an understanding of present arrangements typically demands looking beyond the present to appreciate the conditions that led to the present state. Indeed, a final general observation made by the empirical chapters is that present arrangements are sensitive to economic and political incentives, but these can change rather quickly. For example, if a government-sponsored industrial symbiosis program shifts its metrics for success from the reduction of solid waste to the reduction of greenhouse gas emissions, the participants in such a scheme may change, as may their actions due to shifts in incentives of the participants. This is not to deny the presence and importance of technological lock-in and path dependency, but to point out that companies and individuals do at times appear to 'change on a dime', even if some portion of this change is more rhetorical than fundamental. Path dependency would take account of such shifting incentives, and their effects, along with the role of historical arrangements.

Taken together, these observations help to generate a more general perspective on the dynamics of industrial systems. As touched upon in Chapter 2, and elaborated in several of the empirical chapters, organizational scientists have studied the dynamics of organizational and interorganizational change extensively. They have looked at such interorganizational networks in a dual way (Boons 1998). On the one hand, increasingly rigid networks are the manifestation of lock-in that makes it difficult to change current industrial systems. At the same time, networks are typically more flexible than organizations, and thus they can provide flexible linkages that induce collective learning and innovation. In the regional chapters, we see this dual nature: geographically bounded clusters of actors can be conducive to innovation, but the firms that make up such clusters are also connected into more or less global product chains, which often force them to stay close to current practices.

Nooteboom (1999) explores this dual character in terms of a 'learning cycle', modelling the way in which major innovations in industrial activities emerge and become mainstreamed into global production systems. Such innovations usually emerge in networks of individuals who work in geographical proximity and engage in explorative learning. As activities are scaled up, larger corporations become the dominant organizational form, as they are best able to capture the advantages of economies of scale operating in international markets. Capturing such advantages involves exploitative learning. Interestingly, the learning cycle proposed by Nooteboom connects the regional and product chain varieties of industrial ecosystems into a cyclical process that resembles Holling's (2001) adaptive cycle (see Chapter 2).

In our view, the social science contribution to industrial ecology could be strengthened through a focus on the ways in which the social embeddedness of material and energy flows shapes the dynamics of industrial systems. Incorporating models such as those of Nooteboom and Holling would serve to bring into focus the temporal and spatial dimensions of embeddedness. For example, while path dependency inherently captures a temporal element, it does not explicitly consider how individuals' different time horizons shape their understanding of and engagement in industrial ecology. In the learning cycle, the perception of time is different for exploration and exploitation. Furthermore, time is experienced differently by different people and in different cultures, suggesting that attention to this would reveal further insights beyond those associated with temporal sequencing or pacing. Similarly, spatial aspects are particularly salient to the embeddedness of industrial ecology because flows of material and energy are constrained and significantly influenced by distance. This aspect is recognized in the work on industrial symbiosis and eco-industrial parks, where questions of appropriate scale and boundaries are raised, but it is also present in the work on product chains. For the latter, spatial distribution may also imply cultural and political differences, which further indirectly influence material and energy flows. For example, cultural and political embeddedness may influence who decides on the goals and metrics to be attained, what materials are of interest, etc. Explicit attention to how spatial and temporal aspects of embeddedness operate in industrial ecology, and how these aspects relate to the other mechanisms of embeddedness, would move the field forward, building on the increasingly accepted recognition that social embeddedness 'matters'.

TOWARDS DIALOGUE

The relevance of such future work depends to a great extent on closer collaboration between researchers coming from the social sciences and science, engineering and technology (SET) disciplines. A key aspect of this book has been to invite several prominent scholars to reflect on their own experiences in and with the field of industrial ecology, and to comment on the promise of social science approaches to industrial ecology. Far more than offering summaries or critiques of the other chapters, these elements – the intermezzos, as well as Chapters 3 and 10 – offer fresh and provocative perspectives. Each of the authors is driven by the idea that interdisciplinary approaches that in some way combine social science and technical approaches hold promise for understanding aspects of industrial ecology more richly. A common theme in these contributions is that connecting SET and social science perspectives involves a personal journey, which is demanding because our value as scientists is still mainly determined in terms of the closed boxes of disciplines. As soon as we step out of these, we become to some extent strange outsiders, which is not what most human beings would like to be. Nevertheless, those who have walked such a path seem to enjoy the fruits that they can pick along the way; in that sense, the sharing of experiences by these authors is a welcome invitation. In addition to this personal challenge, they comment on the difficulty of multidisciplinary and interdisciplinary research, share observations of lessons learned through studying and working on industrial ecology, and offer advice for scholars and practitioners in this area. They also recognize the dangers involved in 'tacking on' social dimensions to a set of tools and methodologies developed with other perspectives – like reductionism or optimization – in mind. There is a significant concern that the contributions of scholars from different disciplines will result in the development of 'modular inquiries' that consider either technical or social elements of industrial ecology and fail to offer integrated, coherent analyses (Lifset and Graedel 2002: 15). And the latter is extremely difficult to achieve due to the different stances and standards applied in various disciplines (see Baumann's Chapter 3 and Ehrenfeld's Chapter 10 for insightful discussions of this issue).

In addition, the intermezzos begin to provide insight into some of the hidden assumptions that social scientists may need to confront if they seek to connect to the SET disciplines. Important remarks are made about methodology, which maybe comes as no surprise if we look at scientific research as an inquiry following a specified procedure. Social scientists have to deal with reflexivity: they are human beings studying human beings. This leads to specific methodological issues which are extensively explored in their professional education. When communicating among themselves, they immediately recognize the various strategies that can be adopted towards the reflexive nature of their inquiry, and therefore they do not discuss the rationale behind it explicitly in each paper they write. For those educated in SET disciplines, this taken-for grantedness leads to confusion, or even dismissal of the insights that social scientists have to offer. In this sense, the intermezzos indicate the necessity of making methodological approaches transparent. Of course, this is exactly what can be achieved through dialogue.

So what is an industrial ecologist with an interest in the 'social side' to do? First, researchers and practitioners can be explicit about the approaches they are using, and the assumptions and criteria they carry with them. For example, while engineers might design a program with optimization of material flow in mind, social science contributions suggest that appropriateness of a technology to local conditions might be a better criterion for success. As Baumann notes in Chapter 3, social scientists in general seem to be more open to multiple views than engineers, and more accepting of multiple possible solutions. This does not mean, however, that their perspectives will be the 'right' ones, nor that optimization or efficiency should be abandoned as goals. This leads to a final suggestion which is to use social science perspectives and findings to ask better questions and explore alternative possibilities, rather than expect them to provide universal solutions or strategies. If we accept that no single discipline or method has a monopoly on the 'truth', then we must assess the strengths and contributions of each. The challenge, as others have pointed out in this volume, is that the contributions of different fields are not merely additive.

While it seems almost inadequate as a way to end, perhaps the best suggestion for further including social science insights in industrial ecology is to encourage truly interdisciplinary research teams to form and giving them outlets for publication and practice. While such interdisciplinary teams will continue to cross boundaries and navigate fences, they should, over time, learn together how to integrate the strengths of natural science, engineering and social science perspectives that can inform research and practice. The place for such dialogues is in everyday life, not in the static pages of a book. We hope, however, that this book will serve as a starting point and source of inspiration for such endeavours.

REFERENCES

Allenby, B. (1999), *Industrial Ecology: Policy Framework and Implementation*, NJ: Prentice-Hall.

Arthur, W. (1988), *The Economy as an Evolving Complex System*, New Mexico: Westview Press.

Baumann, Z. (1990), *Thinking Sociologically*, Oxford: Blackwell.

Boons, F. (1998), 'Caught in the web: the dual nature of networks and its consequences', *Business Strategy and the Environment*, 7(4): 204–12.

Boons, F. and N. Roome (2000), 'Industrial ecology as a cultural phenomenon', *Journal of Industrial Ecology* 4(2): 49–54.

Commoner, B. (1997), 'The relation between industrial and ecological systems', *Journal of Cleaner Production*, 5 (1–2): 125–9.

Dosi, G. (1983), 'Technologies as problem-solving procedures and technologies as input–output relations: some perspectives on the theory of production', *Industrial and Corporate Change*, 15(1): 173–202.

Ehrenfeld, J. (2004), 'Can industrial ecology be the science of sustainability?', *Journal of Industrial Ecology*, 8(1–2): 1–3.

Ehrenfeld, J. (2007), 'Would industrial ecology exist without sustainability in the background?', *Journal of Industrial Ecology*, 11(1): 73–84.

Gunderson, L. and C. Holling (eds) (2002), *Panarchy: Understanding Transformations in Human and Natural Systems*, Washington, DC: Island Press.

Holling, C. (2001), 'Understanding the complexity of economic, ecological, and social systems', *Ecosystems*, 4: 390–405.

Lifset, R. and T.E. Graedel (2002), 'Industrial ecology: goals and definitions', in R.U. Ayres and L.W. Ayres (eds), *A Handbook of Industrial Ecology*, Cheltenham, UK and Northampton, MA, USA: Edward Elgar.

Nooteboom, B. (1999) 'Innovation, learning and industrial organization', *Cambridge Journal of Economics*, 23: 127–50.

Index